Animism in Rainforest and Tundra

Animism in Rainforest and Tundra

Personhood, Animals, Plants and Things in Contemporary Amazonia and Siberia

Edited by
*Marc Brightman, Vanessa Elisa Grotti
and Olga Ulturgasheva*

berghahn
NEW YORK • OXFORD
www.berghahnbooks.com

Published in 2012 by
Berghahn Books
www.berghahnbooks.com

© 2012, 2014 Marc Brightman, Vanessa Elisa Grotti and Olga Ulturgasheva
First paperback edition published in 2014

All rights reserved. Except for the quotation of short passages
for the purposes of criticism and review, no part of this book
may be reproduced in any form or by any means, electronic or
mechanical, including photocopying, recording, or any information
storage and retrieval system now known or to be invented,
without written permission of the publisher.

Library of Congress Cataloging-in-Publication Data
Animism in rainforest and tundra : personhood, animals, plants and things in contemporary Amazonia and Siberia / edited by Marc Brightman, Vanessa Elisa Grotti and Olga Ulturgasheva.
   p. cm.
Includes bibliographical references and index.
 ISBN 978-0-85745-468-3 (hardback) -- ISBN 978-0-85745-469-0 (institutional ebook) – ISBN 978-1-78238-524-0 (paperback) – ISBN 978-1-78238-525-7 (retail ebook)
 1. Shamanism--Amazon River Region. 2. Shamanism--Russia (Federation)--Siberia. 3. Human-plant relationships--Amazon River Region. 4. Human-plant relationships--Russia (Federation)--Siberia. 5. Human-animal relationships--Amazon River Region. 6. Human-animal relationships--Russia (Federation)--Siberia. I. Brightman, Marc. II. Grotti, Vanessa Elisa. III. Ulturgasheva, Olga.
 GN564.A47A55 2012
 306.0957--dc23

2011043517

British Library Cataloguing in Publication Data
A catalogue record for this book is available from the British Library

Printed on acid-free paper

ISBN: 978-1-78238-524-0 paperback
ISBN: 978-1-78238-525-7 retail ebook

Contents

List of Figures	vii
Acknowledgements	ix
Foreword *Stephen Hugh-Jones*	xi
Maps	xv

Introduction
    Animism and Invisible Worlds: The Place of Non-humans in Indigenous Ontologies
    Marc Brightman, Vanessa Elisa Grotti and Olga Ulturgasheva
	1

1 Too Many Owners: Mastery and Ownership in Amazonia *Carlos Fausto*	29
2 Revisiting the Animism versus Totemism Debate: Fabricating Persons among the Eveny and Chukchi of North-eastern Siberia *Rane Willerslev and Olga Ulturgasheva*	48
3 Animism and the Meanings of Life: Reflections from Amazonia *Laura Rival*	69
4 Stories about Evenki People and their Dogs: Communication through Sharing Contexts *Tatiana Safonova and István Sántha*	82
5 Making Animals into Food among the Kanamari of Western Amazonia *Luiz Costa*	96
6 'Spirit-charged' Animals in Siberia *Alexandra Lavrillier*	113

7 Shamans, Animals and Enemies: Human and Non-human
   Agency in an Amazonian Cosmos of Alterity   130
   Casey High

8 Expressions and Experiences of Personhood: Spatiality
   and Objects in the Nenets Tundra Home   146
   Vera Skvirskaja

9 Humanity, Personhood and Transformability in
   Northern Amazonia   162
   Vanessa Elisa Grotti and Marc Brightman

10 Masked Predation, Hierarchy and the Scaling of
   Extractive Relations in Inner Asia and Beyond   175
   Katherine Swancutt

Afterword   195
Piers Vitebsky

Notes on Contributors   200

Index   203

Figures

0.1	Lowland South America	xv
0.2	Siberia and Central Asia	xvi
6.1	Evenki taxonomy	118
6.2	The category of wild animals in the taxonomy	120
6.3	Direction of the ritual gestures and invisible acts of the main categories of the taxonomy	121
6.4	The constituents of humans and animals	125
6.5	Worlds of socialization of 'spirit-charged' and other categories of beings	126
8.1	Layout of a choom	151
10.1	The Nuosu soul-spider	182

Acknowledgements

Many of the papers presented in this volume were originally presented at a conference held at the Musée du Quai Branly, Paris, in June 2008. The editors would like to thank warmly the Director of Research at the Musée, Anne-Christine Taylor, as well as Laurent Berger and Myrlande Jean-Pierre, for their financial, logistical and personal support. We would also like to acknowledge the significant contribution made by the four discussants on our panels: Roberte Hamayon, Stephen Hugh-Jones, Anne-Christine Taylor and Piers Vitebsky. Katie Swancutt deserves special thanks for agreeing to contribute a chapter at short notice and for her comments on an early draft of the Introduction. We would like to thank the publishers at Berghahn for their patience and receptiveness, and the anonymous reviewers for their constructive comments. Finally, we are grateful to all of the conference participants for their part in the lively and productive discussion, and we wish especially to mention those who unfortunately were unable to contribute to the present volume: Damien Davy, Andrea-Luz Gutierrez Choquevilca, Mette High, Marc Lenaerts and Emilie Maj, whose presentations and interventions nevertheless formed an important part of the dialogue that grew into this book.

Foreword

Stephen Hugh-Jones

Back in the early 1970s, after a two-year spell of fieldwork in north-west Amazonia and needing somewhere to write her doctoral thesis in social anthropology, my wife Christine was offered desk space at Cambridge University's Scott Polar Research Institute – anything was better than trying to work at home with two small children. Inevitably, this apparently incongruous conjunction between Amazon and Arctic became the subject of frequent jokes by friends and colleagues: 'Bet you're cold in there!', 'Careful, you'll melt the ice', and so on. Little could these jokers have imagined that, forty years on, precisely this conjunction would lead to two international conferences devoted to setting the cultures, societies and current situation of the indigenous peoples of Amazonia and Siberia in comparative perspective. This volume is the outcome of the second conference. Appropriately enough, one of the organiser-editors, Olga Ulturgasheva, did her Ph.D. at the Scott Polar Research Institute under the supervision of Piers Vitebsky; the other two, Vanessa Grotti and Marc Brightman, did theirs in the Department of Social Anthropology at Cambridge and were supervised by myself.

There are several good reasons for bringing Amazonia and Siberia together. To begin with, both are frontier zones associated with extractive economies. In the past, both regions were relatively marginal to global economic processes with large areas inhabited mainly by widely dispersed groups of indigenous peoples, but over time each became an ever increasing focus of economic attention as sources, first of animal skins and forest products, then of oil, gas, minerals and timber, as locations for major hydroelectric schemes and as areas of 'free' or 'unoccupied' land open to exploitation and settlement by people from more crowded parts. These developments have a long history, but in recent years their pace has increased dramatically and their reach has extended to leave no part untouched. Fearing for their lands and livelihoods, and vigorously reasserting their distinctive ethnic and cultural identities, indigenous peoples living in what were once refuge areas have resisted many of these developments, today often in alliance with pro-indigenous and pro-environmental NGOs also concerned with the threat to fragile ecological areas and areas of high biodiversity. These are some of the issues discussed in the proceedings of the first conference mentioned above (Brightman, Grotti and Ulturgasheva 2006/2007).

Secondly, the indigenous inhabitants of the two regions are related: like those throughout the Americas, the peoples of Amazonia are all descended from peoples who crossed in several waves of migration from Siberia sometime between 10,000 and 20,000 years ago.[1] This common prehistory and the intriguing similarities – and differences – between the cultures of the peoples on the two 'sides' have had an influential role in the historical development of anthropology. In their different ways, the pioneering works of Boas and his Russian colleagues, of Hallowell, and then of Lévi-Strauss all dealt with Siberian–American parallels and with the theoretical problems of comparison to which exploration of these parallels gives rise. It was through this line of research that the Siberian-derived term 'shamanism' came to be applied in a North and South American context. Ethnographically, this book is devoted to comparing the shamanistic cosmologies of Siberia and Amazonia. Theoretically it explores the conceptual problems that such cosmologies and comparisons pose.

Siberian and Amerindian peoples share in common a propensity to extend to various non-human entities – animals, plants, objects, spirits – the personhood, agency and intentionality that we would normally see as exclusively human characteristics. Each such person sees from the perspective of their own body but all see through the same lens of human culture. Animistic or perspectival metaphysics of this kind appear to destabilise the theoretical foundations of anthropology as a whole. If others see animals, plants, artefacts and objects as social persons, how then can we square this with theoretical analysis founded on the assumption that 'in reality' such entities are not persons at all but rather parts of one stable and invariant nature? If their animistic reality is not the same as our own naturalistic version, how we can understand it though a theoretical apparatus that assumes that it is? Do we compare epistemologies or world-views or are we dealing with different ontologies? And are ontologies opposed or can they co-exist?

As different parts of the world succeed one another as the dominant foci of anthropological investigation, one region becomes the testing ground for concepts and theories developed in relation to another. In the 1960s, African models of descent were tested against Melanesian ethnography; in the 1970s and 1980s an explosion of research in Amazonia led to a rethinking of models of kinship by setting kinship in the wider context of cosmology. This 'Amerindanization of descent and affinity' (Rivière 1993) led, in turn, to Viveiros de Castro's work on perspectivism, to Descola's similar but not identical reworking of animism and totemism, to the destabilisation of 'nature' as the presumed stable and universal reference point of variable 'culture', and to the current interest in different ontologies – perspectival, animist, totemic, analogical and naturalistic (Descola 2005). There is a convergence between all this and Ingold's (2000) parallel reflections on animism and totemism. Though Ingold draws upon Descola's model, his own version of the animism/totemism contrast has a different, more phenomenological bent. In addition, and crucially for this volume, whereas Viveiros de Castro and Descola are both rooted in Amazonia and structuralism, Ingold's ethnographic roots lie amongst circumpolar peoples, many of whom are reindeer herders. Amazonians keep no true domestic animals other than dogs. Dogs and reindeer figure prominently in this volume and the implications of pastoralism provide a point of tension and contrast on which some of the key debates raised here hinge.

Political factors have meant that, until quite recently, Siberia remained closed to anthropological research. This volume bears testimony to a surge of research and publication on the region over the past decade. By definition fresh and recent, this work reflects some of the major theoretical concerns of contemporary anthropology. It also coincides with an outpouring of work from a second, younger generation of Amazonianists eager to test and refine the arguments of their predecessors. Drawing inspiration from research in both regions, tacking back and forth between data and theory and working together in a critical and comparative dialogue, these younger Siberianists and Amazonianists have now produced a new synthesis, one that might be called the Siberianisation of Amerindian anthropology. One aspect of this involves pitting theoretical abstractions derived from Amazonia against empirical data from various parts of Siberia. Can perspectivism fit the Siberian data and does this produce new insights? What modifications are suggested by this new context? Another aspect involves feeding the answers to these questions back and forth from one empirical context to another, within and between the two regions involved.

Discussions of animist ontologies and shamanic, perspectival cosmologies, revolve around a series of polarised categories such as domesticated/wild, predation/reciprocity, cannibalism/commensality, animism/totemism, horizontal/vertical, equality/hierarchy, endopraxis/exopraxis, and so on. One of the major contributions of this series of essays lies in their fine-grained ethnography, one that returns us to the messy, lived worlds and not always tidy and consistent views of real peoples. This return to the ground not only mediates between structuralism and phenomenology but also reminds us of the limitations of Western categories applied to non-Western contexts – like ships that carry invasive alien species to our shores, these categories sometimes carry unwanted freight.

One aspect of this unwanted freight is our tendency to treat such pairs as mutually exclusive: society A is animist, society B is totemic; the X's 'have' horizontal shamanism, the Y's 'have' vertical shamanism, and so forth. A great virtue of these essays lies in their reminder that such pairs were used originally (or perhaps should have been used) not as polar opposites but rather as ideal types, tendencies or ends of a continuum. In their different ways, the essays all deal with the issue of how such pairs are interrelated and interact – in one society, in different societies within our two regions or across the two. This co-occurrence or co-variation also raises the issue of context: Which animals, plants, objects are endowed with personhood, why and when? How does perspectivism apply to everyday life? And what happens to shamanic cosmologies under the changing historical circumstances of education and missionisation?

These then are some of the issues raised in the essays presented here. If Amazonia and Siberia were once relatively marginal to anthropological debate, today the issues raised by ethnography from these two regions have become central. This volume is an important contribution to these debates and it is one that will set the agenda for the years to come.

Notes

1. There is considerable disagreement about precisely how and when the crossing took place.

References

Brightman, M., V. Grotti and O. Ulturgasheva (eds). 2006/2007. 'Rethinking the "Frontier" in Amazonia and Siberia: Extractive Economies, Indigenous Politics and Social Transformations', *Cambridge Anthropology* 26(2): 1–12.
Descola, P. 2005. *Par-delà nature et culture*. Paris: Gallimard.
Ingold, T. 2000. "Totemism, Animism and the Depiction of Animals", in *The Perception of the Environment: Essays on Livelihood, Dwelling and Skill*. London: Routledge, pp. 112–13.
Rivière, P. 1993. 'The Amerindianization of Descent and Affinity', *L'Homme* 33(2–4): 507–16.

Maps

Figure 0.1: Lowland South America.

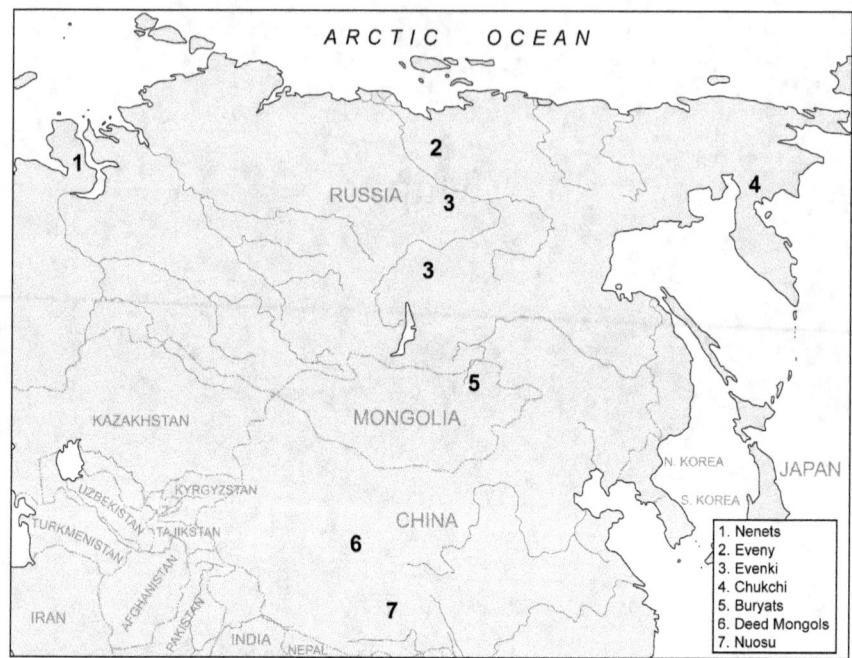

Figure 0.2: Siberia and Central Asia.

INTRODUCTION

Animism and Invisible Worlds: The Place of Non-humans in Indigenous Ontologies

Marc Brightman, Vanessa Elisa Grotti and Olga Ulturgasheva

Shamanic peoples such as the indigenous inhabitants of Amazonia and Siberia frequently appear in the popular imagination as 'living in harmony with nature', and indeed this image has become part of their identity on the global political stage (United Nations 2007). It is therefore not entirely accidental that two thinkers, Rousseau and Marx, had particularly lasting influence over the ethnography of these two regions. Each of them relies in important and divergent ways upon the distinction between nature and culture, and together they have been described as part of the bedrock of modern anthropology (Leach 2000). Rousseau's noble savage, partly inspired by reports of Amazonian Indians, represented humanity before its decisive break with nature, while Marx's vision of human history depends on humanity's ability to act autonomously upon nature as a separate entity.[1] The anthropology of nature has become prominent since the publication by Tim Ingold (1990, 2000), Bruno Latour (1997, 1999) and Philippe Descola (2005) of powerful arguments that the conventional Western nature/culture dichotomy is contingent, historically situated and just one of many other possible and indeed empirically existing modes of understanding relations between humans and non-humans. Many years before them, Edmund Leach, in a wide-ranging discussion of the problem, pointed out that the dichotomy mirrors other recurring themes in the Western history of ideas – for instance, 'the artificial distinction between nature and culture ... which is, from one point of view, a logical derivation from the moral relativism of Locke, is, from another angle, a transformation of the Cartesian opposition between conscious mind and mindless matter. The limitations of the latter dyad apply equally to the former' (Leach 2000: 324). The nature/culture dichotomy is part of the legacy of Western philosophy out of which modern social anthropology has grown, but the very emergence of the anthropology of nature, and its practice, have been dedicated precisely to deconstructing and discrediting the dyad with which they are concerned.[2] This volume is dedicated to the cross-cultural study of relations between humans and non-humans, and focusing on personhood allows us to avoid the trap of criticising the conventional nature/culture dyad without ever being able to escape its terms. Data on personhood in animistic societies have always raised questions about the supposed universal validity of the concept of nature, because they invariably demonstrate that non-human entities may be regarded as social persons.

The study of personhood has a tradition in anthropology going back at least as far as Mauss's 1938 essay on the category of the person (Mauss 1985), in which he argues for the importance of names in ascribing and denoting social roles in a way akin to classical theatrical masks. His argument influenced later authors interested in the relationship between individual and society (e.g., Fortes 1987). Mauss contrasted the 'primitive' person with personhood in modern societies, which he suggested had become associated with individual consciousness (Carrithers, Collins and Lukes 1985). Since Mauss's time, ethnographic data have grown more abundant and, perhaps more importantly, appear different in the light of the abandonment of theories of social evolution. Indeed, the development of the anthropological representation of the non-Western person mirrors in a certain sense the evolution that Mauss took for granted from the person as social object in 'primitive' societies to the person as individual subject in contemporary Western European societies. In accordance with the contemporary view of the anthropological object as 'subject' (Spiro 2006), and following the evidence of their own field data, the contributors to this volume take personhood to be a category of human-like subjectivity. In doing so, we build on an anthropological tradition that arguably begins with Irving Hallowell's essay on Ojibwa ontology, behaviour and world-view, in which he shows that the Ojibwa category of the person 'is by no means limited to *human* beings', and that for a culture such as theirs, 'the concept of "person" is not, in fact, synonymous with human being but transcends it' (Hallowell 1960: 21). Eduardo Viveiros de Castro has described this notion of personhood as follows, and although he refers only to the Americas, his words could equally apply to Siberian societies:

> The ethnography of indigenous America is peopled with these references to a cosmopolitical theory which describes a universe inhabited by diverse types of actants or of subjective agents, human and non-human – gods, animals, the dead, plants, meteorological phenomena, very often objects and artefacts too – all equipped with the same general ensemble of perceptive, appetitive and cognitive dispositions, in other words, of a similar 'soul'. This resemblance includes a shared performative mode, so to speak, of apperception: animals and other non-humans with souls 'see themselves as persons' and therefore, they 'are persons', that is to say: intentional or double-faced (visible and invisible) objects, constituted by social relations and existing under the double pronominal mode of the reflexive and the reciprocal, that is to say of the collective. (Viveiros de Castro 2009: 21)[3]

Thus, certain non-human beings, whether animals, plants or 'things', are regarded by many societies in different regions of the world as having characteristics which conventional Western or Euro-American rationality associates exclusively with human persons: as Hallowell wrote, among such peoples, '[a]nimals are believed to have essentially the same sort of animating agency which man possesses. They have a language of their own, can understand what human beings say and do, have forms of social or tribal organisation, and live a life which is parallel in other respects to that of human societies' (Hallowell 1926: 7).[4] At the dawn of professional anthropology (Bird-David 1999), Tylor assimilated these characteristics with the concept of the soul, and recaptured the term 'animism' from contemporary spiritualists to denote the practice of ascribing souls to non-human entities (Tylor 1913: 428–57). He explained this widespread tendency citing Hume's *Natural History of Religion*:

> There is a universal tendency among mankind to conceive all beings like themselves, and to transfer to every object those qualities with which they are familiarly acquainted, and of which they are intimately conscious ... The *unknown causes*, which continually employ their thought, appearing always in the same aspect, are all apprehended to be of the same kind or species. Nor is it long before we ascribe to them thought and reason, and passion, and sometimes even the limbs and figures of men, in order to bring them nearer to a resemblance with ourselves. (quoted in ibid.: 477)

This manner of 'explaining' religion as a universal human tendency to project human-like agency upon non-human entities has recently been taken up by cognitive anthropologists (Boyer 2003). But, leaving cognitive evolutionary explanations aside, for social anthropology many other questions remain to be answered whose importance lies in their relevance to human, social and environmental interactions: Which objects, animals or plants have these human-like qualities, and what distinguishes them from others? What, indeed, do humanity or subjectivity mean, and are they adequate translations of the qualities that are regarded as shared across species? What do the relationships between human and non-human persons consist of, and what can we learn from them? As Viveiros de Castro puts it, 'What these persons see ... – and therefore what they are as persons – constitutes precisely the philosophical problem posed by and for indigenous thought' (Viveiros de Castro 2009: 21).[5] The point echoes that of Hallowell, who wrote, 'in the metaphysics of being found among these Indians, the action of persons provides the major key to their world view' (Hallowell 1960: 21). Within the anthropology of Amazonia and Siberia, there has been an ongoing and fruitful engagement with such questions, which are raised by and resonate with the ethnography of both regions. However, apart from certain important theoretical borrowings and token ethnographic illustrations, this engagement and the debates surrounding it have hitherto remained largely confined to the literature stemming from each region.

The Comparison between Amazonia and Siberia

This volume seeks to cross-fertilise debate by providing an ethnographic window between the anthropology of Amazonia and Siberia. The specific comparison between Amazonia and Siberia has been brewing for some time in the literature of each region, perhaps most notably in the ongoing dialogue between Philippe Descola and Tim Ingold on animism (Descola 1996; Ingold 2000) – of which, more below. However, while Descola and Ingold have drawn on each other's theoretical reflections, each has continued to pursue his own agenda with little mutual engagement at an empirical level, although the former has recently summoned data from both regions – as well as others – to support his argument (Descola 2005).

An important stimulus for this volume lies in Siberianists' engagement in recent years with theory emerging from Amazonia, particularly Amerindian perspectivism as expounded by Eduardo Viveiros de Castro (1998; see also Århem 1996; Lima 1999). This theory of relative ontologies, based on the ethnography of the Araweté, the Juruna and other native Amazonian peoples, focuses on how 'the different sorts of persons – human and non-human (animals, spirits, the dead, denizens of other cosmic layers, plants, occasionally even objects and artefacts) – apprehend reality from distinct points of view' (Viveiros de Castro 2004: 466). Amerindian perspectivism emerged from a long period of reflection on the nature of personhood in Amazonia, which arguably began with an influential article on the construction of the person in indigenous Brazilian societies (Seeger, Da Matta and Viveiros de Castro 1979). Here it was asserted that personhood and 'corporeality' were fundamental structuring elements in Lowland South American societies which appeared fluid when measured using established anthropological categories: such societies 'are structured in terms of symbolic idioms which ... refer not to the definition of groups and the transmission of property, but to the construction of persons and to the fabrication of bodies' (ibid.: 10).[6] It is worth quoting at length:

> It is not a matter of an opposition between man and animal realized far from the body and through individualizing categories, where the natural and the social repel each other by definition, but of a dialectic in which the natural elements are domesticated by the group and the elements of the group (social elements) are naturalized in the world of animals. The body is the great arena in which these transformations are possible, as is shown by all of South American mythology which must, now, be re-read as stories with a centre: the fundamental idea of corporeality. (ibid.: 14)[7]

Over the ensuing decades, an efflorescence of Lowland South American ethnography has engaged with this challenge (e.g., Carneiro da Cunha 1978; Seeger 1981; Vilaça 1992; Viveiros de Castro 1992; Conklin 1996; Kelly Luciani 2003), forming a significant part of what Peter Rivière has referred to as the 'Amerindianization' of anthropological concepts (Rivière 1993). To take just one especially pertinent example, Anne-Christine Taylor (1996) offers a reflection on what it means to be 'human' for one Amazonian people, and offers a definition of indigenous Amazonian selfhood. She shows that 'the Jivaroan sense of self is predicated on the fusion of a singular though generic body image and other people's emotionally laden perception of this body-image, whereby it comes to be experienced as uniquely personal' (Taylor 1996: 209). It is significant that the 'body-image' refers to the *wakan*, usually translated as 'soul', but which refers 'to the reflected image of a thing, the appearance of someone in a dream as well as the dreamer's consciousness' (ibid.: 206), causing Taylor to remark that 'the Achuar would certainly endorse Wittgenstein's claim that the body is the best image we may have of the soul, not least for its reversibility, since it is equally obvious to them that the soul is also the best image we may have of the body as a generic personalized form' (ibid.: 206). This recalls the idea of the 'eye-soul', which is widespread in Amazonia: the Waiwai, for example, explain it as 'the small person one always sees in the other's eye', and for them 'to see is the same as being seen when it is a matter of supernatural beings' (Fock 1963: 19). For the Trio, although the soul 'is thought to permeate the body with special concentrations at the heart and pulses', they also recognise a 'distinct eye-soul that is extinguished on death' (Rivière 1999: 77). The eye-soul, or the soul as (reflected) body-image, provide a vivid illustration of the reversibility that is a key feature of perspectivism, and which has also been identified in Siberian ethnography (Willerslev 2006).

Perspectivism has been a constant theme in debates in Amazonianist anthropology for many years now, but the question remains open as to how far it can be taken as an analytical device applied to native Amazonian societies. As an illustration of its possible limitations it may be useful to note the variability in the nature and number of souls in Amazonia. Souls or spirits are not necessarily equivalent to subjectivity (Lima 1999) or to vital principle (Vilaça 2005). In addition to the eye-soul, many Amazonian peoples recognise as many as five different souls, discussed by Rivière (1999). For instance, the Yekuana, in addition to the eye-soul, recognise the 'heart soul', the 'soul in the moon' (a receptacle for evil thoughts and actions), the 'soul in the water' (a reflection in the water) and the 'soul in the earth' (the shadow). Souls may also be immortal and retain their identity, as is the case of name-souls among the Barasana instead of their identity being purely relational (ibid.: 80–81). This complexity in the invisible aspects of the human agent, or in the human image, show that the 'double' or binary relationship through which perspectivism has often been discussed is at best only one of its many dimensions (Lima 1999).

Certain authors have pointed directly to the limitations of perspectivism, notably Rival (2005), who has argued that gender differences are prior to and encompass the soul–body relationship, and Turner (2009), who argues that humans and the human body are a privileged kind of person in the Amerindian cosmos, thus placing a limit on the potential for reversibility between human and non-human. On a classificatory level, Descola has argued that perspectivism is a subset of animism, on the grounds that, although for all animist societies non-humans see themselves as humans, for only some such societies do certain non-humans (who see themselves as humans) see humans as non-humans (Descola 2006: 141). The key to resolving such categorical problems may eventually lie in further ethnographic study, especially of communication between humans and non-humans (e.g., Yvinec 2005; Gutierrez Choquevilca 2008).

One of the most interesting challenges for Amerindian perspectivism is an empirical one, set by Césard, Deturche and Erikson (2003). They point out that very few Amazonianist authors have discussed insects, despite the fact that they are not only omnipresent in the environment of the region but play highly significant practical and cultural roles, serving as food, medicine, playthings, fish-hooks, indicators of the quality of land for cultivation or hunting, and stings used in initiation rituals. Sometimes insects are considered to be spirits (ibid.: 391); among Kaingang, mosquitoes or ants are spirits of the dead; shamanic arrows can take the form of insects (cf. High, this volume), and insects often seem to be the tangible manifestation of malign principles, or the desire to do harm. Certain insects, because of the supposed power of their venom, are often among the ingredients of hunting poison. Not always merely instruments, they can be subjective agents: bees may have shamanic powers, and the Matses regard red ants as autonomous subjects with their own agency (Cesard, Deturche and Erikson 2003: 392–93). The Amerindian imagination is especially struck by insects' lack of blood and their desire for the blood of others – blood being associated with vital energy. Despite all of this, the authors point out that indigenous discourses on insects have hitherto been 'surprisingly neglected' in recent debates on both animism and perspectivism, which 'give an eminent place to the relative indifferentiation between the ontological status respectively attributed to humans and to animals, as well as to the notion of metamorphosis and transformability that underpins this' (ibid.: 394).

Lavrillier's chapter in this volume shows that Siberia too has much potential for investigation in a similar direction. For the Evenki, insects are not a generic category, but carrion bugs are said to come from the world of the dead, and the giant woodwasp is said to be the 'soul' of big game such as reindeer or moose; some insects are treated as pets, while others, like spiders, are considered to be ancestor spirits. Beyond Siberia, among the Nuosu, human souls take the form of spiders (Swancutt, this volume), and spiders are so important for them that the Nuosu could even be said to have an arachnidian cosmological idiom. The parallels clearly suggest that this could be fertile ground for further comparison between the regions.

The first attempt to consider the animist cosmologies of North Asia in the light of perspectivist theory was made by Morten Pedersen (2001). Using classic ethnographies of the Siberian Chukchi and Koryak by Bogoras (1909) and Jochelson (1908, 1926), Pedersen pointed to the common elements present in Amazonian and Siberian animist societies such as continuity between humans and non-humans, shamanist cosmology, egalitarian ethos and unbounded potential for identification (Pedersen 2001: 416). Pedersen's attempt to draw an ontological link between North Asia and Amazonia sparked debate on the implications of perspectivist theory for the ethnographies of shamanic societies in and around Mongolia (Pedersen, Empson and Humphrey 2007). The contributors to the latter collection experimented with stretching the original theory that was built on specific ethnographic data while also diverging from it by introducing innovations in the process of its application to the analysis of different cultural settings. This led them to introduce Inner Asian 'transcendental' perspectivism as the characteristic feature of these societies with a hierarchical cosmological order (Holbraad and Willerslev 2007). In this avatar of perspectivism the symmetrical Amerindian model was subverted and all its components were put in vertical terms and presented as ethnographic varieties of inter- and intra-human perspectivisms across Inner Asia.

An important attempt to bring animistic modalities across Siberia, North America and Amazonia into a comparative account has been made by Carlos Fausto, who elaborated on distinctive features of socio-cosmic systems, particularly 'a common mode of identification between humans and non-humans' (Fausto 2007: 498). His endeavour to draw on the ethnographies from what he dubbed the 'Sibero-American' domain highlighted that predation is the 'more productive schema in Amazonia' (ibid.: 498) whereas the progenerative model is dominant in the Siberian and American sub-Arctic (see Brightman 1993; Fienup-Riordan 1990, 1994; Hamayon 1994, 2003; Ingold 2000). His account illustrates that prominent in both Amazonian hunting modalities of predation and commensality, and in Siberian and North American hunter-gathering idioms of love sharing, compassion and reciprocity, are distinctly and dynamically articulated ways of producing people and sociality. The distinction between the models of predation and reciprocity drawn by Fausto appears less sharp in the Siberian and Inner Asian ethnographies of this volume, which show that predatory and extractive relations are also at work but in a less straightforward and even 'masked' manner (Swancutt, this volume; Willerslev and Ulturgasheva, this volume).

No previous volume has compared the ontologies, cosmologies, myth or religion of Amazonia and Siberia, but several previous studies exist of contiguous regions of the Americas, or Siberia and North America.[8] Hallowell's work, especially his doctoral dissertation on bear ceremonialism (Hallowell 1926) and his classic essay on Ojibwa ontology (Hallowell 1960), has been a rich and inspiring resource for scholars such as Descola, Ingold and Viveiros de Castro. Indeed, Viveiros de Castro's most recent project (Viveiros de Castro 2009) could be described as a continuation of Hallowell's pioneering explorations of 'a relatively unexplored territory – ethno-metaphysics' (Hallowell 1960: 20).

Hallowell focuses his 1926 study on cultural practices and beliefs associated with the bear, and thus limits his analysis to the principal geographical distribution of bear hunting, which ranges from northern Europe, across Inner Asia and the American North, to Meso-America. Limiting the comparison to one (albeit culturally very important) species has the advantage of reducing the number of variables. If a similar study were to be conducted for Lowland South America, the species upon which it would focus would undoubtedly be the jaguar, the consummate and iconic predator of the region. No such work exists, but a focused comparison between the symbolism, beliefs and practices associated with jaguars and bears would make a fascinating study. Both animals are large predators that play a central role in the cosmologies of indigenous peoples, who look upon them with a mixture of awed respect and fear. Both are associated with mystical powers and quasi-human qualities. Hunters in both Amazonia and Siberia address jaguars as 'grandfather' or 'grandmother' (Hallowell 1926: 53; Brightman 2007: 265–68), and the ritual and mythological importance of bear and jaguar imagery is vast (Hallowell 1926; Benson 1972; Sullivan 1988). Bears and jaguars are also both closely associated with shamans: they may be said to 'be' shamans themselves, or to be able to transform themselves into humans; shamans are likewise said to be able to transform themselves, or parts of themselves, into shamans or jaguars (Hallowell 1926: 86; Rivière 1994; Costa 2007: 381–83; High, this volume). Perhaps most importantly, both jaguars and bears play key roles in the symbolic organisation of society. In Amazonia there are innumerable pairs of relationships between masters and auxiliaries, in which the jaguar symbolically represents the master 'part', as both tutelary 'fatherhood' and predatory power are expressed as 'jaguarness' (Fausto 2007, this volume). Meanwhile in Siberia, the complex figure of the bear is used in the performance of different forms of alliance: direct exchange (among the Evenks of Iénisséi) is expressed through a ritual hunt, whereas indirect exchange (among the Nivh or Giliak in the region of Amour and Orochon in East Siberia) is expressed through the ritual slaughter of a captive bear (De Sales 1980; Kwon 1999).

On the other hand there are clear differences. Although the flesh of both bears and jaguars is said to be highly potent, for the jaguar there is nothing to compare with the rich variety of ceremonial practices associated with the treatment of the bear carcass and consumption of the meat, and jaguar meat is rarely if ever eaten. Likewise, although a certain amount of respect is shown to the jaguar in general terms, there is nothing in Amazonia to compare with the ritualised respect and 'conciliatory' treatment of the slain bear (Hallowell 1926: 144). It is perhaps therefore on the level of symbolism, ritual and myth that comparisons can be made most fruitfully between indigenous peoples' relationships with jaguars and bears, and this brief consideration of the evidence at hand indeed suggests that on such a level, jaguars and bears are similar kinds of 'person'.

Hallowell's work was based on North American as well as Siberian material, and as this indicates, the limits of a comparative project are, in the end, arbitrary – especially in the absence of a more restrictive theme (such as the bear). It would be reasonable, indeed useful, to extend the comparison offered in the present volume, at least to North America, where the kinds of ontologies and notions of personhood and agency described in this book can also be found, as is clearly shown by the work of authors such as Adrian Tanner (1979), Colin Scott (1989), Robert Brightman (1993), Ann Fienup-Riordan (1994) or Georg Henriksen (2010), and in regionally specific collections (Irimoto and Yamada 1997). Indeed, worthwhile comparisons can be made with other regions further afield, such as South-east Asia (Bird-David 1999; Platenkamp 2007), China and Mongolia (Swancutt, this volume) or Melanesia (Gregor and Tuzin 2001). Viläça has already noted the points of similarity between Amazonian material and Leenhardt's account of the Kanak concept of the human being (Viläça 2005). Clearly, there is rich potential for future comparative projects on the themes of personhood, animism and relations between humans and non-humans.

Siberian Studies and the Amerindian Stimulus under the Soviet Regime

Some of the differences between the characteristics of Amazonian and Siberian ethnography must be attributed to stark contrasts in the historical conditions under which fieldwork was conducted. The history of Amazonian ethnography diverges from that of mainstream anthropology largely in that: firstly, the first systematic studies began to emerge more recently than in other regions, notably Africa; secondly, the presence of French and Latin American practitioners (rather than British and American ones) has traditionally been stronger; and thirdly, the influence of Lévi-Strauss, whose own ethnographic fieldwork was of course carried out in Amazonia, has been more marked and sustained than in other regions. The history of Siberian ethnography differs in important ways because of the hegemony of the Soviet state in the region for most of the twentieth century, precisely the period during which anthropology defined itself as a discipline in the West. Yet before Siberia became closed to researchers who did not operate under the conditions prescribed by the Russian politburo, scientists were already carrying out comparative ethnographic studies as part of an attempt to identify the relationship between populations of the Americas and Northern Asia or Siberia (see Cavalli-Sforza et al.1988; Fortescue 1998). Perhaps most significantly, Franz Boas pioneered an attempt to explore the cultural and physical relationship between inhabitants of the Siberian coast and the Amerindians of the Pacific Northwest.

The project of the Jesup North Pacific Expedition organised in 1897 and led by Boas until 1902 allowed the collection of precious items of material culture as well as linguistic, religious and statistical data from the Siberian North, which still often serve as the only ethnographic source that allows contemporary scholars to observe and reflect on the nature of social transformations and the continuity of certain social and cultural phenomena among Siberian groups over the last century (Pedersen 2001; Willerslev 2007; Willerslev and Ulturgasheva, this volume). The Jesup monographs, which were published as a result of this expedition, gave rise to the academic notion of 'shamanism' that anthropologists began to use to describe the spiritual practices of native populations of Siberia and the Americas.[9] Western scholars, 'who rarely operated with the definition of shamanism prior to 1900, now increasingly began to juxtapose Native American practitioners against their classic "Siberian analogies"' (Znamenski 2003: 17, see also Hultkrantz 1999: 2). At the same time, the scope of literature that documents animistic and shamanic practices in Siberia largely remains unknown to Western scholars and 'lay' audiences (Vasilevich 1936, 1957, 1969; Smolyak 1966, 1974). It is not only that Siberia, as part of the Soviet Union, was inaccessible to Western observers, but there is also a significant language barrier (Znamenski 2003: 31).

While pursuing his interest in remote Siberian ethnic groups, Boas persuaded Morris K. Jesup, a rich American banker, philanthropist and president of the American Museum of Natural History, to fund ethnographic fieldwork on the two coasts of Bering Strait: Siberia and north-western North America (Krupnik and Fitzhugh 2001). This led to work in Siberia that was part of a highly ambitious project that lasted six years from 1898. '[M]uch of the work was carried out by Russian revolutionaries who, during years of political exile in Siberia, had become experts on the ethnology of that region' (Freed, Freed and Williamson 1988: 9). When they joined the Jesup Expedition, Bogoras, Jochelson and Shternberg were already veterans of several years of Siberian research. During their years of political exile in Siberia they made collections, took photographs and anthropometric measurements, and studied the languages of Chukchi, Koryak, Itel'men, Siberian Yupik, Yakuts, Yukaghir, Lamuts (Eveny) and Nivkhi. Their efforts laid the foundations for subsequent ethnographic, linguistic and folklore studies of Siberian indigenous groups.

The Stalinist purge against 'enemies of the people' between 1921 and 1932 brought severe disruption to Siberian ethnographic studies. The campaign against 'non-Marxist' and 'bourgeois' academics declared ethnography a 'tribute to colonialism' (Gagen-Torn 1992,1994) and, as a result, 'museums were closed, scholarly societies disbanded, the teaching of ethnography discontinued, and teachers of ethnography persecuted' (Slezkine 1991: 479). To survive the ideological purge most of the older academics either went completely silent or tried to follow Soviet rule (Bogoras 1931; Ssorin-Chaikov 2003: 97). Under the Communist Party's ideological agenda, ethnography was reduced to the theory of 'primitive communist formation' and the study of any facets of 'primitive' societies had to consist of the task of defining the role of archaic survivals in the subsequent evolution of society, based on the premise that all peoples, including the most backward, were subject to limitless change.

This view contributed to the proliferation of studies of folklore, which have been interpreted as an ideologically safe exercise in the reconstruction of the past (Ssorin-Chaikov 2003: 88), and to the new theory of language, according to which the 'history of language consisted of linear, synthetic, agglutinative, and inflective stages, each corresponding to a specific socioeconomic formation and developing dialectically (i.e. replacing another via a revolutionary "leap")' (Slezkine 1991: 478). Hence, folklorists and students of the oral traditions of various Siberian groups collected folklore items with the aim of exploring a perpetual 'ethnographic past'.

Given these ideological restrictions, it is important to mention that this historical field, which was mostly based on the study of folkloric texts, includes an unforeseeable and, perhaps, unavoidable twist due to the creative endeavours of some remarkable scholars who worked during that period. One of them was Eleazar Meletinsky, who was responsible for substantively forming Siberian folklore studies during the period. Although Russian scholarly literature always highlights the substantial influence of Vladimir Propp on Meletinsky and, although his methodology is undoubtedly significantly shaped by Propp's theory on the morphology of folkloric texts (Propp 1946, 1969), Meletinsky was probably the first and only scholar of the period who took the significant step of openly acknowledging the influence of the work of Claude Lévi-Strauss, particularly, his four-volume *Mythologiques* (1964–1971). This monumental work, in which Lévi-Strauss applies his structural method to hundreds of South and North American Indian myths, became a milestone in the development of Meletinsky's study of myths and the mythological thought of Siberian indigenous groups. Meletinsky discusses Lévi-Straussian theory in his seminal monograph *The Poetics of Myth*, which became a key textbook for several generations of Russian and Soviet scholars of Siberian folklore.[10]

In his discussion of elements of mythological thought, Meletinsky imitates Lévi-Strauss's comparative approach and suggests that it is possible to discern universal models in any 'primitive/archaic' culture through the analysis of the semantic structure of myths (Meletinsky 1998: 60). Though he commends Lévi-Strauss for his detailed examination of the specific characteristics of mytho-logic (its metaphoric nature, the tendency for *bricolage*) and his emphasis on mytho-logic's ability to generalise, classify, and analyse (ibid.: 120), which are particularly suitable to structural analysis, Meletinsky criticises what he took to be his anti-historical viewpoint and considers it as complementary to historical and diachronic approaches to the study of events.[11]

Meletinsky's emphasis on historicism and the search for the mythological origin of modern literature might be explained by the omnipresence of Marxist doctrine in Soviet academia, according to which the evolution of literature was viewed as inseparable from the socio-economic formation in which it existed. This agenda dominates his theory of myth, and consequently his analysis of the mythological thinking of tribal societies is carried out in accordance with Engels's evolutionary thesis on the emergence of statehood in stateless societies (Engels 1970) and the Hegelian distinction between historical and non-historical nations (Hegel 1956).[12]

Given that Meletinsky himself suffered political persecution and imprisonment in Stalinist camps, these latter aspects of his approach can legitimately be understood as an unavoidable product of political censorship from Soviet legal and academic authorities. To secure the chance to publish one's own book or theory one had to pay homage to the Marxist historiographic framework and ensure that the obligatory 'Soviet' terminology was in place (Lanoue 1998: xi). In relation to this, the publication of Russian translations of Lévi-Strauss's work appears as a most extraordinary accomplishment even in view of the fact that it took place at the expense of certain theoretical and analytical contingencies. Soviet versions of *Anthropologie structurale* (1958), *Le Totémisme aujourd'hui* (1962a) and *La Pensée sauvage* (1962b) were first published in the early 1980s (see Lévi-Strauss 1983, 1985b, 1994a, 1994b). It appears that these works of Lévi-Strauss succeeded in presenting themselves as compatible with Russian Soviet scholarly discourse in which the study of the 'otherness' and 'backwardness' of 'aliens' inhabiting remote lands has been viewed as a unique key to understanding the past 'in order for the future to become present' (Slezkine 1992: 57). So the Lévi-Straussian view of 'noble savages' and ethnographic examples from all over the world did not contradict the Soviet ethnographic practice of depicting the lives of 'natural communists' and their mythological way of thinking as synonymous with 'primitive' thinking.

In regard to this, Meletinsky's articles 'Typological Analysis of the Paleo-Asiatic Raven Myths' (Meletinsky 1973) and 'Paleo-Asiatic Myths about Raven and the Issue of the Relationship between North-eastern Asia and North-western America in the Field of Folklore' (Meletinsky 1981) might be viewed as a direct outgrowth of Lévi-Straussian methodology. Meletinsky even devoted the latter article to his theoretical progenitor. In these two articles he uses folkloric texts collected by Bogoras and Jochelson during their fieldwork among the Chukchi, Koryak, Itel'men and Siberian Yupik at the beginning of the twentieth century, and employs them in a typological analysis of the myths collected by Boas among the Tsimshian, Haida, Tlingit and Kwakiutl.

In ethnographic studies of Siberia, Lévi-Strauss's influence is not only limited to the study of narratives and myths. His work on kinship and exchange among Tupian groups of the Brazilian coast (Lévi-Strauss 1969) has greatly shaped Siberian research in France, particularly the works of the prominent French anthropologist Roberte Hamayon. She was among the very few Western anthropologists who managed to gain access to the Siberian field in 1970s and 1980s and conducted research among the Buryat, a large ethnic group of Mongolian origin in the region of Transbaikalia, south Siberia (see Hamayon 1990, 1994, 2003; see also Safanova and Sántha, this volume; Swancutt, this volume). The Lévi-Straussian influence is particularly clear in her study of the notion of exchange in pastoral shamanism in which she presents a thorough examination of Buryat social organisation and kinship (Hamayon 1990, 1994, 2003).

Lévi-Strauss's project was germane not only to a certain tradition of Russian ethnography dedicated to indigenous peoples and their ontologies, but also (and even more so) inspired an entire generation of structuralist anthropologists to study indigenous ontologies in Amazonia. As part of what might be described as the second generation of structuralist-inspired scholars working in this tradition, Viveiros de Castro, whose influence we have discussed above, has recently paid homage to the central role played by Lévi-Strauss's *Mythologiques* in the development of his own thought. In his book *Métaphysiques cannibales* (Viveiros de Castro 2009), which addresses a readership beyond Amazonia and beyond anthropology, Viveiros de Castro discusses his two principal influences: the philosophy of Deleuze and Guattari, and Lévi-Strauss's *Mythologiques*. He attributes to Lévi-Strauss the first correct analysis of native ontologies of the Americas as characterised by 'an economy of *corporeality*' (ibid.: 18),[13] and the first description of:

> an indigenous anthropology formulated in terms of organic flows and material codifications, of significant multiplicities and instances of becoming-animal, rather than

expressed in the spectral terms of our own anthropology which the juridico-theological fog (think of the rights and duties, rules and principles, categories and 'moral persons' that make up our discipline) overcomes through comparison. [*Mythologiques*] made it possible to discern some of the theoretical implications of this unmarked or generic status of the virtual dimension (the 'soul') of each being, which was the chief premise of a powerful indigenous intellectual structure, capable, *inter alia*, of counter-describing its own image as described by Western anthropology, and thus, 'to send back to us an image of ourselves in which we do not recognise ourselves'. (ibid.: 19)[14]

Viveiros de Castro tries to show the possibility of studying 'indigenous anthropologies' rather than merely subjecting data about indigenous peoples to Western theoretical scrutiny. The analysis of mythic transformations has revealed that the key to doing so, at least in the case of so-called 'animist' societies, is to focus on the body and what we refer to as 'personhood'. But, he argues, the structuralist tradition is not to be confused with the phenomenological tradition, which he follows Deleuze and Guattari in criticising:

> By drawing explicitly on the *Mythologiques*, this work [i.e., Seeger, Da Matta and Viveiros de Castro 1979] developed without any connection with the theme of *embodiment*, which would take anthropology by storm in the ensuing decades. The structuralist current in Amerindian ethnology, deaf to the 'at once pious and sensual' appeal of phenomenological Carnism (Deleuze and Guattari 1991: 169) – 'the call of rotten wood', as a reader of *The Raw and the Cooked* might say – has always thought of incarnation from the point of view of the culinary Triangle rather than that of the holy Trinity. (ibid.: 19 n.1)[15]

Drawing both on the legacy of structuralism and phenomenology, the present volume may be viewed as a renewal and reappraisal of both Boasian and Lévi-Straussian traditions in the light of the most recent ethnographic data on topics which include the animistic conceptualisation of property and ownership (Fausto), agency and intentionality (Costa; Grotti and Brightman; Lavrillier; Rival), recursivity and reversibility (High; Willerslev and Ulturgasheva), spirituality and materiality (Skvirskaja) and predation and reciprocity (Safanova and Sántha; Swancutt).

The Limits of Perspectivism and the Limits of Comparison

Some of the limitations of perspectivism as formalised by Viveiros de Castro (1998) – or, perhaps, an indication of how to develop it – are exposed by Santos-Granero's volume on material culture in Amazonia (Santos-Granero 2009). Here, against Viveiros de Castro's claim that humans and animals take primordial forms and plants and objects are derivative (Viveiros de Castro 2004: 477, cited in Santos-Granero 2009: 4–5), it is argued that Amerindian cosmologies have a 'constructional' character and that objects often play a prototypical role in Amazonian ontologies. A similar argument can be made for plants, which are often related to as persons by those who cultivate them (Descola 1986) and by shamans and plant specialists (Lenaerts 2006), and which may have kinship systems of their own (Chaumeil and Chaumeil 1992). Santos-Granero's volume emerges as part of a widespread revival in the study of material culture in the last ten years following the publication of Alfred Gell's *Art and Agency* (Gell 1998), which offered a theory of the attribution of 'agency' and 'intentionality' to human artefacts. We will not discuss here the many fruitful arguments that have followed, and the specific relevance of Gell's theory for Amazonian societies is considered by Laura Rival in her contribution to the present volume. But one point that we would like to take up is that various authors (e.g., Van Velthem 2003; Henare, Holbraad and Wastell 2007) have emphasised the attribution of 'subjectivity' to non-humans other than animals. Animism is, by definition, the attribution of human(-like) subjectivity, agency and emotion to non-humans: in short, non-humans seem to be endowed with personhood. But in animistic societies, are things endowed with the same kind of personhood as humans and animals? The nature of soul (a primary attribute of personhood) in the cosmologies with which we are concerned does not correspond to the conventional Western understanding of the term, which follows Kant in loosely equating it with mind. For the Siberian Chukchi, for example, the word for 'soul' comes from a linguistic root meaning 'body'. Chukchi souls are 'a form of bodies', and body and soul are 'flip sides of each other' (Willerslev 2009: 697). Similarly, among the Wari' in Amazonia, souls are not separate from bodies except when the body becomes attacked by illness, and at this point it is being appropriated by another being – souls in a sense are other bodies. Both regions thus share this materiality and corporeality of the soul (Rivière 1999; Vilaça 2005; Miller 2009). As discussed above, the souls of humans and animals resembles the human or animal body or takes the form of one of its parts. Although the spirit- or animal-masters of plants are often birds (Chapuis and Rivière 2003: 388–89; Gutierrez Choquevilca 2008), the nature of the plant or object soul tends to be less clear.

The ethnographies presented below testify to the importance of other non-humans such as objects, plants and insects (Grotti and Brightman; Rival; Skvirskaja; Swancutt). They challenge some of the conceptual boundaries identifying abstract dichotomies such as animism/totemism, egalitarianism/hierarchy and horizontal/vertical which were conceptual resources for previous anthropological discussions of Amazonian and Siberian societies (Hill 1984; Hugh-Jones 1994; Descola 1996, 2005; Ingold 2000; Pedersen 2001), showing them in dynamic interplay and never as fixed or static.

Many studies of Amazonian sociality have shown the importance of process, especially bodily process, in the constitution of human personhood (Crocker 1985). In an Amazonian world which Fausto (this volume) has described as being made of 'infinite differences characterised by an ontological regime of metamorphosis', babies are 'moulded' into real human beings (Lagrou 2000), and eating together, cooperation, physical contact and verbal interaction are all considered necessary for a person to become, and to remain, human (Vilaça 2000).

There has, however, been less emphasis on the effects that humanising processes can have on non-human actors – on animals and plants, for instance. Nor has there been detailed consideration of where the line is drawn in such processes between personhood (understood as constituted by agentivity, intentionality and subjectivity) and humanity (a special kind of personhood attributed by a group to its members). Descola has written that, at least for the Achuar:

> The hierarchy of animate and inanimate objects … rests upon the variation in the modes of communication which permit the apprehension of unequally distributed sensible qualities. Insofar as the category of 'persons' includes spirits, plants and animals, all endowed with a soul, this cosmology does not discriminate between humans and non-humans; it only introduces a scale of order according to the levels of exchange of information reputed to be feasible. (Descola 2005: 23)[16]

So much for one animistic society. But questioning the distinction between humanity and personhood can be a revealing path of inquiry. The contributors consider processes by which animals, plants and objects become persons, and to what extent they become human. Such processes include the cultivation of manioc (Rival) and the training of hunting dogs (Safanova and Sántha), which are shown to be different processes of kin-making, in which agentive persons are created by humans without becoming fully realised as human beings. Plants and dogs are not fully involved in the processes of human sociality, and, therefore, despite being addressed as kin, are not human (Grotti and Brightman). In analogous cases, Rivière (1994) and Van Velthem (2001) have both independently shown that basket motifs among certain Amazonian peoples can take on personhood, but are kept from fully realising their potential as dangerous and powerful non-human agents by the limits of the basketmaker's skill – though these limits are sometimes said to be self-imposed. In all these cases, human control maintains non-human personhood; human creativity produces a relation of ownership which is exceptional in Amazonian cosmology in that it is not reversible (Fausto, this volume; see also Brightman 2010). Beyond the human social spaces in which manioc, dogs and basketry occur lie non-human others who can in turn 'see' like humans. Here, humanity is subjective.

Death, and the cosmological role and characterisation of the dead, provide fertile ground for comparison between Amazonia and Siberia, and for testing the limits of perspectivism. In Willerslev's ethnography of the Siberian 'hall of mirrors world' – phrasing which echoes Viveiros de Castro's 'forest of mirrors' (Viveiros de Castro 2007) – every relation becomes an inversion of another. The dead have their flesh on the outside of their bodies and their limbs the wrong way round; time for them goes in the opposite direction so that 'before' becomes 'after' and vice versa; 'death' for the deceased is 'birth' for the living, and indeed the living are dead for the dead: when a deceased person dies (s)he returns to the world of the living (Willerslev 2009: 696). However, the deceased are seen as hierarchically superior – suggesting a parallel with the cannibal gods of the Araweté (Viveiros de Castro 1992). Their world is an idealised version of this world, and they are the 'true owners' of reindeer. Here, the role of agency played by the dead can be compared to the masters of animals in Amazonia, who are 'owners' of animal species, and with whom there must be a certain level of reciprocity as they receive human souls with which to replenish their stock. This is why overhunting is commonly said to lead to illness and death: the master of animals is taking back souls (for a similar Amazonian case, see Costa, this volume). Among the Chukchi, there is a 'fixed pool of souls that simply go round in an endless circle' (Willerslev 2007: 697), recalling the north-west Amazonian Makuna's conception of the cosmos as an interlinked web in which energy and souls are perpetually exchanged and regenerated (Århem 1996). Even if the hierarchically superior nature of the deceased noted by Willerslev is in marked distinction to the classic Amazonian type of animist society, exemplified by the Achuar (above), in which humanity is the index of superiority, the Araweté case suggests that the distinction is not so clear cut.

Among the Chukchi, humans are in a relationship of 'unconditional indebtedness toward the deceased' (Willerslev 2009: 698) rather than being involved within a network of gift exchange or mutual obligation. In Amazonia, the dead matter, in the sense that all dead (humans as well as non-humans) matter, but relations with them are kept to a safe minimum, they are not individualised, and indebtedness is strongly avoided (see High, this volume). But there are exceptions to this, which Viveiros de Castro has analysed in terms of Hugh-Jones's distinction between 'vertical' and 'horizontal' shamanism (Hugh-Jones 1994): if horizontal shamanism corresponds to the classic Amazonian model in which animals and the dead are assimilated as the 'other' of humanity, and vertical shamanism results from the 'divorce between the dead and animals, the former remain human, or even become superhuman, and the latter begin to cease to be human, moving towards a sub- or anti-humanity' (Viveiros de Castro 2009: 127).[17] Viveiros de Castro attaches great importance to this, associating the former, horizontal type with 'exopraxis' and the vertical type with 'endopraxis', and suggesting that the former is 'anterior – logically, chronologically and cosmologically – to endopraxis, and that it remains always operational, even in more hierarchical formations such as those in north-west Amazonia, in the manner of a residue that blocks the constitution of chiefdoms or of States equipped with a complete metaphysical interiority' (ibid. :127; cf. Clastres 1974).[18] This suggests that a possibility for further comparison with Siberia may lie in examining the 'residue' of exopraxis in societies characterised by vertical shamanism.

Animism and Totemism: Complementary Models (and Only Models)

Animism and totemism have been defined as modes of relationship with nature (Descola 1986). But for totemism this is not necessarily so.[19] The defining characteristic of totemism for Lévi-Strauss is the metaphorical transposition of an ensemble of relationships between elements in a classificatory system; it is arguably of secondary importance that this transposition tends to occur between nature and culture (Lévi-Strauss 1962b: 160). For animism, as we have seen, certain characteristics of personhood can be attributed to cultural artefacts, suggesting that the nature/culture dichotomy (of which Descola is himself a prominent critic) does not hold in the case of animism either. However, Descola himself proposes a stricter definition of animism: for him the non-human 'persons' within animistic systems are regarded as having 'social attributes – a hierarchy of positions, behaviours based on kinship, respect for certain norms of conduct' (Descola 1992: 114). In recent years he has also revised his characterisation of totemism and animism derived from relationships between nature and society, choosing instead to define them in terms of the relationship between 'interiority' and 'physicality', corresponding to Husserl's 'intentionality' and 'body' respectively (Descola 2006: 138). It is consequently more difficult to distinguish Descola's animism from perspectivism, for the 'social attributes' of non-humans in such a system tend to be identical to those of the culture to which the system belongs, and these attributes tend to be said to be present from the point of view of non-humans as subjects. However, Viveiros de Castro has taken pains to distinguish the two, writing as follows to define perspectivism: 'Neither animism – which would assert a substantial or analogical resemblance between animals and humans, nor totemism – which would assert a formal or homological resemblance between intra-human differences and inter-animal differences, perspectivism asserts an intensive difference which brings the human/non-human difference *to the interior of each being*' (Viveiros de Castro 2009: 36).[20]

All the chapters of this volume show that the current tendency to classify societies according to their 'ontologies' – totemistic, animistic or other – may create problems especially when it comes to interpreting ethnographic elements that do not fit such neat categories – although one of the most interesting lines of inquiry of Descola's monograph on the subject (Descola 2005) is the discussion of the ways in which these categories are blurred by ethnographic facts. One of the lessons of perspectivist theory itself is that some societies define themselves precisely by their transformability, their inconsistency and their instability (Vilaça 2005; Grotti and Brightman, this volume).

In his discussion of the distinctions between totemism and animism, Descola points out that some societies combine degrees of both analytical constructs (Descola 1996: 88). He derives this point from Århem's account of the Makuna (Århem 1996) in which he suggests that 'intellectually, totemism and animism are complementary and commensurate strategies for comprehending reality and relating humans to their environment (Århem 1996: 186)'. Willerslev and Ulturgasheva (this volume) go further, arguing that the combination of animistic and totemic features should not be treated as an exception but as a rule. They suggest that animism and totemism 'shade into each other rather than appear as two opposites of one dichotomy'. Hence, if these categories are to be maintained, it is mutual implication, interdependence and 'shading' that should be taken as the main conceptual components for the perception of complex and incommensurate ethnographic data.

In a similar vein Swancutt effectively introduces in this volume a 'scaling' mode that is analytically necessary for the consideration of ontological differentiations between predation and hierarchy. Swancutt's emphasis on the potential for movement not only between different ontological registers but also between differently scaled elements within any given ontology enforces a particular analytical pattern that enables one to grasp and uncover ethnographic expressions of social relations which are veiled or masked. In her analysis of ethnographic data from different sites in south-west China and Mongolia she elaborates on cases where people who explicitly emphasise their social hierarchies also make efforts to mask their predatory motives. Among the Buryats of north-east Mongolia and the Deed Mongols of Qinghai, China, the scaling of hierarchy and predation, which is masked under seemingly selfless and virtuous acts of Buddhist offerings and blessings, tips increasingly towards the pole of explicit predation. In the same fashion, her Nuosu case study shows that the sliding scale implies a movement along different degrees of 'overlap' between hierarchy and predation so it is a 'loophole' in the Nuosu's masked hierarchy, which takes the form of a vestigial slavery, that even gives rise to more explicit predation.

In his discussion of mastery and control, Ingold draws a straightforward distinction between two modes of hunter–animal relations: one relies on the mutual trust common among egalitarian hunter-gatherers and the other is based on coercion exercised by hierarchical cattle-breeding pastoralists (Ingold 2000: 61–76). According to Ingold, in the case of pastoralists, 'the attempt to extract by force represents a betrayal of trust' and there is an automatic movement from trust to domination or hierarchy (ibid.: 71). This involves ontological ramifications, particularly those related to the notion of domestication, that implies 'a kind of mastery and control similar to that entailed in slavery' (ibid.: 73). Such a clear-cut categorisation of 'hierarchy' as absent in hunter-gatherer ontologies can only appear valid on a macro scale of analysis. Closer examination of indigenous practices reveals that the distinction is far from clear. As studies of mastery and control, and of pets, in Amazonia have shown, the taming of animals constitutes a counterpoint to predation (Erikson 2000) and a reiteration of the hierarchical relations that it enacts (Fausto, this volume). The control devices and forms of manipulation to which Ingold is referring seem to derive from a Western preoccupation with mechanical, instrumental and social domination and do not really account for the more intricate details of indigenous socio-cosmologies.

Hierarchy is an important part of the cosmological systems of all of the groups presented in this volume (cf. Descola 2005: 24; Brightman 2007; Kohn 2007: 17). In contrast to Ingold's treatment of mastery and hierarchy, Fausto's analysis of the plural and altering nature of Amazonian mastery shows that practices of enslavement and ownership are also involved in the construction of social relations between humans and non-humans, and he argues that mastery operates at multiple cosmological scales. Once again, here 'hierarchy' slides along scales from authority and control to enmity and filiation, which is why 'captives, orphans and pet animals often receive treatment that veers between care and cruelty' (ibid.; cf. Erikson 2000).

Conclusion

In a passage praising Descola's recent study of different ontologies (Descola 2005), Bruno Latour muses, '[w]hereas for its first century, anthropology could multiply "cultures" while nature remained the non-coded category in contrast to which cultures could be defined, it is fair to say that, in this century, anthropology will go on multiplying the ways in which former cultures and natures (now in the plural) become coded categories' (Latour 2009: 466). The work presented here shows that this may raise the old ethnological problem of the tension between generalisation and the integrity of individual cases. But cross-regional comparison may highlight potential connecting points between seemingly unrelated ontologies. In conclusion we would like to stress that this remains a study of classic themes within two regional contexts, and that this volume should be considered as a first attempt to engage comparatively with the contemporary shamanic cosmologies of Amazonia and Siberia. A fruitful addition to this initial comparative presentation of the entanglement of relations between humans and non-humans would be one which grapples with the additional transformations of the lived environment of native Siberians and Amazonians, such as the depletion of natural resources, changes in the practical involvement with ecosystems through migration to urban centres or sedentarisation processes, or transformations of the symbolic engagement with other living beings, through conversion to national or alien modes of being, such as Christianity or 'nationalisation'. Further clues should be sought as to the management of these various 'perspectives' and what that can tell us of ideas of change and continuity. The contributors to the present volume all conducted their ethnographic fieldwork among peoples undergoing such transformative processes, and they have described here fundamental relational modes which have been tested in the face of change. Indeed, in the 'relational spaces' (García Hierro and Surrallés 2005) in which the indigenous peoples of Amazonia and Siberia live, they are the medium through which such changes are experienced.

Notes

1. This could be seen as another example of 'Whitehead's "fallacy of misplaced concreteness"', the confusion of abstractions with real phenomena, of which Bateson accused Marxist historians for believing that 'economic "phenomena" are "primary"' (Bateson 1972: 64).
2. The Cartesian dichotomy may in fact be more robust than that of nature and culture. Descola has argued that his concepts of 'interiority' and 'physicality', corresponding to Husserl's 'intentionality' and 'body', 'are not Western constructs generated by the marriage of Greek philosophy with Christian theology and subsequently raised under the rigorous ferule of a long line of Cartesian tutors. According to developmental psychology,

the awareness of this duality is probably innate and specific to the human species, a point confirmed by ethnographic and historical accounts' (Descola 2006: 139).
3. 'L'ethnographie de l'Amérique indigène est peuplée de ces références à une théorie cosmopolitique qui décrit un univers habité per divers types d'actants ou d'agents subjectifs, humains et non humains – les dieux, les animaux, les morts, les plantes, les phénomènes météorologiques, très souvent les objets et les artefacts aussi –, tous munis d'un même ensemble général de dispositions perceptives, appétitives et cognitives, autrement dit, d'une "âme" semblable. Cet ressemblance inclut un même mode, pour ainsi dire performatif, d'aperception: les animaux et les autres non-humains pourvus d'âme "se voient comme des personnes" et donc, ils "sont des personnes", c'est-à-dire: des objets intentionnels ou à deux faces (visible et invisibles), constitués par des relations sociales et existant sous le double modes pronominal du réflexif et du réciproque, c'est-à-dire du collectif'. All translations by Marc Brightman.
4. However we are aware of the danger of essentialising the nature of human–animal relations in 'the West', which are highly complex and diverse, and the subject of sophisticated analyses in their own right (see, e.g., Haraway 2007).
5. 'Ce que ces personnes voient, cependant – et donc ce qu'elles sont en tant que personnes – constitue précisément le problème philosophique posé par et pour la pensée indigène'.
6. 'se estruturam em termos de idiomas simbólicos que ... não dizem respeito à definição de grupos e à transmissão de bens, mas à construção de pessoas e à fabricação de corpos'.
7. 'Não se trata de uma oposição entre o homem e o animal realizada longe do corpo e ao longo de categorias individualizantes, onde o natural e o social se auto-repelem por definição, mas de uma dialética onde os elementos naturais são domesticados pelo grupo e os elementos do grupo (as coisas sociais) são naturalizados no mundo dos animais. O corpo é a grande arena onde essas transformações são possíveis, como faz prova toda a mitologia sul-americana que deve, agora, ser relida como histórias com um centro: a idéia fundamental de corporalidade'.
8. See Hallowell (1926), Lévi-Strauss (1964, 1966, 1968, 1971, 1975, 1985a, 1991), Irimoto and Yamada (1997), Sullivan (1988) and Laugrand and Oosten (2007).
9. 'Shaman' is a Tungus word for a person chosen and trained to work for the community by engaging with significant other-than-human persons (Vitebsky 1995; Harvey 2003). On the Jesup Expedition, see Boas (1905), and for monographs, see Jochelson (1908, 1926) and Bogoras (1909, 1910). In addition, see Shternberg (1925, 1933, 1936).
10. Meletinsky's book was first published in Russian as *Poetika Mifa* (1976), and later in English translation (Meletinsky 1998).
11. See Gow (2001) for a criticism of similar readings of the relationship between myth and history in Lévi-Strauss's *Mythologiques*.
12. Meletinsky's historicism could also conceivably have been a reaction against the lack of historicism (in a conventional sense) of Lévi-Strauss's *Mythologiques*, in which there is less emphasis on dynamic processes than in the later 'petites mythologiques' (Lévi-Strauss 1975, 1985a, 1991). We are grateful to Katherine Swancutt for suggesting this point.
13. 'Une économie de la *corporalité* au coeur même des ontologies qui venaient d'être redéfinies ... comme *animistes* (par Descola)'.
14. 'une anthropologie indigène formulée en termes de flux organiques et de codages matériels, de multiplicités sensibles et de devenirs-animaux, plutôt qu'exprimée dans les termes spectraux de notre propre anthropologie que la grisaille juridico-théologique (songeons aux droits et aux devoirs, aux catégories et aux "personnes morales" qui façonnent notre discipline) accable par comparaison. Ensuite, il permettait d'entrevoir

certaines des implications théoriques de ce statut non marqué ou générique de la dimension virtuelle (l'"âme") des existants, prémisse capitale d'une puissante structure intellectuelle indigène, capable, *inter alia*, de contre-décrire se propre image dessinée par l'anthropologie occidentale, et, par là, "nous renvoyer de nous-même une image où nous ne nous reconnaissons pas"'.

15. 'En s'appuyant explicitement sut les *Mythologiques*, ce travail s'est développé sans aucune connexion avec le thème de l'*embodiment*, qui prendrait l'anthropologie d'assaut dans les décennies suivantes. Le courant structuraliste de l'ethnologie amérindienne, sourd à l'appel "pieux et sensuel à la fois" du Carnisme phénoménologique (Deleuze et Guattari 1991: 169) – "à l'appel du bois pourri", dirait un lecteur de *Le cru et le cuit* – a toujours pensé l'incarnation du point de vue du Triangle culinaire plutôt de celui de la sainte Trinité'.

16. 'La hiérarchie des objets animés et inanimés … s'appuie sur la variation dans les modes de communication qu'autorise l'appréhension de qualités sensibles inégalement distribuées. Dans la mesure où la catégorie des "personnes" englobe des esprits, des plantes et des animaux, tous dotés d'un âme, cette cosmologie ne discrimine pas entre les humains et les non-humains; elle introduit seulement une échelle d'ordre selon les niveaux d'échange d'information réputés faisables'.

17. 'avec le divorce entre morts et animaux, les premiers restent humains, ou deviennent même des surhumains, et les seconds commencent à cesser de l'être, en dérivant vers une sous- ou une anti-humanité'.

18. 'Je suggère qu'en Amazonie indigène l'exopraxis est antérieur – logiquement, chronologiquement, et cosmologiquement – à l'endopraxis, et qu'elle reste toujours opérationnelle, même dans ces formations plus hiérarchiques telles que celles du Nord-Ouest amazonien, à la manière d'un résidu qui bloque la constitution de chefferies ou d'États pourvus d'une intériorité métaphysique achevée'.

19. Descola's totemism is more narrowly defined than that of Lévi-Strauss. As Viveiros de Castro has pointed out, Descola divides Lévi-Strauss's totemism into two sub-types: 'totemism *sensu* Descola' and 'analogism' (Viveiros de Castro 2009: 50).

20. 'Ni animisme – qui affirmerait une ressemblence substantielle ou analogique entre animaux et humains –, ni totémisme – qui affirmerait une ressemblance formelle ou homologique entre différences intrahumaines et différences inter-animales –, le perspectivisme affirme une différence intensive qui porte la différence humain/non-humain à l'intérieur de chaque existant'. Elsewhere, Viveiros de Castro distinguishes perspectivism from animism by saying that for the former all creatures are human (i.e., they share a human subjectivity), whereas for the latter, they all have spirit (Stzutman 2008: 6). For a measured and more sustained criticism of Descola's approach as an amplification in 'extension' of Lévi-Strauss's structuralism, in contrast to his own perspectivism as an interpretation in 'intensity' of the same, see Viveiros de Castro (2009: 47–51).

References

Århem, K. 1996. 'The Cosmic Food Web: Human–Nature Relatedness in the Northwest Amazon', in P. Descola and G. Pálsson (eds), *Nature and Society: Anthropological Perspectives*. London: Routledge, pp. 185–204.

Bateson, G. 1972. 'Culture Contact and Schismogenesis', in *Steps to an Ecology of Mind*. New York: Ballantine, pp. 201–27.

Benson, E. (ed.) 1972. *The Cult of the Feline*. Washington, DC: Dumbarton Oaks Research Library and Collection.

Bird-David, N. 1999. '"Animism" Revisited: Personhood, Environment and Relational Epistemology', *Current Anthropology* 40: 67–91.
Boas, F. 1905. 'The Jesup North Pacific Expedition', in *Proceedings of the 13th International Congress of Americanists*. New York, pp. 91–100.
Bogoras, W. 1909. *The Chukchee. Jesup North Pacific Expedition, Memoirs of the American Museum of Natural History, vol. 7*. New York: G.E. Sterchert.
——— 1910. Chukchee Mythology. In *Jesup North Pacific Expedition*, Vol. 8, Part 1. Leiden & New-York: American Museum of Natural History, pp. 1–197.
——— 1931. 'Klassovoje rassloenie u chukoch-olenevodov', *Sovetskaya Etnographija* 1–2: 93–116.
Boyer, P. 2003. 'Religious Thought and Behaviour as By-products of Brain Function', *Trends in Cognitive Sciences* 7: 119–24.
Brightman, M. 2007. 'Amerindian Leadership in Guianese Amazonia', Ph.D. thesis. Cambridge: Cambridge University.
——— 2010. 'Creativity and Control: Property in Guianese Amazonia', *Journal de la Société des Américanistes* 96(1): 135–68.
Brightman, R. 1993. *Grateful Prey: Rock Cree Human–animal relationships*. Berkeley: University of California Press.
Carneiro da Cunha, M. 1978. *Os mortos e os outros: uma análise do sistema funerário e da noção da pessoa entre os Índios Krahó*. São Paolo: Hucitec.
Carrithers, M., S. Collins and S. Lukes (eds). 1985. *The Category of the Person: Anthropology, Philosophy, History*. Cambridge: Cambridge University Press.
Cavalli-Sforza, L., A. Piazza, P. Menozzi and J. Mountain. 1988. 'Reconstruction of Human Evolution: Bringing together Genetic, Archeological, and Linguistic Data', *Proceedings of the National Academy of Sciences* 85(16): 6002–6.
Césard, N., J. Deturche and P. Erikson. 2003. 'Les insectes dans les pratiques médicinales et rituelles en Amazonie indigène', in E. Motte-Florac and J. Thomas (eds), *Les Insectes dans la tradition orale/Insects in Oral Literature and Traditions*. Paris: Peeters, pp. 395–406.
Chapuis, J., and H. Rivière. 2003. *Wayana eitoponpë: (Une) histoire (orale) des Indiens Wayana*. Paris: Ibis Rouge.
Chaumeil, B., and J.-P. Chaumeil. 1992. 'L'oncle et le neveu: la parenté du vivant chez les Yagua (Amazonie péruvienne)', *Journal de la Société des Américanistes* 78(2): 25–37.
Clastres, P. 1974. *La société contre l'Etat*. Paris: Minuit.
Conklin, B. 1996. 'Reflections on Amazonian Anthropologies of the Body', *Medical Anthropology Quarterly* 10: 373–75.
Costa, L. 2007. 'As faces do jaguar: parentesco, história e mitologia entre os Kanamari da Amazônia Ocidental', Ph.D. thesis. Rio e Janeiro: PPGAS-Museu Nacional, Universidade Federal do Rio de Janeiro.
Crocker, J.C. 1985. *Vital Souls: Bororo Cosmology, Natural Symbolism, and Shamanism*. Tucson: University of Arizona Press.
Deleuze, G., and F. Guattari. 1991. *Qu'est-ce que la philosophie?* Paris: Minuit.
De Sales, A. 1980. 'Deux conceptions de l'alliance à travers la fête de l'ours en Sibérie', *Etudes mongoles et sibériennes* 11: 147–213.
Descola, P. 1986. *La Nature domestique: symbolisme et praxis dans l'écologie des Achuar*. Paris: Maison des Sciences de l'Homme.
——— 1992. 'Societies of Nature and the Nature of Society', in A. Kuper (ed.) *Conceptualizing Society*. London: Routledge, pp. 107–26.

――― 1996. 'Constructing Natures: Symbolic Ecology and Social Practice', in P. Descola and G. Pálsson (eds), *Nature and Society: Anthropological Perspectives*. London: Routledge, pp. 82–102.
――― 2005. *Par-delà nature et culture*. Paris: Gallimard.
――― 2006. 'Beyond Nature and Culture', *Proceedings of the British Academy* 139: 137–55.
Engels, F. 1970[1884]. *The Origin of the Family, Private Property, and the State*. New York: International Publishers.
Erikson, P. 2000. 'The Social Significance of Pet-keeping among Amazonian Indians', in A. Podberscek, E. Paul and J. Serpell (eds), *Companion Animals and Us: Exploring the Relationships between People and Pets*. Cambridge: Cambridge University Press, pp. 7–26.
Fausto, C. 2007. 'Feasting on People: Eating Animals and Humans in Amazonia', *Current Anthropology* 48(4): 497–530.
Fienup-Riordan, A. 1990. 'Original Ecologists? The Relationship between Yup'ik Eskimos and Animals', in *Eskimo Essays: Yup'ik Eskimos and How We See Them*. New Brunswick, NJ: Rutgers University Press, pp. 138–57.
――― 1994. *Boundaries and Passages: Rule and Ritual in Yup'ik Eskimo Oral Tradition*. Norman: University of Oklahoma Press.
Fock, N. 1963. *Waiwai: Religion and Society of an Amazonian Tribe*. Copenhagen: National Museum.
Fortes, M. 1987[1973]. 'On the Concept of the Person among the Tallensi', in *Religion, Morality and the Person: Essays on Tallensi Religion*, ed. J. Goody. Cambridge: Cambridge University Press, pp. 247–86.
Fortescue, M. 1998. *Language Relations across the Bering Strait: Reappraising Archaeological and Linguistic Evidence*. London: Cassell.
Freed, S., R. Freed and L. Williamson. 1988. 'Capitalist Philanthropy and Russian Revolutionaries: The Jesup North Pacific Expedition (1897–1902)', *American Anthropologist* 90(1): 7–24.
Gagen-Torn, N.I. 1992. *Soprotivlenie v Gulage: Vospominanija. Pis'ma. Dokumenty*. Moscow: Vozvrashenije.
――― 1994. *Memoria*. Moscow: Vozvrashenije.
García Hierro, P., and A. Surrallès. 2005. 'Introduction', in A. Surrallès and P. García Hierro (eds), *The Land Within: Indigenous Territory and the Perception of the Environment*. Copenhagen: IWGIA, pp. 8–21.
Gell, A. 1998. *Art and Agency: An Anthropological Theory*. Oxford: Clarendon.
Gow, P. 2001. *An Amazonian Myth and Its History*. Oxford: Oxford University Press.
Gregor, T., and D. Tuzin (eds). 2001. *Gender in Amazonia and Melanesia: An Exploration of the Comparative Method*. Berkeley: University of California Press.
Gutierrez Choquevilca, A.-L. 2008. 'Note sur le rôle de l'imaginaire acoustique dans l'apprentissage d'une ontologie animiste chez les Quechua d'Amazonie péruvienne (Pastaza)', unpublished paper presented at the Musée du Quai Branly, 10 June.
Hallowell, A.I. 1926. 'Bear Ceremonialism in the Northern Hemisphere', *American Anthropologist* 28: 1–175.
――― 1960. 'Ojibwa Ontology, Behavior, and World View', in S. Diamond (ed.), *Culture in History: Essays in Honor of Paul Radin*. New York: Octagon Books, pp. 19–52.
Hamayon, R. 1990. *La Chasse à l'âme: esquisse d'une théorie du chamanisme sibérien*. Nanterre: Société d'Ethnologie.
――― 1994. 'Shamanism: A Religion of Nature?' in T. Irimoto and T. Yamada (eds), *Circumpolar Religion and Ecology: An Anthropology of the North*. Tokyo: University of Tokyo Press, pp. 109–23.

───── 2003. 'Game and Games, Fortune and Dualism in Siberian Shamanism', in G. Harvey (ed.), *Shamanism: A Reader*. London: Routledge, pp. 63–68.

Haraway, D. 2007. 'Cyborgs to Companion Species: Reconfiguring Kinship in Technoscience', in L. Kalif and A. Fitzgerald (eds), *The Animals Reader*. Oxford: Berg, pp. 362–74.

Harvey, G. 2003. *Shamanism: A Reader*. London: Routledge.

Hegel, G.W.F. 1956. *The Philosophy of History*. New York: Dover Publications.

Henare, A., M. Holbraad and S. Wastell (eds). 2007. *Thinking Through Things: Theorising Artefacts Ethnographically*. New York: Routledge.

Henriksen, G. 2010. *Hunters in the Barrens: The Naskapi on the Edge of the White Man's World*. Oxford: Berghahn.

Hill, J. 1984. 'Social Equality and Ritual Hierarchy: The Arawakan Wakuenai of Venezuela', *American Ethnologist* 11(3): 528–44.

Holbraad, M., and R. Willerslev. 2007. 'Transcendental Perspectivism: Anonymous Viewpoints From Inner Asia', *Inner Asia* 9(2): 329–45.

Hugh-Jones, S. 1994. 'Shamans, Prophets, Priests, and Pastors', in N. Thomas and C. Humphrey (eds), *Shamanism, History, and the State*. Ann Arbor: University of Michigan Press, pp. 32–75.

Hultkrantz, A. 1999. 'The Specific Character of North American Shamanism', *European Review of Native American Studies* 13(2): 1–10.

Ingold, T. 1990. 'Society, Nature and the Concept of Technology', *Archaeological Review from Cambridge* 9(1): 5–17.

───── 2000. *The Perception of the Environment: Essays on Livelihood, Dwelling and Skill*. London: Routledge.

Irimoto, T., and T. Yamada (eds). 1997. *Circumpolar Animism and Shamanism*. Sapporo: Hokkaido University Press.

Jochelson, W. 1908. *The Koryak*. New York: American Museum of Natural History.

───── 1926. *The Yukaghir and the Yukaghized Tungus*. New York: American Museum of Natural History.

Kelly Luciani, J. 2003. 'Relations within the Health System among the Yanomami in the Upper Orinoco, Venezuela', Ph.D. thesis. Cambridge: Cambridge University.

Kohn, E. 2007. 'How Dogs Dream: Amazonian Natures and the Politics of Trans-species Engagement', *American Ethnologist* 31(1): 3–24.

Krupnik, I., and W. Fitzhugh. 2001. *Gateways: Exploring the Legacy of the Jesup North Pacific Expedition, 1897–1902*. Washington, DC: Arctic Studies Centre, National Museum of Natural History, Smithsonian Institution.

Kwon, H. 1999. 'Play the Bear: Myth and Ritual in East Siberia', *History of Religions* 38(4): 373–87.

Lagrou, E. 2000. 'Homesickness and the Cashinahua Self: A Reflection on the Embodied Condition of Relatedness', in J. Overing and A. Passes (eds), *The Anthropology of Love and Anger: The Aesthetics of Conviviality in Native Amazonia*. London: Routledge, pp. 152–69.

Lambert, J.-L. 2002/2003. 'Essai sur le chamanisme nganassane (Arctique sibérien)', *Etudes mongoles et sibériennes*: 33/34: 563–65.

Lanoue, G. 1998. 'Preface to the Russian Edition', in E. Meletinsky, *The Poetics of Myth*. New York: Garland Publishing, pp. vii–xvi.

Latour, B. 1997. *Nous n'avons jamais été modernes: essai d'anthropologie symétrique*. Paris: La Découverte.

───── 1999. *Politiques de la nature: comment faire entrer les sciences en démocratie?* Paris: La Découverte.

―――― 2009. 'Will Non-humans Be Saved? An Argument in Ecotheology', *Journal of the Royal Anthropological Institute* 15(3): 459–75.
Laugrand, F., and J. Oosten (eds). 2007. *La Nature des esprits dans les cosmologies autochtones*. Montréal: Presses de l'Université Laval.
Leach, E. 2000[1977]. 'Anthropos', in S. Hugh-Jones and J. Laidlaw (eds), *The Essential Edmund Leach*. New Haven, CT: Yale University Press, pp. 324–80.
Lenaerts, M. 2006. 'Substances, Relationships and the Omnipresence of the Body: An Overview of Ashéninka Ethnomedicine (Western Amazonia)' *Journal of Ethnobiology and Ethnomedicine* 2(49). Retrieved 16 February 2011 from: http://www.ethnobiomed.com/content/2/1/49.
Lévi-Strauss, C. 1958. *Anthropologie structurale*. Paris: Plon.
―――― 1962a. *Le Totémisme aujourd'hui*. Paris: Presses Universitaires de France.
―――― 1962b. *La Pensée sauvage*. Paris: Plon.
―――― 1964. *Le Cru et le cuit*. Paris: Plon.
―――― 1966. *Du miel aux cendres*. Paris: Plon.
―――― 1968. *L'Origine des manières de table*. Paris: Plon.
―――― 1969. *The Elementary Structures of Kinship*, rev. edn. Boston: Beacon Press.
―――― 1971. *L'Homme nu*. Paris: Plon.
―――― 1975. *La Voie des masques*. Geneva: Skira.
―――― 1983. *Strukturnaya antropologiya*. Moscow: Nauka.
―――― 1985a. *La Potière jalouse*. Paris: Plon.
―――― 1985b. 'Kak Umirayut Mify', in *Zarubezhnyie Issledovania po Semiotike Folklora*. Moscow: Nauka, pp. 77–88.
―――― 1991. *Histoire de lynx*. Paris: Plon.
―――― 1994a[1983] 'Totemizm Segodnya', in *Pervobytnoye Myshlenije*. Moscow: Respublika, pp. 37–111.
―――― 1994b[1983]. 'Nepriruchennaya Mysl', in *Pervobytnoye Myshlenije*. Moscow: Respublika, pp. 111–337.
Lima, T.S. 1999. 'The Two and Its Many: Reflections on Perspectivism in a Tupi Cosmology', *Ethnos* 64(1): 107–31.
Mauss, M. 1985. 'A Category of the Human Mind: The Notion of Person; the Notion of Self', in M. Carrithers, S. Collins and S. Lukes (eds), *The Category of the Person: Anthropology, Philosophy, History*. Cambridge: Cambridge University Press, pp. 1–25.
Meletinsky, E. 1963. *Proiskhozhdeni'e Geoiricheskogo Eposa: Rannt'e Formy i Arkhaicheski'e Pamyatniki*. Moscow: Izdatel'stvo Vostochnoi Literatury.
―――― 1973. Typological Analysis of the Paleo-Asiatic Raven Myths, in *Acta Ethnographica Academiae Scientiarum Hungaricae*, Vol. XXII pp. 107 – 155
―――― 1981. Paleo-aziatsky epos o vorone i problema otnosheniy Severo-Vostochnoi Aziyi i Severo-Zapadnoi Ameriki v oblasti pholklora, in *Traditzyonnyie kul'tury Severnoi Sibiri i Severnoi Ameriki*. Moscow: Nauka, pp. 182– 200.
―――― 1998. *The Poetics of Myth*. New York: Garland Publishing.
Miller, J. 2009. 'Things as Persons: Body Ornaments and Alterity among the Mamaindê (Nambikwara)', in F. Santos Granero (ed.), *The Occult Life of Things: Native Amazonian Theories of Materiality and Personhood*. Tucson: University of Arizona Press, pp. 69–97.
Pedersen, M. 2001. 'Totemism, Animism and North Asian Indigenous Ontologies', *Journal of the Royal Anthropological institute* 7(3): 411–27.
Pedersen, M., R. Empson and C. Humphrey (eds). 2007. 'Perspectivism', *Inner Asia*, special issue 9(2).

Platenkamp, J. 2007. 'Spirit Representations in Southeast Asia: A Comparative View', in F. Laugrand and J. Oosten (eds), *La nature des esprits dans les cosmologies autochtones*. Montréal: Presses de l'Université Laval, pp. 99–129.
Propp,V. 1946. *Istoricheskye Korni Volshebnoi Skazki*. Leningrad: Izdetsl'stvo Leningradskogo Universiteta.
—— 1969. *Morphologiya Skazki*. Moscow: Nauka.
Rival, L. 2005. 'Soul, Body and Gender among the Huaorani of Amazonian Ecuador', *Ethnos* 70(3): 285-310.
Rivière, P. 1993. 'The Amerindianization of Descent and Affinity', *L'Homme* 126–128: 507–16.
—— 1994. 'WYSINWYG in Amazonia', *Journal of the Anthropological Society of Oxford* 25(3): 255–62.
—— 1999. 'Shamanism and the Unconfined Soul', in M. James and C. Crabbe (eds), *From Soul to Self*. London: Routledge, pp. 70-88.
Santos-Granero, F. (ed.) 2009. *The Occult Life of Things: Native Amazonian Theories of Materiality and Personhood*. Tucson: University of Arizona Press.
Scott, C. 1989. 'Knowledge Construction among Cree Hunters: Metaphors and Literal Understanding', *Journal de la Société des Américanistes* 75: 193–208.
Seeger, A. 1981. *Nature and Society in Central Brazil: The Suyá Indians of Mato Grosso*. Cambridge, MA: Harvard University Press.
Seeger, A., R. Da Matta and E. Viveiros de Castro. 1979. 'A construção da pessoa nas sociedades indígenas brasileiras', *Boletim do Museu Nacional* 32: 2–19.
Shternberg, L.Y. 1925. *Kul't Orla u Sibirskikh Narodov*. Leningrad: Nauka.
—— 1933. *Gilyaki, Orochi, Gol'dy, Negidal'tsy, Ainy*. Khabarovsk: Khabarosvkoije Knizhnoije Izdatel'stvo.
—— 1936. *Pervobytnaija Religija v Svete Etnographii*. Moscow: Nauka.
Slezkine, Y. 1991. 'The Fall of Soviet Ethnography, 1928–38', *Current Anthropology* 32(4): 476–84.
—— 1992. 'From Savages to Citizens: The Cultural Revolution in the Soviet Far North, 1928–1938', *Slavic Review* 51(1): 52–76.
Smolyak, A.V. 1966. *Ulchi*. Moscow: Nauka.
—— 1974. 'Novyie Dannije po Animizmy i Shamanizmy u Nanaitsev', *Sovetskaya Entsiklopedija* 2: 106–13.
Spiro, M. 2006. 'Postmodernist Anthropology, Subjectivity and Science: A Modernist Critique', in H. Moore and T. Sanders (eds), *Anthropology in Theory: Issues in Epistemology*. Oxford: Blackwell, pp. 523–37.
Ssorin-Chaikov, N. 2003. *The Social Life of the State in Subarctic Siberia*. Stanford, CA: Stanford University Press.
Stzutman, R. (ed.) 2008. *Encontros: Eduardo Viveiros de Castro*. Rio de Janeiro: Azougue.
Sullivan, L. 1988. *Icanchu's Drum: An Orientation to Meaning in South American Religions*. London: Macmillan.
Tanner, A. 1979. *Bringing Home Animals: Religious Ideology and Mode of Production of the Mistassini Cree Hunters*. London: Hurst.
Taylor, A.-C. 1996. 'The Soul's Body and Its States: An Amazonian Perspective on the Nature of Being Human', *Journal of the Royal Anthropological Institute* 2(2): 201–215.
Turner, T. 2009. 'O corpo além do corpo: dimensões fisiológicas, sociais e cosmológicas da corporalidade em uma sociedade indígena amazónica', unpublished paper delivered at the

conference 'Corpos Nativos: Perspectivas Comparativas', 4th Congress of the Portuguese Anthopological Association, 11 September.

Tylor, E.B. 1913[1871]. *Primitive Culture: Researches into the Development of Mythology, Philosophy, Religion, Language, Art and Custom.* London: John Murray.

United Nations. 2007. 'United Nations Declaration on the Rights of Indigenous Peoples', UN General Assembly A/61/L.67. Geneva: United Nations.

Van Velthem, L. 2001. 'The Woven Universe: Carib Basketry', in C. McEwan, C. Barreto and C. Neves (eds), *Unknown Amazon: Culture in Nature in Ancient Brazil.* London: British Museum Press, pp. 198–213.

——— 2003. *O belo e a fera: a estética da produção e da predação entre os Wayana.* Lisbon: Assírio and Alvim

Vasilevich, G.M. 1936. *Materialy po Evenkiyskomy (Tungusskomy) Folklory.* Leningrad: Nauka.

——— 1957. *Drevnije Okhotnichji i Olenevodcheskije Obryady Evenkov,* Tome 17. Leningrad: Museum of Anthropology and Ethnography of AN SSSR.

——— 1969. *Evenki: Istoriko-Etnographitecheskiye Ocherki (XVIII- Nachala XX vv.).* Leningrad: Nauka.

Vilaça, A. 1992. *Comendo como gente: formas do canibalismo wari.* Rio de Janeiro: Editora Da Universidade Federal do Rio de Janeiro.

——— 2000. 'Making Kin Out of Others in Amazonia', *Journal of the Royal Anthropological Institute* 8(2): 347–65.

——— 2005. 'Chronically Unstable Bodies: Reflections on Amazonian Corporalities', *Journal of the Royal Anthropological Institute* 11: 445–64.

Vitebsky, P. 1995. *Shaman.* London: Duncan Baird Publishers.

Viveiros de Castro, E. 1992. *From the Enemy's Point of View: Humanity and Divinity in An Amazonian Society.* Chicago: University of Chicago Press.

——— 1998. 'Cosmological Deixis and Amerindian Perspectivism', *Journal of the Royal Anthropological Institute* 4: 469–85.

——— 2004. 'Exchanging Perspectives: The Transformation of Objects into Subjects in Amerindian Ontologies', *Common Knowledge* 10(3): 463–84.

——— 2007. 'La forêt des mirroirs: quelques notes sur l'ontologie des esprits amazoniens', in F. Laugrand and J. Oosten (eds), *La Nature des esprits dans les cosmologies autochtones.* Montréal: Presses de l'Université Laval, pp. 45–74.

——— 2009. *Métaphysiques cannibales.* Paris: Presses Universitaires de France.

Willerslev, R. 2006. 'Theory of Conceptive Economy: Reversibility among the Siberian Yukaghir', unpublished paper delivered at 'The "Frontier" in Amazonia and Siberia: Extractive Economies, Indigenous Politics and Social Transformations', Scott Polar Research Institute, Cambridge University, 26 June.

——— 2007. *Soul Hunters: Hunting, Animism, and Personhood among the Siberian Yukaghirs.* Berkeley: University of California Press.

——— 2009. 'The Optimal Sacrifice: A Study of Voluntary Death among the Siberian Chukchi', *American Ethnologist* 36(4): 693–704.

Yvinec, C. 2005. 'Que disent les tapirs? De la communication avec les non-humains en Amazonie', *Journal de la Société des Américanistes* 91(1): 41–70.

Znamenski, A. 2003. *Shamanism in Siberia: Russian Records of Siberian Spirituality.* Dordrecht: Kluwer/Springer.

Chapter 1
Too Many Owners: Mastery and Ownership in Amazonia

Carlos Fausto

This chapter discusses an indigenous Amazonian category – usually translated as 'owner' or 'master' – which far transcends a simple expression of a relation of ownership, authority or domination.[1] The category and its reciprocal terms designate a widespread mode of relationship that applies to humans, non-humans and things. I argue here that it comprises a key category for our comprehension of indigenous socio-cosmologies, despite receiving relatively little consideration thus far. Three decades ago, Seeger called our attention to this disregard: 'The concept of the owner-controller permeates Suyá society, even though there is relatively little property in the material sense of the word … it is a fallacy of ethnocentrism to maintain that ownership and property are unimportant' (Seeger 1981: 181–82).

The reason for this omission is the widespread view of the South American lowlands as a realm of equality and symmetry, in contrast to Andean hierarchy and asymmetry. This horizontal conception of social relations – conceived either as socio-political equality or symmetrical reciprocity – has marked the literature from the early chroniclers to modern ethnology. The notion of owner fits uncomfortably into this socio-political imagery, not only because of the asymmetry of the relation that defines it, but also because of its potential evocation of private property. Consequently, the mastery relation has ended up consigned to ethnographic footnotes, or reduced to a simple ontological category.

This article aims to show that, on the contrary, mastery is as central to understanding indigenous socio-cosmologies as affinity. Here I return to a problem that I first attempted to examine via the notion of 'familiarising predation' – a schema through which predatory relations are converted into asymmetric relations of control and protection, conceptualised as a form of adoption (Fausto 1997). Here I propose imagining the Amerindian world as a world of owners and the owner as a model of the magnified person (Strathern 1991).

The Owner-master Category

All Amazonian languages possess a term that designates a position involving control and/or protection, engendering and/or possession, and that applies to relations between persons (human or non-human) and between persons and things (tangible or intangible). This term is highly productive and applies to a wide spectrum of semantic fields.

Seeger writes that for the Suyá: 'most things have owner-controllers: villages, ceremonies, songs, houses, gardens, belongings, pets and so forth. The importance of *kande* is pervasive' (Seeger 1981: 182). The term *kande* ('owner-controller') not only refers to the possession of tangible and intangible wealth (such as ritual knowledge) but also to the potential ability to produce it. It also forms expressions designating social functions endowed with prestige and political power. Seeger states that *kande* is 'the most important concept in Suyá thinking about power' (ibid.: 181).

The category is also central in the Upper Xingu multilingual system. Viveiros de Castro claims that it constitutes 'a fundamental notion of Xinguano culture', applicable to a wide range of contexts, its concrete model being paternity (Viveiros de Castro 2002: 82–83). Among the Kuikuro, a Carib people of the region, the category *oto* applies to a large semantic field, taking the paternal/maternal bond as its main schema: parents are 'our owners' (*kukoto*) because they care for us and feed us. The owners of collective structures (the ritual path, the men's house, the central plaza and the village itself) mobilise communal work and feed the people who help them to take care of their 'things'. The owner-master category also applies to the depositaries of intangible knowledge, and characterises the relation between a ritual sponsor and his festival.[2]

Among Tupi-Guarani peoples, the vernacular terms for the category 'owner' are cognates of **jar*. The Araweté *ñã* connotes ideas such as 'leadership, control, representation, responsibility, and ownership of some resource or domain' (Viveiros de Castro 1992: 345). Among the Parakanã, the most common reciprocal term of *-jara* is 'pet', and the concrete schema for the ownership relation is familiarisation of the young of animal prey (Fausto 2001a: 347–48). This is also true for other Tupi-Guarani peoples, such as the Wayãpi, for whom 'all jar have "their young", which they treat like *eima*, or wild pets' (Gallois 1988: 98).

Panoan languages employ very similar cognates to designate the owner-master. In Sharanahua, *ifo* refers to the genitor in relation to his children, the chief in relation to his people, the owner in relation to the objects in his[3] possession, and the owner in relation to domestic animals. The term *ifo* connotes authority, genesis and feeding (Déléage 2005: 189–91). *Ifo* also designates a particular type of entity: the masters of animals and plants with whom shamans interact.

This category of owner-master is widespread in the region and corresponds to what Hultkrantz (1961) termed 'the supernatural owners of nature'.[4] Until recently, ethnology limited itself to these figures when speaking of owners or masters, depicting them as hyperboles of the species they represent or the anthropomorphic form through which they appear to shamans. These figures need to be reinserted in the overall set of ownership relations, since, as Cesarino notes in relation to another Panoan people, the masters of animals 'replicate the same configuration that characterises the Marubo maloca owners (*shovō ivo*): both are chiefs of their houses, in which they live with their families and have their own ways of being' (Cesarino 2008: 25). The animal masters are owners in their own environment, containing a species-collectivity within themselves.

Among the Katukina-speaking Kanamari, recursivity is the main trait of the category *warah-*, meaning owner, chief, body, trunk and main river. Costa emphasises its intrinsic relationality: 'a person is always a "chief/body/owner" in relation to something, someone or some people' (Costa 2007: 63). *Warah* expresses a relation of container-contained, singularity-plurality, such that 'the name of a person followed by *–warah* designates not only that person's body, but also, in the case of chiefs, all those people who call that person "my body-owner" ("my chief"), along with all the belongings of the person whose name forms the noun phrase "X-*warah*"' (Costa 2010: 172). This structure is replicated at different scales: between the soul and its body, between a people and their chief, between the village chief and the chief of a hydrographic network, and so forth.[5]

What general features of the owner-master category can we extract from these examples? First of all, we need to shift our emphasis from the entity to the relation it implies (Déléage 2005: 191). The owner-master reciprocal category is usually 'child' or 'pet animal', both implying the idea of adoption. The prototypical relation of mastery-ownership is adoptive filiation, a relation that is not given but constituted through a dynamic I have called familiarising predation. Such a dynamic accounts for relations as diverse as those between the shaman and auxiliary spirits, the warrior and the captive child, the killer and the victim's spirit, or the ritual officiant and ceremonial objects (Fausto 1999). Combining the findings of my earlier works with the examples given above, we can infer that the mastery-ownership relation has the following characteristics:

1. It frequently applies to the possession of certain material items (mainly ceremonial objects) and immaterial items (especially ritual knowledge);
2. It does not always designate the parent–child relation, although it almost always applies to the relation between parents and adoptive children, in particular war captives;
3. It never applies to autonomous living enemy persons, but it may designate the relation between the killer and their victim after the killing;
4. It never applies, either, to game animals, although it designates the relation to pets and, very frequently, to the shaman's relation to auxiliary spirits;
5. It often applies to the relation between chiefs and their followers and, as we shall see later, was used to designate new relations in the context of conquest and colonisation;
6. It does not apply solely to relations between humans (or humans and non-humans), but also designates relations internal to the non-human world.

An important feature of this relation is its asymmetry: owners control and protect their creatures, being responsible for their well-being, reproduction and mobility. This asymmetry implies not only control but care. Hence, the master of animals among the Chimane is defined as *chojca-csi-ty*, 'the one who watches over them ..., who cares for them'(Daillant 2003: 317). From the perspective of whoever is captured-adopted, being or placing oneself in the position of an orphan or a wild pet is more than just a negative injunction: it may also be a positive way of eliciting attention and generosity. The asymmetry of the ownership relation is often conceived as a form of encompassment, expressed as a relation between container and contained. For example, the masters of animals usually keep their 'children' in an enclosure, releasing them slowly to be hunted by humans (ibid.: 303). An Arara shaman once explained to Teixeira-Pinto that the owners of animal species keep their 'creatures' in a box, like the cupboards used by whites (Teixeira-Pinto 1997: 97).

Shamans also store their auxiliary spirits in containers. Some keep them inside baskets and feed them with tobacco; others insert them into their own body in the form of resins or stones. The Wayãpi *ōpi-wan* caterpillars, who are the shaman's auxiliary spirits, are contained within his body, wrapped in tiny slings, just as the shaman himself is wrapped in the webs linking him to the masters of animals (Gallois 1996: 46–47). This is likewise the case of the Kanamari *dyohko*, solidified bits of plant resin that are kept by shamans within their own bodies, but may also be placed in baskets to be thrown as magic darts or to wander in the forest in the form of jaguars (Costa 2007: 381–83). The topology is always complex since the shaman's auxiliaries appear, simultaneously, as internal and external parts of the owner-master, as if his body was a Klein bottle.

This topology involves an interplay between singularity and multiplicity: the owner is a plural singularity, containing other singularities within himself as a body (Costa 2007) or a maloca (Cesarino 2008). The owner-master is the form through which a plurality appears as a singularity to others. That is why a chief is an owner. When speaking in the central plaza, the Kuikuro chief refers to all the inhabitants of his village, irrespective of sex or age, as his children. All other distinctions are obviated for him to appear as an inclusive singularity, a magnified person (Heckenberger 2005: 259–63). The chief-form – the body, the bow in the hand, the speech commemorating the unique history of the Kuikuro people (Franchetto 1993) – appears to the eyes of the messengers from other villages as a people, an *otomo* (the collectivised form of the term 'owner'). In this sense, rather than being a representative – that is, someone occupying the place of another – the master-chief is the form through which a collectivity is constituted as an image: it comprises the form in which a singularity is presented to others.[6]

As a singular image of a collectivity, the master-chief-form also applies to the owners of animals. The prototypical example is the master of peccaries, who contains a collectivity conceived as his children or pets. For the master to appear as a magnified singularity, the band must appear as an anonymous collectivity without its own agency. This is why I have argued that the master represents the jaguar-part, while the band represents the game-part, the passive aspect of the peccaries (Fausto 2007: 509). In Amazonia, every magnified singularity appears to the eyes of others as a predator, usually as a jaguar, anaconda or harpy eagle.

The owner is, then, a double-sided figure: in the eyes of his children-pets, a protective father; in the eyes of other species (especially humans), a predatory affine.[7] Jaguarness is one of the traits associated with the figure of the master in Amazonia. Even the mild-tempered Upper Xingu chief covers himself in parts of a jaguar body when he ritually greets dignitaries from other villages: a belt and hat made from the animal's pelt, a necklace made from its claws. In a sense, every master is a jaguar. It is easy to understand why: the main device for producing encompassment and hence for magnifying the person is cannibal incorporation. Predation is an asymmetric vector of identification-alteration: by eating, one contains the other and its alterity within oneself.

Possessive (In)dividualism

The absence of private ownership over important material resources has blocked our conceptual imagination of ownership relations in Amazonia, as though their sole model was exclusively private property in goods, corresponding to a consumerist and expansive *conatus*. In the Amerindian case, the possession of objects must be seen as a particular case of the ownership relation between subjects, and the thing-artefact as a particular case of the person-artefact. As Sztutman writes, mastery is 'a cosmological notion that is reflected on the socio-political plane, referring in very general terms to this capacity to "contain" – to appropriate or dispose of – persons, things and properties, and to constitute domains, niches and groups' (Sztutman 2005: 261).

If Amerindian ownership relations are not to be confused with our conception of property relations, how should we compare them? How do we speak of owners and ownership without reviving the spectre of possessive individualism that so much of contemporary anthropology strives to exorcise? I lack the space here for an exhaustive comparison, so I shall concentrate instead on an emblematic author: John Locke.[8]

I begin with the double problem confronted by Locke in his refutation of absolutism and patriarchalism in *Two Treatises of Government* (1689): on one hand, he looked to lay the foundations for individual freedom and the limits of government; on the other, he sought to base private property on natural law, despite positing an originary state in which the world was given in common to all. Locke located the solution to both problems in the concept of self-ownership, the originary and exclusive relation of a person to his own self, which simultaneously founds both freedom and property: 'Though the Earth, and all inferior Creatures be common to all Men, yet every Man has a *Property* in his own *Person*. This no Body has any Right to but himself' (Locke 1988: 287).

If self-ownership makes despotism and slavery contrary to natural law, how do we pass from this self-relation to the relation between persons and things? How are legitimate claims established between a subject and an object to the exclusion of other subjects? For Locke, the extension of self-ownership to things is achieved through labour. Objects are 'contaminated' by the action of the body, an action that belongs to the agent and that removes things from their natural state and annexes them to the self as its exclusive property. This reasoning, known as the labour-mixing argument, implies that labour is mixed with things, adding to them something that belongs to the subject of the action (ibid.: 288).

Such a theory of ownership presupposes a theory of personal identity that accounts for the person's persistence across time and space. Locke founds personal identity on the continuity of consciousness, on the subject's reflexive relation with himself. A person is a 'thinking intelligent being, that has reason and reflection, and can consider itself as itself, the same thinking thing, in different times and places' (Locke 1995: 246). Here sameness and selfhood merge, since both depend on a relation to self, a self-identity. *Mêmeté et ipseité*, to use Ricoeur's vocabulary (Ricoeur 1990), become indissociable in the construction of the person. The self must be identical to itself in order for it to become the object of a judgment: without identity the pairing of moral responsibility and legal accountability cannot be constructed; without reducing difference to zero, sociability cannot be founded on appropriative individuals who are free because they own themselves.

Locke's theory of property activates a series of cosmological and anthropological premises. We have a divinity who fabricates a world peopled by subjects (human beings) and useful things (animals, plants, land) given in common to humanity. These subjects have two main attributes: firstly, a self-identity that is maintained over time and makes their acts accountable (to God and to Men); secondly, they are owners (the cause) of their acts by being owners of their own body, which is the means by which these acts have efficacy on the world. Actions on the world – conceptualised under the category of labour – lead to the appropriation of useful things, meaning that what was given in common becomes individuated and owned by some to the exclusion of others. In social life, this process leads to a distinction between owners and non-owners where the former, through their ownership of things that are added to their own body, acquire a surplus of agency. The owner becomes the model of the agent and appropriated goods are transformed into indices of the person's capacity for agency.

How would an indigenous narrative compare with this Lockean account of the constitution of the person and society, of freedom and obligation? Were we to narrate it in an Amerindian key, what kind of world would emerge?

A World of Owners

In the beginning, the world was not given by a divinity to all humans in common for them to appropriate it. The ontology of mythic time does not establish two major classes of beings: autonomous subjects (self-owners), and appropriable things (potential property). No given separation exists between subjects and objects. The mythic world is pervaded by a background of continuous subjectivity, a communicational flux involving all entities. In contrast to the original identity with God-Substance, this state is, as Viveiros de Castro argues, a state of infinite differences characterised by an ontological regime of metamorphosis (Viveiros de Castro 1998: 41).

In this primordial state, difference is presupposed, though not yet posed, since what myth narrates is precisely the positing of difference – that is, the production of discontinuities between species, between human collectivities, between sky and earth, day and night – differences that, combined, will constitute the world as we know it. It is the owners-to-be, beings with creative and transformative capacities, that will engender-fabricate the post-mythic world through their actions and their lapses.

> The First People lived just as shamans do today, in a polymorphous state in which no boundaries yet existed. It was the time of origins … when Heaven and Earth were still connected and the distinctions between species not yet recognised. Only when these divisions solidified did the First People finally remove themselves from Earth, leaving their forms behind as reminders of what this Dream Time had been like. After their withdrawal from the Earth, each of the First People became the 'Master' or *arache* of the species they engendered. (Guss 1989: 52)

Not only are 'natural' attributes defined in this process of speciation, but so too are the 'cultural' attributes of each species, which often results from a transfer of ownership. Indigenous etiological myths narrate not so much a genesis as the way in which attributes that typify human sociality are appropriated from animals.[9] The world that emerges from this initial dynamic is comprised of multiple domains, so much so that one of the premises informing human action over what we call the 'natural world' is, precisely, that everything has or can have an owner. As Descola (1986) has shown, nature is domestic because it is always the *domus* of someone. For the Achuar, the forest is the plantation of Shakaim, wild animals are the young kin of the mothers of the game, and cultivated plants are cared for by Nunkui, the spirit-woman who gave rise to cultigens. The non-human world does not belong to everyone, nor is it no one's land. As the Kuikuro would say, the world is not *tatutolo engü*, 'everyone's thing', which would be the same as saying 'there's nobody to care for it'.

If this is a world of owners, what kind of domains do they own? Referring to the Guarani-Kaiowá, Mura suggests: 'From the viewpoint of the tradition of indigenous knowledge, it is impossible to imagine the existence of places, paths, living beings and inanimate beings as neutral, autonomous and owner-less. All the elements composing the current Cosmos possess owners, constituting domains and reflecting an extremely significant logic in the Universe's hierarchisation' (Mura 2006: 234–35).

The world consists of different domains pertaining to humans and non-humans, each with its own masters. In order to live, humans infringe on their limits. The

Miraña, for example, conceive the forest to be the domain of the animal masters, who 'reign there in the same way that the human maloca masters reign over their people' (Karadimas 2005: 342). Human intrusions into this space 'are perceived as bellicose acts against animals, undertaken in an identical fashion to the war expeditions of the past' (ibid.: 344). Even the production of certain artefacts can be dangerous. Before Yekuana men can take the canes used to make their famous bicolour flat baskets, they must ask a shaman to negotiate with Yododai – the master who plants the canes and protects them (Guss 1989: 106–7).

Everything in principle has or may have an owner: the forest, animals, rivers and lakes, but also an animal species, another plant species or a particular stand of bamboo, a curve of the river, a certain tree, a particular mountain. Claiming that the current cosmos is structured by ownership relations, however, does not mean conceiving it to be organised exhaustively into discrete spaces (territories and jurisdictions), as though resulting from a series of enclosure acts decreed at the end of mythic time. The passage from the continuous to the discrete, described in Amerindian mythology, implies the constitution of a world traversed by ownership relations, but not a cosmic cartography of finite and exclusive properties. These ownership relations are multiple and potentially infinite. Neither are they given once and for all: they have a post-mythic dynamic in which beings and things can appropriate or become appropriated, inserting themselves within a new ownership relation: objects are fabricated, children are engendered, capacities are acquired, animals are captured, enemies are killed, spirits are familiarised, human collectivities are conquered.

This dynamic operates in the macro-relations between collectivities and in the micro-production of the person, which is constituted and deconstituted continually by appropriating others and being appropriated in turn. This person is not a unitary self-identical self. It does not suffice to say, though, that it is a 'distributed' or 'relational' person. Locke's theory of personal identity is not based on a self-enclosed individual in contrast to the relational person of Amazonia, Melanesia or wherever. As Balibar points out, Locke takes identity to be a relation, which implies 'that it presupposes difference, or that it is … a certain way of dealing with difference … by reducing it to zero' (Balibar 1998: 247). Locke's model implies a distributed person (Gell 1998) insofar as property-objects are indices of agency. The Lockean proprietor is a magnified person to the extent that, thanks to a relation to himself, the world can be appropriated. The own-self (guaranteed by self-consciousness) and ownership (based on the private property of the body) lead to appropriation, which magnifies persons by extending them to things and annexing things to persons.

The crucial distinction in terms of Amazonian indigenous peoples is the fact that, here, the founding relation is not self-identity: the Self and the Same do not merge in the construction of the Amerindian person. The multiplicity and fractal nature of ownership relations imply internally composite subjects, 'self-different' persons (Viveiros de Castro 2002: 377). The model of the agent is not that of the owner who annexes things to an immutable self, but the master who contains multiple singularities. While both the Lockean and Amerindian models are appropriative, the risk of the former is, as Kant would say, the 'a-social sociability' (Kant 1985: 15) of possessive individualism, while the risk of the latter is the cannibal sociality of possessive singularity. The mechanisms for limiting appropriation also differ: on one hand, the moral responsibility of the forensic person; on the other, the sociality of kinship and the body of kin.

Magnification and Power

Just as the spectre of private property has blocked our conceptual imagination of ownership relations, so our capacity to think of power in the South American lowlands has been obscured by the state model and the focus on coercion. It is as though we were forced to choose between an anti-state model (negatively obsessed with the state) and a model of teleological centralisation (positively obsessed with the state). We need to construct an ethnographically informed language to conceptualise asymmetric relations in the region without dissolving them into a swamp of symmetry, or transforming them into seeds containing the protoplasm of a state apparatus.[10]

As an alternative, I suggest mastery as a relational schema for producing magnified persons that contains the mechanisms both for generating potency and for undermining power. In the micro-analysis of this relation, it is crucial to identify the mechanisms for constituting and deconstituting relations that imply control. This is a fundamental step if we are to escape Clastres' essentialist language, in particular his metaphysics of primitive society qua the absolute.[11]

The term control is open to misunderstanding. Control devices are an obsession in our mechanical, psychic and social engineering: our relations are pervaded by an 'imperative of control'. As Strathern suggests, notions of control and property are strongly associated in Euro-American thought: 'This notion of control implies something like an exercise of proprietorship, either over attributes "belonging" to one self or else over attributes "belonging" to others and yielded by them. The concept already prejudges the manner in which persons impinge upon one another' (Strathern 1988: 141).

If indigenous ownership relations do not demand this same normative imagery of social control, nor its complementary notion of deviance, this should not prevent us from investigating, in each ethnographic context, how persons impinge upon one another. The verb 'impinge' means to 'to go against', 'to impose', whose participle is 'impact'. We can ask then: what impact do masters have?

If the classical Weberian definition of power as 'the possibility of imposing one's own will within a social relation despite any resistance' (Weber 1984: 43) fails to apply adequately to the Amerindian context, this stems more from the notion of 'own will' than 'imposing'. Magnified persons are constituted by incorporating relationships with alien-subjects endowed with other-wills. The master's potency is the capacity to extract an action from his wild pet. This is coercion, as Strathern (1988: 272) would say. But here we find an ambivalence, since it is impossible to know who caused the action and who is acting. Who is the agent of the Araweté warrior's song, the killer or his victim (Viveiros de Castro 1992: 241–45)? Who is the Parakanã curer, the dreamer or the dreamt enemy (Fausto 2001a: 357–69)?

This paradoxical image, in which antagonistic elements are condensed and appear to be simultaneously singular and multiple, is the very source of the ritual efficacy of these figures (Severi 2007). In Amazonia, this efficacy suffers from a constitutive instability, since we can never know who adopted whom and who controls whom: to be powerful, shamans and warriors must ensure that the subjectivity of their wild pets is preserved, which means that they can never become entirely tamed (Fausto 1999: 949). This explains the ambivalence of shamans and warriors, forever on the verge of adopting the perspective of the others contained within themselves.

The alteration induced by mastery (the fact that the master is inevitably 'affected' by his wild pet) combines with the multiple relations contained within a magnified person, which produces the latter's relational dispersion. As Rodgers states, 'the shaman is a multiple being, a micro-population of shamanic agencies sheltering within a body: hence neither are his "intentions" exclusively "his," nor can he ever be certain of his own intentions' (Rodgers 2002: 121). This plurality also characterises the killer, who contains relations with human-others (his victims), but also with non-humans, since his predatory potency must be fabricated before the homicidal act through a process of 'jaguarisation'.[12]

The fact that the plural and altering nature of Amazonian mastery produces an instability in the ownership relation helps explain why it has rarely crystallised into an institutional locus of power. The very constitution of these functions seems to contain the means for undermining them, since potency depends on an uncertain relation with other subjects who are never entirely loyal. It would be a mistake, though, to ignore the fact that there were (and still are) institutionalised forms of chiefdom in the region. The question resides in knowing how the centrifugal tendencies of the mastery relation can be blocked, turning them into a mechanism for concentrating and localising power.

My suspicion is that this happened where a limit was posed to the multiplicative and other-oriented logic of warfare and shamanism. Indigenous warfare involves an almost unlimited expansion of the number of killers and vital attributes that can be obtained and transmitted by warriors (Fausto 2001a: 305–6, 330–31). This amplification is linked to the low hierarchisation of men in terms of warfare exploits, since warfare, rather than ranking men according to their predatory power, focuses on multiplying the regenerative capacities to be captured. Significantly the highest crystallisation of power is found where this logic is curtailed, turning a mechanism of dispersion into a mechanism of concentration.[13]

Similar processes may well have occurred in the transition from shamanic systems to temple-priest systems, a transition in which the emergence of vertical shamanism, associated with ancestrality, was perhaps an intermediary phase (Hugh-Jones 1994; Viveiros de Castro 2002: 471–72). If so, spatial territorialisation (the temple) and temporal territorialisation (ancestrality) would have corresponded to the conversion of multiple ownership relations into a pyramidal system of domination. This hypothesis helps us to conceptualise the past existence of predatory mega-machines in the Americas – state theocracies that conserved the cannibal principle as a constitutive element of power, subsuming ancestrality and predation within a single hierarchical structure.

Masters in History

The mastery relation served Amerindians as a way of thinking about and acting within the asymmetries that have marked colonial and postcolonial history, especially in their interactions with missionaries, slave raiders, rubber bosses and government agents. Initially, the mastery relation served as a pivot connecting indigenous war captivity with the colonial slavery system, just as it would later serve in the debt-peonage relations of the rubber economy (Karadimas 2001; Santos-Granero 2005). It articulated a system focused on extracting the regenerative capacities of persons with another one focused on extracting labour to produce goods. The hierarchical structure of mastery with its double face (predation and protection) also made thinkable the structures of colonial power, especially in the context of mission settlements and, later, the tutelary apparatus of nation-states.

Contemporary ethnographic literature presents us with many instances in which relationships with whites are assimilated to a master–pet relation.[14] The Arawá-speaking Paumari tried to control the whites' predatory potential by granting them the dominant position in such a relational scheme. They designate all whites *Jara*, a term borrowed from the Amazonian *língua geral*, meaning 'owner-master'.[15] Such a strategy contains a lure, since it is a way of eliciting the action corresponding to the owner position (Bonilla 2005: 58). The masters live in a world of abundance, and people expect that if they do not behave as predators they will behave as providers. However, whites do sometimes act as predators, capturing children's souls (just like any other non-human master), thus obliging shamans to work to recuperate them.

Mastery relations tend to traverse different socio-cosmic domains, never being circumscribed to a single visible socio-political arena. That is why the historical relations of work and dependency on white people also inflect indigenous shamanic concepts. In the words of a Paumari shaman: 'The shaman is the father of the *itavari* [auxiliary spirit]. He's like a governor. Whatever the shaman tells him, he must do and obey, like an employee' (Bonilla 2007: 355).

This resonance between historical relations of power and exploitation and indigenous cosmology is also found among the Ávila Runa of Ecuador (Kohn 2002, 2007). Here the animal masters express different figures of authority from the precolonial, colonial and postcolonial past. The world in which they live is described as an urban network with its own hierarchy: the main owners live in a kind of 'Quito in the forest,' located within the Sumaco volcano, linked by roads to other smaller towns where less important owners live. Another image employed to describe this world is that of the haciendas of the rubber era with their bosses and their domestic animals kept in corrals. Both towns and haciendas are imagined as places of abundance in which the most powerful masters walk around with jaguars by their side like pet dogs (Kohn 2007: 109–20).[16]

Mastery was not only productive in terms of conceptualising and acting upon the asymmetries between Amerindians and whites, or humans and non-humans. It was also an important mechanism structuring hierarchical relations between different indigenous groups, a fact we can still observe today in some regional systems. This appears to be the case of the asymmetric relation between the Maku and the dominant Tukanoan and Arawakan peoples on the Upper Rio Negro (Ramos, Silverwood-Cope and Oliveira 1980), as well as between the Guaná 'serfs' (Terena and Kinikinau) and the Mbayá-Guaykuru (Kadiwéu), historical evidence of which dates back to Ulrich Schmidel's voyage in the first half of the sixteenth century (Cardoso de Oliveira 1976: 31–32).

From this same period comes the first information on the Chiriguano, a people formed by the asymmetric fusion of the Guarani and the Arawak-speaking Chané. In the sixteenth century, the Chané were cannibalised and incorporated into a subordinate position, being defined as 'slaves' (*tapii*) to the Guarani, called reciprocally their 'masters' (*iya*) (Combès and Lowrey 2006: 692).[17] From the nineteenth century onwards, the Izoceños, a people of Chané descent, began to reverse this asymmetry, proclaiming themselves Iyambae: 'those-without-masters' (Combès and Villar 2004). This term, initially used as a surname by a dynasty of Izoceños chiefs, has today been converted into a new ethnic marker, providing the name for a territory called the 'land without owner' (*Ivi Iyambae*) and a foundation by the same name. Despite its evocative flavour, which serves Izoceños goals well among outsiders, one should not readily conflate this designation with the society-against-the-state and the land-without-evil scenarios. By calling themselves 'without owner', Izoceños are both refusing the condition of *tapii*, and postulating the status of magnified people for themselves (Combès and Lowrey 2006: 700–1), making a new turn within the mastery relation.

Conclusion

I would like to conclude this chapter by evincing the gist of my argument on mastery in Amazonia. The very first paragraph of this text may have already betrayed my intentions to certain readers. It paraphrases a passage from Lévi-Strauss's essay 'The Social Use of Kinship Terms among Brazilian Indians' (Lévi-Strauss 1943), which inaugurated a whole literature on the brother-in-law relationship (Coelho de Souza and Fausto 2004). In my view, mastery operates as a 'cosmological operator' in tandem with symmetric affinity (Viveiros de Castro 1993, 2001). If Amazonian socio-cosmologies posit an 'affinity without affines' (intensive and potential), they also posit a cosmopolitical and interspecific filiation (a metafiliation) in which adoption is the crucial element. I hope to have given enough evidence of this fact in the pages above. A question remains, though: Could we say the same of other relational modalities, like asymmetric affinity (the father-in-law/son-in-law relationship) or symmetric consanguinity (siblinghood)?

In Amazonia, siblinghood, particularly same-sex, is often taken to be the core of identity and limited to the sociological domain. There is no meta-siblinghood as found in India (Jamous 1991) or universal brotherhood of the Christian kind.[18] Whenever siblinghood emerges as a socio-cosmic idiom, an asymmetry based on birth order must be introduced. This is the case of the twin sagas analysed by Lévi-Strauss (1991), as well as the myths on the origin of the difference between Amerindians and white people, equated with an inversion of seniority between brothers (D'Abbeville 1975[1614]: 251–52; Hugh-Jones 1988: 143–44). Birth order can also serve as a socio-cosmic ruler for marking hierarchical differences between segments of the same people, as occurs in the Upper Rio Negro system, or between siblings descending from chiefs, as happens in the Upper Xingu. As an identity relation, however, siblinghood does not constitute a generalised cosmopolitical idiom, despite the fact that the sibling group is a fundamental unit in the structuration of intra-village political dynamics.

The father-in-law/son-in-law relation lies at the opposite pole to siblinghood. It is constituted on two superimposed differences: that between wife-givers and wife-takers, and between generations. The relation is overly potent and veers towards figures of power and cannibal voracity. Not by chance, the two preeminent images of this relation are the overworked son-in-law and the jaguar father-in-law.[19] As Turner (1979) and Rivière (1984) show, this is the only kinship relation that involves the substitution of one person's work by another, a fact that derives from marriage itself. According to them, this relation is a mechanism for controlling persons with repercussions on the formation of leaders and on the autonomy of adult men in general. Even though important variations exist in terms of its structural effects, if ethnologists had to identify one kinship relation involving authority and control in Amazonia, nine out of ten specialists would pick the relation between father-in-law and son-in-law. However, it does not provide a general idiom for schematising relations as diverse as those between shamans and auxiliary spirits, warriors and victims, captors and captives, masters and pets – despite the fact that the son-in-law's position in an uxorilocal regime is frequently compared to that of a captive enemy or a pet animal. The difference between a master and a father-in-law is that the former is always double-sided (a voracious jaguar for others and a protective fathers for their own) whereas the latter tends to be all too jaguar. Taken together, thus, neither symmetric consanguinity nor asymmetric affinity reach the level of generality of symmetric affinity and asymmetric consanguinity. They occupy the polar positions of identity and difference, tending to slip either into the sterile fixity of the same or into the uncontrollable potency of the cannibal.

But what about women? What can we say about maternity and matrimony? Maternity seems to be a particular case of the mastery relation in which the male owner's genitor function is foregrounded and female-gendered. It is notably expressed via entities called mothers of the game animals or plants (especially hallucinogens). These, however, are not as widely distributed as the male-master, nor does motherhood apply to such a number of different relationships as is the case of mastery. Matrimony, in turn, seems to be a more productive relation. In mythology, interspecific marriages are a central mechanism in the passage from one kinship situation to another. In addition, some indigenous peoples conceive the shaman's relation with his auxiliary spirits as a matrimonial bond: shamans constitute spirit families by marrying a spirit and engendering spirit-children. Even in these cases, however, there is, on the one hand, an emphasis on paternity (a man begins his shamanic life as a husband and ends up as a father, a bond conceived to be more stable and secure); and, on the other, a relative de-emphasis of affinity (D'Anglure and Morin 1998: 67; Fausto 2001b; Daillant 2003: 313, 325; Miller 2007: 200). It is as though matrimony itself converged towards adoption rather than alliance, in contrast to Siberian hunting shamanism (Hamayon 1990).

In sum, none of the relations analysed above have the same degree of generality as symmetric affinity and asymmetric consanguinity. The first combines difference and symmetry; the second, identity and asymmetry. The overlapping of new differences (of gender or generation) is limited in terms of both ethnic and spatial distribution, as well as socio-cosmic domains. Meta-affinity and meta-filiation are both elective, dispensing with any other prior relation: one can be an enemy/brother-in-law of anyone, just as one can adopt any enemy one wishes. We are not talking about just any adoptive filiation, though, or just any brother-in-law relation. The latter, in its intensive modality (potential affinity), is a figure of enmity, while the former is a figure of ownership, of the asymmetric relation between the owner-master and his children-pets. This form of socio-cosmic adoption is, so to speak, an incomplete filiation. It does not produce full identity but an ambivalent relation in which the substrate of enmity is obviated, yet not neutralised. The master's double face is matched by the pet's wildness: the latter is an 'other' and will never cease to be so entirely.[20]

To conclude, let me paraphrase once more Claude Lévi-Strauss (1943: 409) to whom I dedicate this text, by stating that a sufficient number of convergent indications have been recorded so that we may consider the outstanding character of the mastery relationship a specific feature of Amerindian socio-cosmology, configuring a world of owners and enemies, but not necessarily one of domination and private ownership.

Translated by David Rodgers

Notes

1. This chapter is a revised version of 'Donos demais: maestria e domínio na Amazônia', *Mana* 14/2 (2008), pp. 329–66. I thank the editors for the opportunity of organising ideas that have been buzzing round my head for many years. I am also grateful for the

comments of Aparecida Vilaça, Cesar Gordon, Federico Neiburg, Luiz Costa, Marina Velasco, Marnio Teixeira-Pinto and Marc Brightman.
2. Among another Carib people, the Trio, we find the cognate *entu*, which 'carries the sense of both "owner" and "boss"', and applies to 'temporary controlled possession' (Brightman 2007: 83). According to Brightman, this is the key idiom of leadership and political organisation. *Entu* also means 'tree trunk' and 'foothill,' whose connotation of 'to be the base of' reappears in other ethnographic contexts.
3. The 'owner' is almost always gendered as male.
4. The author refers to North American peoples, but we can also apply it to Siberian hunters, where these masters are called in Russian *Khoyzayn* (Vitebsky 2005: 262) or *Khoziain* (Willerslev 2007: 42).
5. I employ here the concept of singularity to designate an internally multiple and non-self-identical unity, following its contemporary usage, inspired by Deleuze (1968). Sometimes I also use the composite expression 'plural singularity'. As Viveiros de Castro (2007) points out, in anthropology the concept resonates with the proposals of Strathern (1988, 1992) and Wagner (1991) for redefining the relation between part/whole and particular/collective at different scales (from the micro-constitution of the person to the macro-constitution of the social). Though I cannot develop the point here, it is important to note that the type of sovereignty implied by the Amazonian notion of 'owner' differs from that implied by our own concept of political body; in other words, the chief-owner-body is not a Leviathan.
6. The reification of the chief-form, which makes him the singular image of an owner-master, also makes him something that belongs to the community: 'Persons are owned as things through a political-ritual fabrication that presents the person being claimed by another as singular, entire and *whole*' (Strathern 2005: 120). Entire and whole, but simultaneously singular and plural, since here the individual is not opposed to the collectivity: 'for whether we see a man or a clan is in one sense irrelevant: collective action aggrandises each man's performance but is no different in kind from his own aggrandisement as a single person' (Strathern 1999: 37).
7. See Willerslev on the hunters 'double perspective' among the Siberian Yukaghirs: 'Nested within the hunters' perspective of the animal master-spirits as generous parents … is a sort of counter-perspective, the spirits as predators who seek to trick and kill humans in order to satisfy their selfish love for them' (Willerslev 2007: 4).
8. I focus only on the *Second Treatise of Government* and Chapter 27, Book 2, of *An Essay Concerning Human Understanding*. Locke's work contains another model of the person, described as a passive repository of capacities, that characterises his ideas on education (Tully 1993: 88).
9. Culinary fire is the most famous example: in Tupi-Guarani myths, the theft of the fire owned by vultures makes humans become eaters of cooked meat in opposition to necrophagy; in Gê myths, the theft of fire from jaguars leads to the distinction between a raw (cannibal) diet and cooked food, capable of producing identity between kin (Fausto 2007).
10. See Brightman (2007: 2–4, 236–45) on the shortcomings of political anthropology (particularly with regard to notions of power and hierarchy when applied to Amazonian indigenous peoples), and the need for a new approach to the theme in the region.
11. I am referring here above all to Clastres's *Society Against the State* in which 'primitive society' appears as a kind of Gulag-like nightmare (pictured as a dream) 'from which nothing escapes … since all exits are closed' (Clastres 1978: 147–48).

12. Among the Jívaro, success in warfare depends on the prior encounter with the *arutam*, the image of an ancestor with a jaguar affection, which 'will lodge in the recipient like an internal double' (Taylor 2003: 237).
13. Among some Chacoan peoples, membership of the warrior rank was limited to those who had actually scalped an enemy. The victim could be handed over to a companion, but each trophy corresponded to just one warrior (Clastres 1982: 222). In the Aztec case, with a much more rigid class system, passing on a sacrificial captive to another person was a crime punishable by death (Clendinnen 1991: 116).
14. Elsewhere, I have described how the western Parakanã equated whites with powerful dream enemies, who are conceived as the dreamer's pets (Fausto 2002a, 2002b).
15. Amazonian *língua geral* or *nheengatu* refers to a Tupi-based lingua franca that emerged from the interactions between indigenous peoples, and state and church agents during colonial times. In some cases, it came to replace the language originally spoken by indigenous peoples in the region.
16. The association between dog and jaguar occurred in some parts of the Americas reflecting not only morphological and behavioural similarities, but also the status of dogs as ferocious domesticated animals under the control of an owner. This enabled them to be associated with the (invisible) jaguars familiarised by shamans and warriors.
17. The translation of *tapii* as 'slave' should be considered carefully (Combès 2005: 60–68). Among the coastal Tupi, the term designated non-Tupi peoples but did not indicate a relation of submission, as appears to have happened in the Chiriguano case. For a survey of forms of subordination among Amerindian peoples, see Santos-Granero (2008).
18. In Amazonia, siblinghood only connects wider domains where religious conversions have taken place, especially with regard to forms of evangelism (Vilaça 1996).
19. See, for example, the Yekuana myths in which the son-in-law has to carry out superhuman tasks to avoid being devoured by his cannibalistic father-in-law (Guss 1989: 80, 94).
20. This may explain why captives, orphans and pet animals often receive treatment that veers between care and cruelty.

References

Balibar, E. 1998. 'Introduction: le traité lockien de l'identité' and 'Glossaire', in J. Locke, *Identité et différence: l'invention de la conscience*. Paris: Points, pp. 9–101 and 183–261.
Bonilla, O. 2005. 'O bom patrão e o inimigo voraz: predação e comércio na cosmologia paumari', *Mana* 11(1): 41–66.
——— 2007. 'Des proies si désirables: soumission et prédation pour le Paumari d'Amazonie brésilienne', Ph.D. thesis. Paris: Ecole des Hautes Etudes en Sciences Sociales.
Brightman, M. 2007. 'Amerindian Leadership in Guianese Amazonia', Ph.D. thesis. Cambridge: Cambridge University.
Cardoso de Oliveira, R. 1976. *Do índio ao bugre: o processo de assimilação dos Terêna*. Rio de Janeiro: Livraria F. Alves Editora.
Cesarino, P.N. 2008. 'Oniska: a poética do mundo e da morte entre os Marubo da Amazônia ocidental', Ph.D. thesis. Rio de Janeiro: PPGAS-Museu Nacional, Universidade Federal do Rio de Janeiro.
Clastres, P. 1978. *A sociedade contra o estado*. Rio de Janeiro: Francisco Alves.
——— 1982. *Arqueologia da violência: ensaios de antropologia política*. São Paulo: Brasiliense.

Clendinnen, I. 1991. *Aztecs: An Interpretation*. Cambridge: Cambridge University Press.
Coelho de Souza, M., and C. Fausto. 2004. 'Reconquistando o campo perdido: o que Lévi-Strauss deve aos ameríndios', *Revista de Antropologia* 47(1): 87–131.
Combés, I. 2005. *Etno-historias del Isoso: Chané y Chiriguanos en el Chaco boliviano (siglos XVI a XX)*. La Paz: Fundación PIEB, IFEA.
Combés, I., and K. Lowrey. 2006. 'Slaves without Masters? Arawakan Dynasties among the Chiriguano', *Ethnohistory* 53(4): 689–714.
Combés, I., and D. Villar. 2004. 'Aristocracias chané: "casas" en el Chaco argentino y boliviano', *Journal de la Société des Américanistes* 90(2): 63–102.
Costa, L. 2007. 'As faces do jaguar: parentesco, história e mitologia entre os Kanamari da Amazônia Ocidental', Ph.D. thesis. Rio e Janeiro: PPGAS-Museu Nacional, Universidade Federal do Rio de Janeiro.
——— 2010. 'The Kanamari Body-Owner. Predation and Feeding in Western Amazonia', *Journal de la Société des Américanistes* 96(1): 169–192.
D'Abbeville, C. 1975[1614]. *História da missão dos padres capuchinhos na ilha do Maranhão e terras circunvisinhas*. São Paulo: Itatiaia/Edusp.
Daillant, I. 2003. *Sens dessus dessous: organisation sociale et spatiale des chimane d'Amazonie bolivienne*. Nanterre: Société d'ethnologie.
D'Anglure, B.-S., and F. Morin. 1998. 'Marriage mystique et pouvoir chamanique chez les Shipibo et les Inuit', *Anthropologie et Sociétés* 22(2): 49–74.
Déléage, P. 2005. 'Le chamanisme sharanahua: enquête sur l'apprentissage et l'épistémologie d'un rituel', Ph.D. thesis. Paris: Ecole des Hauts Etudes en Sciences Sociales
Deleuze, G. 1968. *Spinoza et le problème de l'expression*. Paris: Editions de Minuit.
Descola, P. 1986. *La nature domestique: symbolisme et praxis dans l'écologie des Achuar*. Paris: Maison des Sciences de l'Homme.
Fausto, C. 1997. 'A dialética da predação e da familiarização entre os Parakanã da Amazônia oriental: por uma teoria da guerra ameríndia', Ph.D. thesis. Rio de Janeiro: PPGAS-Museu Nacional, UFRJ.
——— 1999. 'Of Enemies and Pets: Warfare and Shamanism in Amazonia', *American Ethnologist* 26(4): 933–56.
——— 2001a. *Inimigos fiéis: história, guerra e xamanismo na Amazônia*. São Paulo: Edusp.
——— 2001b. 'La conversion des ennemis: un rêve amazonien', unpublished paper presented at the École Pratiques des Hautes Études, Paris.
2002a. 'The Bones Affair. Knowledge Practices in Contact Situations Seen from an Amazonian Case', *Journal of the Royal Anthropological Institute* 8(4): 669–90.
——— 2002b. 'Faire le mythe: histoire, récit et transformation en Amazonie', *Journal de la Société des Américanistes* 88: 69–90.
——— 2007. 'Feasting on People: Cannibalism and Commensality in Amazonia', *Current Anthropology* 48(4): 497–530.
Franchetto, B. 1993. 'A celebração da história nos discursos cerimoniais kuikúru (Alto Xingu)', in M. Carneiro da Cunha and E. Viveiros de Castro (eds), *Amazônia: etnologia e história indígena*. São Paulo: Núcleo de História Indígena e do Indigenismo da USP/FAPESP, pp. 95–116.
Gallois, D. 1988. 'O movimento na cosmologia waiãpi: criação, expansão e transformação do mundo', PhD. thesis. São Paulo: Universidade de São Paulo.
——— 1996. 'Xamanismo waiãpi: nos caminhos invisíveis, a relação I-Paie', in J. Langdon (ed.), *Xamanismo no Brasil: novas perspectivas*. Florianópolis: UFSC, pp. 39–74.
Gell, A. 1998. *Art and Agency: An Anthropological Theory*. Oxford: Clarendon Press.

Guss, D. 1989. *To Weave and Sing: Art, Symbol, and Narrative in the South American Rain Forest*. Berkeley: University of California Press.

Hamayon, R. 1990. *La chasse à l'âme*. Paris: Mémoires de la Société d'Ethnologie, Nanterre.

Heckenberger, M. 2005. *The Ecology of Power: Culture, Place, and Personhood in the Southern Amazon, AD 1000–2000*. New York: Routledge.

Hugh-Jones, S. 1988. 'The Gun and the Bow: Myths of White Men and Indians', *L'Homme* 27(2/3): 138–55.

────── 1994. 'Shamans, Prophets, Priests and Pastors', in N. Thomas and C. Humphrey (eds), *Shamanism, History and the State*. Ann Arbor: Michigan University Press, pp. 32–75.

Hultkrantz, A. 1961. 'The Owner of the Animals in the Religion of North American Indians', in A. Hultcrantz (ed.), *The Supernatural Owners of Nature*. Stockholm: Almqvist and Wiksell, pp. 53–64.

Jamous, R. 1991. *La relation frère–sœur: parenté et rites chez les Meo de l'Inde du Nord*. Paris: Editions de l'Ecole des Hautes Etudes en Sciences Sociales.

Kant, I. 1985[1784]. 'Idea for a Universal History from a Cosmopolitan Point of View', in *On History*, 5th edn, trans. L.W. Beck. Indianapolis, IN: Bobbs-Merrill, pp. 11–26.

Karadimas, D. 2001. 'Parenté en esclavage: pratiques matrimoniales et alliances politiques chez les Miraña d'Amazonie colombienne', *Droit et Cultures* 39: 81–100.

────── 2005. *La raison du corps: idéologie du corps et représentations de l'environnement chez les Miraña d'Amazonie colombienne*. Paris: Peeters.

Kohn, E. 2002. 'Natural Engagements and Ecological Aesthetics among the Avila Runa of Amazonian Ecuador', Ph.D. thesis. Madison: University of Wisconsin.

────── 2007. 'Animal Masters and the Ecological Embedding of History among the Ávila Runa of Ecuador', in C. Fausto and M. Heckenberger (eds), *Time and Memory in Indigenous Amazonia: Anthropological Perspectives*. Gainesville: University Press of Florida, pp. 106–29.

Lévi-Strauss, C. 1943. 'The Social Use of Kinship Terms among Brazilian Indians', *American Anthropologist* 45: 398–409.

────── 1964. *Mythologiques: le cru et le cuit*. Paris: Plon.

────── 1991. *Histoire de lynx*. Paris: Plon.

Locke, J. 1988[1689]. *Two Treatises of Government*. Cambridge: Cambridge University Press.

────── 1995[1691]. *An Essay Concerning Human Understanding*. Oxford: Clarendon Press.

Miller, J. 2007. 'As coisas: enfeites corporais e a noção de pessoa entre os Mamaindê (Nambiquara)', Ph.D. thesis. Rio de Janeiro: PPGAS-Museu Nacional, UFRJ.

Mura, F. 2006. 'À procura do "bom viver": território, tradição de conhecimento e ecologia doméstica entre os Kaiowá', Ph.D. thesis. Rio de Janeiro: PPGAS-Museu Nacional, UFRJ.

Ramos, A., P. Silverwood-Cope and A.-G. Oliveira. 1980. 'Patrões e clientes: relações intertribais no Alto Rio Negro', in A. Ramos (ed.), *Hierarquia e simbiose: relações intertribais no Brasil*. São Paulo: Hucitec, pp. 135–82.

Ricoeur, P. 1990. *Soi-même comme un autre*. Paris: Seuil.

Riviére, P. 1984. *Individual and Society in Guiana: A Comparative Study of Amerindian Social Organisation*. Cambridge: Cambridge University Press.

Rodgers, D. 2002. 'A soma anômala: a questão do suplemento no xamanismo e menstruação ikpeng', *Mana* 8(2): 91–125.

Santos-Granero, F. 2005. 'Amerindian Torture Revisited: Rituals of Enslavement and Markers of Servitude in Tropical America', *Tipití* 3(2): 147–74.

────── 2008. *Vital Enemies: Slavery, Predation and the Amerindian Political Economy of Life*. Austin: University of Texas Press.

Seeger, A. 1981. *Nature and Society in Central Brazil: The Suyá Indians of Mato Grosso*. Cambridge, MA: Harvard University Press.
Severi, C. 2007. *Le principe de la chimère: une anthropologie de la mémoire*. Paris: Presses de l'Ecole Normale Supérieure/Musée du Quai Branly.
Strathern, M. 1988. *The Gender of the Gift: Problems with Women and Problems with Society in Melanesia*. Berkeley: University of California Press.
——— 1991. 'One Man and Many Men', in M. Godelier and M. Strathern (eds), *Big Men and Great Men: Personifications of Power in Melanesia*. Cambridge: Cambridge University Press, pp. 197–214.
——— 1992. 'Parts and Wholes: Refiguring Relationships in a Post-plural World', in A. Kuper, (ed.), *Conceptualising Society*. London: Routledge, pp. 75–104.
——— 1999. *Property, Substance and Effect: Anthropological Essays on Persons and Things*. London: Athlone.
——— 2005. *Kinship, Law and the Unexpected: Relatives Are Always a Surprise*. New York: Cambridge University Press.
Sztutman, R. 2005. 'O profeta e o principal: a ação política ameríndia e seus personagens', Ph.D. thesis. São Paulo: Departamento de Antropologia, Universidade de São Paulo.
Taylor, A.-C. 2003. 'Les masques de la mémoire: essai sur la fonction des peintures corporelles jíbaro', *L'Homme* 164: 223–48.
Teixeira-Pinto, M. 1997. *Ieipari: sacrificio e vida social entre os índios Arara (Caribe)*. São Paulo: Editora Hucitec/ANPOCS/Editora UFPR.
Tully, J. 1993. *An Approach to Political Philosophy: Locke in Context*. Cambridge: Cambridge University Press.
Turner, T. 1979. 'The Gê and Bororo Societies as Dialectical Systems: A General Model', in D. Maybury-Lewis (ed.), *Dialectical Societies: The Gê and Bororo of Central Brazil*. Cambridge, MA: Harvard University Press, pp. 145–78.
Vilaça, A. 1996. 'Cristãos sem fé: alguns aspectos da conversão dos Wari (Pakaa Nova)', *Mana* 2(1): 109–37.
Vitebsky, P. 2005. *Reindeer People: Living with Animals and Spirits in Siberia*. Boston: Houghton Mifflin.
Viveiros de Castro, E. 1992. *From the Enemy's Point of View: Humanity and Divinity in an Amazonian Society*. Chicago: University of Chicago Press.
——— 1993. 'Alguns aspectos da afinidade no dravidianato amazônico', in: M. Carneiro da Cunha e E. Viveiros de Castro (eds.), *Amazônia: etnologia e história indígena*. São Paulo: NHII/USP – FAPESP, pp. 149–210.
——— 1998. 'Cosmological Perspectivism in Amazonia and Elsewhere', Simon Bolivar Lectures. Cambridge: Department of Social Anthropology, University of Cambridge.
——— 2001. 'Gut Feelings about Amazonia: Potential Affinity and the Construction of Sociality', in L. Rival and N. Whitehead (eds), *Beyond the Visible and the Material: The Amerindianisation of Society in the Work of Peter Rivière*. Oxford: Oxford University Press, pp. 19–43.
——— 2002. *A inconstância da alma selvagem*. São Paulo: Cosac and Naify.
Wagner, R. 1991. 'The Fractal Person', in M. Godelier and M. Strathern (eds), *Big Men and Great Men: Personifications of Power in Melanesia*. Cambridge: Cambridge University Press, pp. 159–73.
Weber, M. 1984[1922]. *Economia y sociedad: esbozo de sociología comprensiva*. Mexico City: Fondo de Cultura Económica.
Willerslev, R. 2007. *Soul Hunters: Hunting, Animism, and Personhood among the Siberian Yukaghirs*. Berkeley: University of California Press.

Chapter 2
Revisiting the Animism versus Totemism Debate: Fabricating Persons among the Eveny and Chukchi of North-eastern Siberia

Rane Willerslev and Olga Ulturgasheva

This chapter explores hunting and pastoralist ontological models, essential to the construction of human personhood among two Siberian indigenous groups, the Eveny and the Chukchi. Besides speaking distinct languages that belong to totally different language groups, the greatest difference between the two groups rests on their modes of subsistence and the environments they inhabit: whereas the Eveny inhabit forested and mountain regions and live by a combination of small-scale reindeer herding and hunting, the Chukchi inhabit the treeless tundra and live either as large-scale reindeer herders in the interior or as sea-mammal hunters on the Arctic seashore.

Despite these obvious differences in economy and geography, the two groups share many common aspects of cosmology, especially with regard to their ideas about the fabrication of persons. We discuss their concepts of personhood, spiritual beings and their practices of naming children in order to argue that totemism and animism, rather than being understood in terms of an antinomy between two opposed ontological principles, should perhaps better be seen as facets of one and the same mode of being. Thus, we propose refashioning certain influential theoretical ideas about animism and totemism, which have often been discussed in terms of rather fixed typologies, and suggest that in Siberia relations are multifarious and less rigidly defined.

Animistic and Totemic Typologies

The idea of contrasting totemic and animistic systems was first proposed by Philippe Descola (1996: 78–88), who based his argument on ethnographic examples from Amazonian Indian societies.[1] Following the classic study of Claude

Lévi-Strauss (1966), Descola conceived of totemism as a classificatory project that seeks to confer conceptual distinctions on human society on the basis of given discontinuities between species in nature. By contrast, he argued, animism endows natural beings with human dispositions and social attributes to establish relations between human beings and natural species. Thus, Descola proposed that 'in totemic systems non-humans are treated as signs, [while] in animic systems they are treated as the term of a relation' (Descola 1996: 88). Although lately Descola has shifted the emphasis from 'stabilised relational systems' towards ontological realities which are categorised in terms of the variable modalities of the relationships between 'interiority' (mind) and 'physicality' (body) (Descola 2006: 2), here we offer a more radical treatment of two social modalities and view them as co-implicated in and dependent on each other rather than as combinatorial or interacting 'between the two planes' (ibid.: 3).

Tim Ingold (2000a), who has taken inspiration from Descola's earlier model (Descola 1996), has furthered this contrast by drawing on ethnographies from Australian Aborigines and indigenous circumpolar peoples. He proposes that the most fundamental distinction between the two rests on the ways corporeality and vitality are construed. In the totemic ontology of Australian Aborigines, the vital force or the same essence is shared by all beings and is drawn from the features, textures and contours of the land, which, 'in turn, embodies the creative powers of the ancestors' (Ingold 2000a: 113). By contrast, the animist societies of the circumpolar North draw not upon such shared substance or essence of being, but upon the relative positioning of self and other, human and non-human, in social contexts of inter-species dialogue. Of paramount importance to the animist ontology, Ingold claims, is the maintenance of a balance in the exchange of vital energy between the human and non-human worlds. Shape-shifting and 'crossing over' to the other side by shamans on both sides is the paradigmatic animist tool by means of which humans and non-humans secure the continuation of this crucial balance. Such inter-species transformations are entirely alien and also unnecessary in totemic societies for whom, as Ingold suggests, the ancestral world-creation, along with its inherent distinctions, is always already in place and complete. Thus totemism, Ingold ventures to suggest, can only really flourish where social relations as a whole are of a vertical or hierarchical character, marked by an essential asymmetrical relationship to the ancestors as the source of all life. By contrast, the animist ontology is essentially horizontal and egalitarian in its social relationship with other beings.

Recently, Morten Pedersen (2001) has attempted to synthesise the various indigenous ontologies of North Asia by ranging them in terms of the apparent presence of animist versus totemist principles. He proposes that the further north one moves the more animistic in scale indigenous societies become (ibid.: 413). Thus, the purest form of animism is to be found in north-eastern Siberia, among groups such as the Chukchi, Koryak and Yukaghirs, with all that this entails of social relations of an essentially horizontal and analogous character. By contrast, in the southern parts of Siberia and Mongolia, the totemic principle dominates along with its principle of vertical social relations of a homologous character (ibid.: 417). This distinction, Pedersen ventures to suggest, is perhaps most clearly reflected in the types of 'perspectivism' – the notion that beings can take on the viewpoint of others (see Viveiros de Castro 1998) – operating in the two regions:

> As one moves across North Asia, the relative importance of human ancestor spirits and nonhuman animal spirits undergoes an inversion similar to the inversion of the internal hierarchy of animism and totemism that occurs over this region ... while the animist principle dominant in NNA [north North Asia] gives rise to a primary extra-human perspectivism, the totemist principle dominating SNA [south North Asian] ontologies produces a perspectivism primarily concerned with inter-human metamorphosis ... [As such,] the shamans of SNA are much more interested in seeking to take the perspective of past humans (ancestors). (Pedersen 2001: 423–24)

The overarching analytical models of Descola, Ingold and Pedersen are thus based on a principle of mutual exclusion, constructed around a number of interrelated dichotomies. Thus, the dichotomy between animism and totemism has, as we have seen, been arranged next to those between relations versus sign, extra-human versus inter-human perspectivism, egalitarianism versus hierarchy, homologous relations versus analogous relations, and, above all, horizontal versus vertical social relationships. But how valid are these dichotomies really and how robust are the ethnographic assumptions on which they rest? For we may ask: Is it really reasonable to argue that animism and totemism are fundamentally opposed so that the presence of one automatically excludes the other or, at most, limits it to sheer negligibility?

We do not think so. In our view, all three theories underline the over-simplification and danger of assuming the predominance and exclusiveness of one ontological model. Although all three authors claim that their typologies are not absolute and that mixtures of the two exist, none of them actually provides any actual ethnographic examples of such hybrids or how they might possibly work. However, in Siberia, the combination of animistic and totemic features appears to be the rule rather than the exception. In what follows, we give our claim ethnographic substance by turning to our studies of the Eveny and Chukchi. As we shall see, both of these groups are marked by an essentially crossbred or composed ontology that takes on features of both animism and totemism. In fact, we intend to show how each typology is essentially dependent on the other and cannot exist without the other. As such, the essentially dualist typology proposed by the generalising analytic models described above collapses in the face of our Siberian ethnographic data. This makes us question the analytic value of the terms totemism and animism. Perhaps the two should be understood in terms of their complementarity and intersection rather than in terms of binarism. They shadow and shade into each other rather than appear as two opposites of one dichotomy. Our first ethnographic case, which will exemplify this, is the Eveny.

The Eveny

Child, Guardian Reindeer and Name in the Construction of Human Personhood

The small group of Eveny reindeer herders and hunters discussed here is based in the settlement Topolinoye, in the Verkhoyansk mountains in the Sakha Republic of Yakutia. The Eveny (singular Even) belong to the so-called Tungus-speaking group. By virtue of their reindeer-herding activity and nomadic mode of life the Tungus peoples expanded and occupied an enormous area of the mountain and taiga zone of north-east Asia. All of these Tungus groups share similar features, including languages with common roots, a shamanic cultural complex and traditional economies based mostly on reindeer herding and hunting. The Eveny are the most northerly group of Tungus origin, and have close relations with and are influenced by neighbouring Paleo-Asiatic groups, such as the Yukaghir and Chukchi, who occupy the northern part of the Kolyma river basin and northern Kamchatka (Tugolukov 1997: 27; Willerslev 2007, 2009). About half the Eveny population is scattered around the Arctic districts of the Republic of Sakha (Yakutia) and other parts of north-east Siberia.

In this part of the discussion, we focus on the cultural practices of having a guardian reindeer and the naming of children, both of which the Eveny maintain in order to ensure the safe social moulding of a child's personhood.

Within the domain of human spiritual beings there are particular kinds of spirits that are neither incarnated in the body of other animate beings (such as a bear or fox), as in the straightforward model of animism, nor entirely metamorphosed into the immobile features of the landscape, as in the totemic model (Ingold 2000a: 113). Indeed, it seems that the features of the mode in which these ancestral spiritual beings interact with their living kin does not fit a purely vertical or horizontal model. Let us illustrate this.

The ancestral spirits that reside in the landscape affect the well-being of the human collective by controlling the disposition of both domestic and wild animals. Though their influence can be affected by minor sacrifices on the part of humans or by respectful behaviour, the overall assumption is that these spirits will prey on the youngest and the most vulnerable human beings, as the spirits long for the souls of their living kin.[2] For this reason, the ancestor spirits that attack the most vulnerable and inflict misfortune on the living human community are referred to as *magdili* or 'evil spirits'.

One of the most precarious stages in the human life cycle is that of early childhood. Generally, the young child is viewed as fragile and volatile, and thus unable to resist attacks by malevolent spirits. Because of this, the personhood of newly born children is understood as moulded by social relations with various other-than-living agents of both the human and the non-human world. This particular stage in the human life cycle is perceived as the most precarious and is expressed in the concept of an 'open body' (*angati aertang*).[3] The 'open body' is thus an essentially frail body of a newly born child, which requires such means of protection as *khavek*, the guardian reindeer, and a proper name. Owing to its precarious 'openness', the 'child' soul is viewed by non-human spirits as an animal prey to be killed and consumed, and by the spirits of the ancestors as an absent kin who needs to be brought back to the land of the dead. In particular, danger comes from the ancestral spirit whose name was given to the child. The ancestral namesake of the child strives to get hold of the child's 'open body' and continues to do so until the body 'closes' – that is, when it separates from the deceased ancestor. At this stage the child is more its deceased namesake than its own individual being. Hence this asymmetry between the inferior position of the child and the domination of the predatory spirit points to a totemic type of relationship between the living and the dead.

According to Mikhail Neustrojev, an elderly Eveny reindeer herder and hunter, the spirits of the dead are mobile and act as a neighbouring social group that exists in parallel to the ever mobile camp of its living kinsmen. While speaking about the spirits of the dead, he recalled the following situation from his life:

> It was a very cold winter. One night everyone was asleep in the tent but I could not sleep for a long time, and when I was half-asleep I suddenly heard some reindeer sledges arriving in our camp. I heard how people unloaded their things off the sledges and brought them into the tent, which they put up next to us. Then, they suddenly packed and promptly left. I guessed that perhaps it was my uncle who had died not long ago. I was anxious, since I thought that perhaps it was me he was coming to take along. But later on, our youngest son Vas'ka [a two-year-old boy], whom we adopted after his parents had died, fell ill with severe pneumonia. We couldn't save him and due to a heavy snowstorm the helicopter was incapable of reaching our camp. He died that winter. They [the spirits] called for him (*Nongartan arittaen*).

This story illustrates the outcome of the contact between living humans and the ancestral predatory spirits who caused the death of Mikhail's adopted son and took him away from his living family. According to Mikhail, the boy was not strong enough to resist their 'calling' as his body was still 'open', and it was his adopted son's namesake, grandfather Vasily, who took his grandson away to the land of the dead. So it was the spirit of the deceased that caused the boy's illness and blocked any help among the living humans, including the arrival of a helicopter. In this case, we observe a key relationship of non-reciprocity and asymmetry between the living and the dead – a relationship in which the latter holds a critical position of domination and control. This dangerous relation of predatory asymmetry comes to the forefront as the dead affect the child's body and cause his deadly illness.

If we were to follow the animist typology proposed by Pedersen (2001: 414), the relation should be of an analogous character. However, contrary to this model, the predatory relation described is not aimed at a horizontal exchange of bodies, since the dead person, who holds the more powerful position of the two interlocutors, comes to take control over the child's body. The child's state of having an 'open body' is dangerous as it has not yet reached the firmness and stability of a 'closed body' (*dakhupti artaeng*) and this allows for the spirit's non-reciprocal act of predation.

Having a 'closed' body is crucial as it serves as a protective shield against dangerous contact with the spirit world. The 'closing' ensures that the spirits cannot enter the person's body. The 'closing' or sealing of the child's body is not achieved immediately and is done in the course of one's lifetime by protective means, most notably one's individual name and the help of a guardian reindeer. Let us consider the latter first.

The Eveny distinguish wild (*buyun*) and domesticated reindeer (*oron*). One type of reindeer belonging to the *oron* category is termed *khavek*, which means 'double soul', and it serves to guard a young child (Ulturgasheva 2008). The *khavek* may stand in for the young child with its 'open' and vulnerable body, and take his or her place when the child is attacked by malevolent spirits. Since a newborn's body does not fully belong to the human world or to the animal world, but shares a vital relationship with both, it may be identified as being betwixt and between. The guardian reindeer disguises the child's human identity in the eyes of the spirits, which may take it for a reindeer. In a story told by an old Eveny woman in Topolinoye, a reindeer carrying a human baby on its back lagged behind the caravan and got lost. In order to save the baby, the reindeer brought it to one of the most dangerous ancestral spirits, the owner of the mountain, and asked the spirit to raise the baby as its offspring. The spirit took the child to be a reindeer and thus raised it as its domesticated reindeer. After a year, the reindeer took the child back to its real human parents.

In our understanding, this story emphasises the following social aspects of a reindeer: first, the reindeer's protective agency and its ability to negotiate and find a path between non-human and human domains; second, a conceptual equivalence of child and reindeer – that is, their mutual reversibility. While, the child-reindeer story fits Pedersen's analytic model of 'animist analogous identification' (Pedersen 2001: 416) and Descola's proposition that non-humans are treated in animist systems in terms of a 'social relation' (Descola 1996: 88), we need to keep in mind that human individuality begins in a fundamentally asymmetrical relation with the spirits of the dead as 'open body', which in the process of growing up becomes symmetrical and 'closed'. In this sense, the starting point for the human–spirit relation is not simply symmetry and analogous identification but is intersected by a basic principle of vertical social relations of an essentially homologous character. In this sense, it could be deemed totemic rather than animistic.

On a certain level, Alfred Gell's notion of distributed personhood (Gell 1998) may be used as a possible interpretation of the Eveny concept of child-reindeer: a child is viewed as an extension of a domestic reindeer and vice versa. In the human world it is essentially shape, or more accurately appearance, that differentiates them, but in the animal-spirit world child and reindeer are viewed as two parts of one whole – that is, a child's personhood. This may also go together with Pedersen's observation, which points to the logic of endless substitution common throughout North Asian communities, namely that 'every element can be interchanged with another' (Pedersen 2001: 416; see also Willerslev 2007: 25). However, what we shall see in the case of the child's first hunt and the child and ancestor-spirit relationship is that human and non-human components not only substitute for each other but also move within the spectrum of relations from hierarchical predation to horizontal exchange and between the symmetry of human and non-human components and their asymmetry.

If we follow Ingold's theory of pastoralist societies (Ingold 2000b), Eveny society might be classified as pastoralist. However, the concept of a 'guardian' reindeer may not easily fit this argument due to its emphasis on the protective agency of a reindeer. The ethnographic details presented above may put in doubt Ingold's argument about all pastoralist societies. He argues that the human protection of cattle common to pastoralist societies points to the mode of domination in which human control over domestic animals turns the latter into 'inanimate and insentient beings' (ibid.: 73). Although Ingold does not explicitly state this, he implies that the element of human control over animals removes the power of intentionality from reindeer, and thus ascribes this mode of human–reindeer relationship to totemism. According to this argument, the human–reindeer component should instantiate totemic operation and metaphorical assimilation. This proposition may work well for the part of the world where Ingold conducted fieldwork, but our ethnographic data from Topolinoye portray reindeer as sentient and agentive beings. In addition, the agency of guardian reindeer among the Eveny of Sebyan has been eloquently emphasised by Piers Vitebsky in his discussion of *kujjai*. He writes: 'Only a reindeer could sacrifice itself knowingly and intentionally … Beyond allowing itself to be harnessed, ridden, or eaten, this was surely the deepest expression of the contract that was proposed to us by the first pair of reindeer: to stand for a human, and to die in the human's place, of its own free will' (Vitebsky 2005: 279).

This implies that the element of a domesticated reindeer involved in the constitution of human personhood reproduces a type of human–animal relationship which might be characterised as animistic. Moreover, the concept of 'open body' points to the premise that, among the Eveny, totemism is the starting point on which the animistic type of relationship is built. It suggests that totemism and animism operate together as two sides of the same coin.

This suggests that the Eveny view of animal guardianship does not follow consistently and strictly one model – that is, animist or totemist. In the animal-spirit world, a reindeer or other animal – such as a dog or horse (see Vitebsky 2005) – takes the guise of a human under attack, and, by doing so, receives the attack, which is meant for the human whose guise it took. Here the child and the guardian reindeer are two reversible elements: from the spirits' perspective, the child's body is the reindeer soul; from a human perspective, the child's soul is the reindeer body. That is why, among Eveny, the guardian reindeer is referred to as a 'double soul' or *khavek*. Here, Lévi-Strauss's observation regarding the Nuer substitution of a cucumber for an ox (see Evans-Pritchard 1956) is apposite: it is 'a cucumber which is sacrificed if there is no ox but the sacrifice of an ox for want of a cucumber would be an absurdity' (Lévi-Strauss 1966: 224). In the case of human–reindeer relations the act of substitution is unidirectional too – that is, the reindeer can stand for the human but the human cannot stand in for the reindeer. Hence, we observe how analogous and horizontal relations are working towards the outcome, which is of totemic character – that is, of homologous and vertical differentiation. The substitution is based on the principle of reversibility, but the process of substitution is directed towards an essentially asymmetrical and hierarchical outcome.

Using the Child as a Substitute in Hunting

People also operate with the concepts of 'open' and 'closed' bodies during hunting, which is perhaps the most intense contact of humans with the non-human spirit world. Here the child with its 'open body' plays a key part. At the age of six or seven, the child is already skilful in riding a reindeer and strong enough to participate in hunting trips, which can last several days. Most importantly, the child's body is still more or less 'open', and this condition of the child's personhood is used as a sort of bait for an animal spirit. The child's involvement in the hunt is of paramount importance to the adult hunter's contact with the animal and its associated spirit, as theirs is 'closed' and needs to 're-open' in order to establish social contact with the prey.[4] So, it is the child, whose body is 'open', which comes to substitute for the hunter's 'closed body' and allows contact to be established. The reason is that the game will 'give itself up' only when the relation between hunter and prey is hierarchical, as with the relation between a newborn child and the spirit of the dead. Indeed, this asymmetry is reflected in the fact that the hunter at the end of the hunt will declare: 'You came to me out of your own free will, please have pity on us and do not harm us'.

During a child's first hunt, two important components of its personhood are at work, namely the child's 'open body', which substitutes for the adult hunter's 'closed body', and the guardian reindeer, which also allows the hunt to be completed successfully. Let us have a closer look at this latter aspect. After the adult hunter shoots a large game animal, such as a snow ram or a wild reindeer, it is the young child who carries the killed game on their reindeer's back to the human encampment. The replacement of the hunter by the child implies that, in its attempt to take revenge for the killing, the spirit of the animal will not attack the adult hunter but instead see the child as the killer. Hence, by blaming the child for the killing, the horizontal character of the relation between adult hunter and prey is transformed into an essentially asymmetrical relation of the child and the spirit, which in turn allows for the event of the kill to be conceived of as a voluntary sacrifice on the part of the animal and its spiritual being – that is, the animal was not taken by force but was a voluntary gift, given by the superior spirit to the inferior child.

Furthermore, the guardian reindeer serves to ensure the child's safety in case the angry animal spirit would attack the child anyway. The reindeer stands in for the child in much the same way as the child stands in for the adult hunter. The chain of substitutions or replacements based on a movement away from dangerous symmetry towards still greater asymmetry is essentially what allows a safe hunt to take place. Contrary to Pedersen's logic of substitution, the switch between positions receives here a different twist, since in the sequence of substitution the subject to be substituted and the substitute switch from symmetry to asymmetry in order to establish a vertical exchange between hunter and prey.

The stage of adolescence signifies that a person's body is 'closed'. This suggests that reaching the stage of adulthood or acquiring a 'closed body' represents a movement from a totemic to an animistic mode of relation with the spirits. Achieving the safe condition of a 'closed' body is the point when homologous relations get transformed into analogous ones. Hence, it is possible to observe a switch between totemic and animistic modes of identification. Such a switch from asymmetry to symmetry and from predation to reciprocity is meant to 'close' the child's body and make it less fragile. What this evokes is that people and spirits move in and out of homologous and vertical relations and analogous and horizontal relations, rather than being fixed in one or the other as in Pedersen's generalised account of animism and totemism (Pedersen 2001: 416).

Naming Children

The practice of having a guardian reindeer or 'double soul' also corresponds to naming practices among Eveny. As was shown above, the reindeer serves as a guardian at the time when the child's body is still 'open' – that is, the child's personhood still needs to be consolidated. The body and soul of a newly born child are especially fragile, since body and soul have not yet reached their proper connection and the child's body and soul are therefore still subject to reversals and transformations. The child is still an object for the ancestors' longing and they have the power to kill the child before its body 'closes', as happened in the above story of Mikhail. Therefore, such protective means as employing a guardian reindeer and providing the child with a protective name make the child's body 'as if' closed. In other words, they create an illusion of a 'closed body'.

The practice of creating 'name' twins or 'name' doubles – that is, having children with the same name – serves the same end as a guardian reindeer. In this sense the 'name' twin works to minimise the effect of evil spirits' attacks. While identifying a victim of their attack, malicious spirits choose a particular child with a particular name, but if several children have the same name the spirits get confused and their attack is diminished. This practice was especially common at the time of epidemics and famine. For example, one Eveny couple survived epidemics of flu, hepatitis and smallpox but all their children unfortunately died. Despite the tragic loss of children they again gave birth to a girl and named her Sasha. There was no one among their relatives or deceased ancestors who had that name. Two years later they gave birth to a boy and they gave him the same name as his elder sister: Sasha. Out of all the children this couple had, it was these two children with the same name who survived a sequence of epidemics and happily reached maturity.

Nowadays, though the stock of individual names is small, and fairly homogeneous throughout the ethnic group, infants are also often given the name of a known living person within the social universe of the parents. Although people do name their children after their deceased parents or grandparents, there is no special demand to give the name of a deceased ancestor to a newly born child as with, for example, the Chukchi (about which more below) and Inupiat (Bodenhorn 2006: 148). The meaning of naming among the Eveny is always contingent and does not rest solely upon the necessity of invoking a particular human identity with a set of relationships in which 'the past is brought into the future' (ibid.: 148). The practice of creating namesakes or name duplicates works towards a production of ambiguity and uncertainty by means of producing doubles (twins), triples (triplets) and so forth. An exposed single identity is dangerous at this stage of the human life cycle, so the fabrication of homonymy and multiplicity is meant to secure a child stays in the world of living humans.

As we have seen, both the name and a guardian reindeer deal with the fragility of personhood. The name protects the child from the ancestor spirits by diffusing their attention, while the reindeer interacts with animal spirits on the child's behalf. They serve as two substitutes that generate the child's protection and diminish the negative impact of the spirits' attack until a person acquires a relative invulnerability ('closed body') which is manifested in physical agility and strength. If by late adolescence – that is, around fifteen to seventeen years of age – the body of a child remains unclosed, the person will stay susceptible to various kinds of danger, including the effect of malevolent spirits throughout their life.

Another clear-cut distinction between animism and totemism which does not fit well with our ethnographic data lies in the ways the relationship between the living and the dead is construed. In totemism the relationship is socially discontinuous, as the final forms the ancestral beings take are inanimate entities (mountains, cliffs, amulets). Thus, people know and experience the land, and the ancestral spirits that shaped it, only by their final immobile forms (Ingold 2000a: 128). By contrast, in animist society human ancestor spirits take on a guise of non-human entities that reside immanently 'within the manifold appearances of the lifeworld' (ibid.: 130). However, our ethnographic data provide us with a less coherent picture when it comes to the locality of the dead.

There is no explicit theory about where the dead reside and Eveny explanations become extremely vague when it comes to the point of clarification. Among some local Eveny the body of an animal (white ermine, bear, eagle) is a destination of a shaman after his death which, if we follow Pedersen, points to the presence of so-called 'extra-human perspectivism' and the horizontal type of human–animal relations in this group. However, the ethnographic reality offers a less coherent picture as there are cases which undermine this view. For example, in the area of Topolinoye there are two mountains which are viewed by locals as post-mortem forms of two shamans. The story is that two dead shamans turned into mountains after a very long fight, during which they both took different forms; they started fighting as humans, but after a while they transformed themselves into bears, then continued as elks, wild reindeer and lynx. Finally, they got exhausted and turned into two mountains called Daik and Darpir.

So, given the unsystematic and incoherent view about the locality of the spirits of the dead among the Eveny, we suggest that this should be considered in terms of a plurality of connections which emphasises that one mode of identification does not necessarily exclude another one (see Vitebsky 2005: 307). Moreover, things that conceptually overlap and conflict acquire hybrid form and, as a result, horizontal relations may involve elements of asymmetry and verticality and an animist model may also be built on the totemic mode of relations.

The Chukchi

Name, Ancestor, Sacrifice and Personhood

Let us now move from the mountain forest of the Sakha Republic to northern Kamchatka and Chukotka, which is the home of the Chukchi. As with the case of the Eveny, the Chukchi do not easily fit into the respective typologies of animism versus totemism. Rather, they move in and out of the two ontologies as a means of surviving their precarious relationship with the 'deceased ancestors' (*pene'elin*, 'the ancient ones'), who are the main focus of Chukchi religious life.

In constructing our argument we draw on ethnographic information collected among a small group of Chukchi reindeer herders in the village of Achaiyayam in northern Kamchatka. The village, which is home to about four hundred people, is close to the border between Kamchatka and Chukotka, and the people speak for the most part a dialect of the Koryak language (*Chavchuven*). This has led certain Russian scholars to classify them as Koryak (e.g., Gorbacheva 1985). However, the people virtually all refer to themselves as Chukchi (Plattet 2005: 72), which is why we refer to them by this name.[5]

A remarkable feature of this group of Chukchi is that they were never converted to Christianity, and permanent socio-economic relations with Russia were established relatively late, in the 1930s and 1940s (ibid.: 135). Perhaps this is one important reason why they have kept strong indigenous ideas about the circulation of souls between the worlds of the living and the dead. When a person dies or an animal is sacrificed, their soul (*uvi'rit*) goes to the next world, where it is reclothed with flesh. Each family group (*va'rat*) is said to have an ancestral counterpart in the next world, and every newcomer joins their own relatives, just as any reindeer slaughtered joins the family herd. The deceased, the Chukchi say, are always eager to receive the souls of the dead, because from their viewpoint this is experienced as the physical return of a long-deceased relative. The same goes for the souls of the deceased, who upon 'death', conversely, return to this world through an act of spontaneous rebirth. As soon as a child is born its family members will ask 'what relative has come back' and seek to discover the child's true identity. A child will be given an official Russian name and up to five indigenous names. However, only one of these indigenous names will be the child's 'real' name – that is, the name of the deceased ancestor who has returned in the child, and the latter will then take, at least formally, the deceased's place within the wider network of kin. This can be illustrated with a story told by a young Chukchi mother:

> When my son, Misha [the child's official Russian name], was born we started searching for his real [Chukchi] name with the help of an *anipel* [divining stone]. We placed two driving sticks [for reindeer sledges] in the ground and hung the stone between them. And then this old woman, Kukaka, asked the stone and found three names for Misha from [dead] relatives on my father's side. Then Misha was given one name of these names. But the same week he became seriously ill. And his right ear ached terribly. Well, we had already seen how his right ear kind of stood out. Then the old woman, Kukaka, who had been searching for the name, saw in a dream that her mother, Kachytvava, lived at our place. She came to us early in the morning and whispered to Misha in his left ear – she whispered the name Kachytvava. It turned out that this was the right name, his true name. Her [Kachytvava's] right ear had been aching strongly too. In fact, part of her ear had been rotting away. Misha got well in a few days. Now Misha is very close to Kul-u [whose mother returned in him]. They drink tea together, speak kindly to each other and do all of the things a mother and her daughter do together.

It follows from this story and many others like it that among the Chukchi no insuperable barrier exists between the living and the dead or male and female. Quite the opposite: there seems to be an almost unbounded potential for identification with others: the dead transform into the living, and one gender turns into another. As Pedersen puts it with regard to the animist principle of 'analogous identification': 'There are no radical discontinuities here, only continuous substitutions of Same becoming Other, and visa versa (Pedersen 2001: 416). Likewise, death among the Chukchi is seen as an integral and necessary part of the creative circle of renewal: just as the living depend on the deceased for their supply of souls, so the deceased depend on the mortality of the living, who ensure their reproduction in the other realm. One could easily interpret this continuity of soul exchange between the living and the dead along the lines of Ingold (1986, 2000a: 115) and Descola (1996) – that is, as the direct result of the reciprocal and symmetric obligation to exchange life energy with the spirit world, typical of animist societies.

However, the Chukchi relationship with the deceased is in fact a good deal more complicated than this. On closer inspection it turns out that the exchange relationship between the two realms is mediated by fundamental aspects of asymmetry and hierarchy. First, the deceased are assigned a permanently superior status in that their world is seen to be an exact replica of this world, minus its troubles and sins. Thus, it is said that in the world of the dead people live in strict accordance with tradition and in perfect harmony, and there are no Russian elements, such as alcohol, canned food and Russian-style clothing. Moreover, and even more importantly, the deceased are believed to be the ultimate authority over the life-giving souls. This was made clear by a Chukchi herder, who explained it this way: 'It happens that a hundred or more heads of reindeer just disappear. They are not to be found anywhere. I tell you, it is the deceased, who have taken back their property, for they are the true "owners" (Russian: *khoziain*) of the herd. If they want to, they can take away all the reindeers just like that'.

Let us explain the meaning of this statement, which provides important insight into Chukchi ideas about possession and ownership. When a child is born, a close relative of the deceased person who is believed to have returned in the child will normally – but without being obliged to – give the child a reindeer doe, so that the recipient can start building up their own private herd. The animal given, along with all of its offspring and their offspring and so forth, will be given the private earmark of the recipient, who can do with the animals as they please. However, when the original donor of the doe dies and a sacrificial animal is needed to accompany them to the next world, their family will demand that the recipient provides an animal for slaughter, taken from the stock of animals that originated from the doe. This is because the original donor is understood to be the 'true owner' of these animals, although the recipient holds the right to use them. So, the reindeer are at once a 'property' and a 'possession', at once 'given' and 'kept' (Weiner 1992). What is kept is the ownership; what is given is its possession, all of which means that ownership over herds is ultimately traced back to the initial donors, the deceased ancestors, who originally gave their reindeer to their living kin without the latter ever having asked (just as the newborn child does not ask for the reindeer given to it). Moreover, just as the ancestors were not obliged to give in the first place, so they are not obliged to accept or to give in return, because the debts owed to them can never really be cancelled, or even 'balanced out'.

We take this last point from Maurice Godelier (1999: 186), who criticises Marcel Mauss for reducing sacrifice to a 'contractual' bond that humans are said to hold over their deities. Thus, according to Mauss: 'The purpose of destruction by sacrifice is precisely that it is an act of giving that is necessarily reciprocated' (Mauss 1990: 20). However, what Mauss fails to take into account, Godelier rightly argues, is 'that the men approaching the gods are already in their debt, since it is from them that they have already received the conditions for their existence' (Godelier 1999: 30). This argument may also be levelled as a criticism against Pedersen (2001) and Ingold (2000a), who in their overarching and rather totalising description of animism in North Asian and Arctic hunting and herding societies describe the exchange as reciprocal and horizontal. However, as should be clear by now, this exchange is not between genuinely equal partners and cannot, therefore, be reciprocal and horizontal, since, among the Chukchi at least, the spirits remain the true owners of the souls and they have both the right and the power to repossess their property at any given moment.

The ancestral owner appears to be represented by the family wooden fireboard, the most sacred of the Chukchi idols. The fireboard is roughly carved in human form and among the Chukchi of Achaiyayam it is called *gichgei* or *qaya'-eti 'nvila'n*, 'master of the herd' (Jochelson 1908: 34; Ragtytval' 1986: 105). Each board goes with a private herd of reindeer and signifies that its proprietary right has a double aspect of which one is its human 'possessor' and the other its ancestral 'owner' to whom the herd ultimately belongs. Thus, when someone experiences a decline in their number of livestock due to disease, bad weather or other misfortunes, it is understood to be the result of the ancestor taking back their property. This fear is further intensified by the fact that souls are conceived of in terms of a limited number. Indeed, as Lee Guemple describes it with regard to the Inuit, but which also holds true for the Chukchi, 'the system ... is regarded as a closed "circle": no new spiritual components can enter, and none are ever lost' (Guemple 1994: 118). We are, therefore, at least in principle, dealing with a fixed pool of souls that simply go round and round in an endless circle. This means that when the deceased have plenty of reindeer they are scarce among the living, and vice versa (Bogoras 1904–1909: 330). Both parties cannot be rich in reindeer at the same time.

There is an important sense in which the deceased represent a prototypical notion of the spirit world as 'experience reversed' (Leach 1976: 81–93). Thus, they are said to live in *irangas* (skin tents) with their families, just as the living do, and they also keep herds of domesticated reindeer; yet from the perspective of the living basic things are turned upside-down and inside-out: When it is night here, it is day there, and the same goes for winter and summer. Moreover, the bodies of the deceased are turned the 'wrong' way round, so that they have the colour of raw meat, while their heads and feet bend backwards. To speak of the 'deceased' and the 'living' is, however, not quite correct, because from the viewpoint of each of these categories of beings they are the living while the others are seen as the dead ones (Bogoras 1904–1909: 331). Moreover, while the deceased are generally described as dwelling in the 'upper world', this is not to be misunderstood as literally meaning the sky. Rather, the deceased are often conflated with other beings, such as the spirits of the mountains, lakes and rivers, and even with the *ke'let*, the evil spirits that are said to dwell everywhere in the landscape.

So, despite a considerable overlap and confusion between different spirit categories, the deceased among the Chukchi represent in an important sense the prototypical totemic principle of higher-ranked ancestors that dwell in the landscape and whose life-giving energy needs to be transferred directly to their living kin through the continuous rebirth of souls, most notably signified by the incarnation of ancestral names. A Chukchi person's identity, therefore, is defined by an essentially vertical relation to their incarnation and this relation is both unique and exclusive – that is, homologous. Although the Chukchi, as we shall see below, also hold that humans and animals may take the place of one another (as in the sense of Amazonian perspectivism), this so-called 'extra-human perspectivism' – humans becoming non-humans and vice versa (Pedersen 2001: 421) – is not the basic principle. Rather, it is 'inter-human perspectivism' (humans becoming other humans) that predominates among the Chukchi: The starting point of personhood, as we have seen, is literally to see '*through the eyes of other people*, people who [are] dead and [have] become spirits' (ibid.: 423, original emphasis and insertions) – what Pedersen in his typology brings under the rubric of totemism.

Ritual Blood Sacrifice and the Separation of Perspectives

With these observations in mind, let us turn to the topic of ritual blood sacrifice, the main feature of Chukchi ritual life. First, we need to ask what the living could possibly give to the deceased so that the latter will allow the former to keep most of the souls to themselves. The answer is that the victim of the sacrifice, which prototypically is a reindeer; 'stands-in' for the person or persons who are making the sacrifice or upon whose behalf the sacrifice is made. As Evans-Prichard puts it with regard to the Nuer: 'When [they] give their cattle in sacrifice they are very much, and in a very intimate way, giving a part of themselves' (Evans-Prichard 1954: 27). This is clearly true of the Chukchi as well, who identify very strongly with their livestock. All reindeer have their own particular earmark that identifies them as belonging to an individual owner. Moreover, during the autumn festival, which is accompanied by offerings of sacrifice to the dead, the blood of the first reindeer slaughtered, which is a fawn, is used to paint designs on the faces of all the members of the family. The idea is to make the face of the wearer look like that of a reindeer (Bogoras 1904–1909: 360). Although the designs are quite simple, indicating the animal's eyes, ears and mouth, they clearly suggest that the sacrificer here takes on the identity of the animal victim, so that what is consecrated and sacrificed is in some symbolic sense themselves.

At times, however, it is not even a real animal but a substitute for the beast that is sacrificed. The prototypical substitute is a sausage (*zyozyat*) made by stuffing the third stomach of a reindeer with fat from its intestines (Plattet 2005: 194), but a fish or a stone might also serve as a substitute. Even a small wooden image of the sausage may be used, making the substitution triple (Bogoras 1904–1909: 369). Each substitute is regarded as taking the place of a real reindeer and is, therefore, stabbed with a knife to represent an actual slaughter.

What appears to be the underlying logic here is that these surrogate victims are made into 'signs' of the sacrificer. Chukchi sacrifice is, therefore, really about the symbolic displacement of ritual violence from the human donor to the animal and further to an almost endless chain of substitutions. The sacrificer seeks to postpone for as long as possible their own death or that of their relatives by offering substitutes in the place of real human lives. In a fundamental sense then, ritual blood sacrifice fits neatly into Pedersen's description of animism as based on 'an unbounded potential for identification' in which 'a logic of endless substitutions seems intrinsic' (Pedersen 2001: 416), although, as has already been pointed out in the Eveny case, it is unidirectional – that is, the reindeer can stand for the human but the human cannot stand in for the reindeer.

Does this then mean that Chukchi sacrifice seeks to generate a predominantly animist ontology? The answer is no. Sacrifice constitutes a necessary element in the construction of the essentially vertical and homologous relation with the deceased. Let us explain this. We have already seen that the Chukchi do not postulate an insuperable ontological barrier between the living and the dead. Quite the opposite: Through acts of spontaneous rebirth, people share from the outset an unstable condition in which the life essence or soul of their ancestral relatives is mixed with their own – that is, no clear differences or divisions between humanity and divinity are yet apparent. This, however, does not mean that the Chukchi are not preoccupied with differentiating themselves from the deceased. On the contrary, the lack of any guaranteed a priori difference means that difference has to be created constantly through everyday ritual practices that demonstrate it. Sacrifice, we suggest, is such a display of difference. It creates the social separation between the two realms, making them distinct from one another, which in turn is the precondition for living human existence, because, without such distinction, there is no life for humanity.

This can perhaps best be illustrated by taking a look at how suicide, which mainly involves young people (Pika 1993), is conceived by the Chukchi. The suicidal person is understood to be controlled and subordinated to the soul of the dead ancestor they are said to be. This finds expression in strange and anti-social behaviour, such as when a youngster starts babbling unintelligibly, threatening others with personal violence or roughly insulting them, before eventually going on and killing themselves (Willerslev 2009). The suicidal person is effectively acting in accordance with the social and moral code of the deceased, who, as we have already described, from the viewpoint of the living is a direct inversion of ordinary social behaviour. Thus, the suicidal youngster is effectively dominated by confused identifications with their deceased ancestor or namesake. We might say that the youngster is caught in an enclosed, circular relationship with their deceased double, making any relations with a 'third' – that is social relations – impossible. Social relations depend on the mediation of this dyadically enclosed relationship in which the living person is held in thrall by their deceased kinsmen. This mediation is accomplished through the way each apex in the sacrificial triangle – described by Henri Hubert and Mauss as including a 'sacrificer', a 'deity' and a 'victim' (Hubert and Mauss 1964: 100) – comes to mediate the dual relationship between the other two.

First, by virtue of the basic use of a substitute, the sacrificer is set apart from the victim that stands in their place. Moreover, the sacrificial destruction of the victim creates a separation between the living as donor and the deceased as recipient – that is, humanity and divinity become defined in respect to one another. This very fact signifies that the interests of the two parties are no longer the same, because they have by means of their separation come to possess different and socially stratified positions in the transaction from which they now perceive one another (see Strathern 1988: 177). Indeed, this is contrary to the suicidal person, who remains trapped in a dyadic and symmetrical relationship of immediate identification with the dead, thus acting in accordance with the deceased's perspective and intent.

It should be clear by now that we need not get very deep into the analysis of Chukchi sacrifice to realise that it quite crucially serves to detach the deceased, in that it effectively asks the dead 'to turn away from the living rather than seeking closer union with them' (Beattie 1980: 38). This in turn allows for hierarchical social relations to occur between the two realms.

The Switch from Totemism to Animism and Back Again

We are now in a position to turn to the key issue that interests us, namely the extent to which the diverse beliefs and practices that have traditionally been brought under the respective rubrics of totemism and animism apply to Chukchi ideas about the fabrication of personhood. We have seen that for Chukchi the starting point is a situation in which living humans are believed to be the direct incarnations of their deceased ancestors. Thus, it is not simply the case that particular individuals are associated with particular ancestors, whose name they adopt; they are essentially conceived of as partaking in the same life essence or energy as these ancestors, which means that the ancestors dwell at the very core of their being. It is to this linkage that the concept of totemism has come to refer, and in this sense the Chukchi are predominantly totemic in the classical sense of the term. However, the trouble is that for the Chukchi this condition of truly totemic relations with the ancestors is ultimately unsustainable and indeed self-destructive. It always ends in madness and death – as in the case of suicides – rather than in fullness of life. On the whole, therefore, the ancestors are viewed negatively: they stand for the loss of agency and ultimately for death, because without their detachment, there is no life for the living.

The Chukchi solution is to accentuate difference by transforming their essentially totemic relations with the ancestors, along with all this entails of a sociality, defined by fundamentally vertical and homologous relations, into an animist one, marked as it is by social relations of a horizontal and analogous character. The means of this transformation is the practice of ritual blood sacrifice. As Brian K. Smith and Wendy Doniger point out: 'It is substitution that defines sacrifice as sacrifice. Sacrifice is essentially a game of displacement and replacement in that anything one sacrifice is a surrogate substitute for the ultimate paradigm underlying all sacrifices, the sacrifice of oneself' (Smith and Doniger 1989: 190–91).

Sacrifice then is in some fundamental sense based in the animist principle of an unbounded potential for identification. To reiterate Pedersen's key statement: 'a logic of endless substitutions seems intrinsic to animist thought, the principle that every element … can be interchanged with another' (Pedersen 2001: 416). What is interesting, however, is that Chukchi sacrifices to the ancestors, despite being animist in character, result not in an animist modality but rather in a transformed totemic one, which has the distinction of perspectives at its core. That is, through the introduction of surrogate victims and their destruction, the primordial condition of 'oneness' or 'sameness' with the deceased is displaced, which in turn allows for a disruption of their respective subjective perspectives:

the living become 'donors' and therefore inferior, while the dead become 'takers' and superior. Thus, differentiation, hierarchy and discontinuity now become key aspects of the relationship between the two realms. This situation of dissimilarity with one's ancestor and namesake allows for further manipulations of the relationship: through continuous acts of sacrifice, a person can now postpone for as long as possible their own death by offering substitutes to the deceased. Thus, it is in fact the key element of non-coincidence or difference between the two realms that allows the sacrificial act to be calculated action, a technology of time manipulation, so to speak, in that the delay or time lag generated through the killings of substitutes is what allows human life to happen. This suggests that to reach the status of a truly living human person among the Chukchi requires a movement from a totemic to an animistic mode of relation with the deceased in order to be transformed back to a totemic relation based on the differentiation of perspectives.

Conclusion

The two case studies discussed, those of the Eveny and the Chukchi, show that, in Siberian indigenous cosmologies, things, bodies and people are rarely just themselves but always something else as well – that is, one ontological model duplicates itself all along with another model, which, as a kind of twin or doppelgänger, 'ghosts' its presence (Corsín Jiménez and Willerslev 2007). At certain moments, what appear to be predominantly 'vertical' and 'egalitarian' social relations with the spirit world cross over to the 'other side', so to speak, and become 'horizontal' and 'hierarchical' or vice versa – all of which makes it difficult, in fact impossible, to specify if we are here dealing with animistic or totemic social formations. There are two key aspects to this: Firstly, among the Eveny and Chukchi, and quite possibly elsewhere, totemism and animism are essentially relative or more precisely deictic phenomena, which implies that their respective presence depends on who is looking and from where. This was perhaps most clearly illustrated in the Eveny case, where the prey will 'give itself up' freely only when the relation between hunter and animal is hierarchical – as with the relation between the newborn child and the spirits of the dead. Thus, from the child's perspective, the relation to prey has a totemic character, whereas, for the adult hunter, the relation is animistic, and each may trade places with the other.

Secondly, the study of animism and totemism in Siberia cannot escape the key element of time – that is, the fact that no ontological form is ever permanent. Thus, rather than being fixed in one ontology or the other – as in Descola's, Ingold's and Pedersen's generalised accounts of animism and totemism – the Siberian case studies quite clearly show how people tend to move in and out of homologous and analogous types of relations, and how these transformations in time are integral rather than exceptional to their strategies of survival when interacting with the spirit world. Among other things, this is illustrated by the Chukchi case, where a person's relationship with their incarnations at the outset takes an essentially totemic character, marked by a 'oneness' of perspectives of self and ancestor. The impossibility of this unity, however, gives way to a process of detachment in which the use of an essentially animist logic of sacrificial substitution plays a key part. The result is a kind of transformed totemism, based in a principle of differentiation of perspectives. Thus, over time, we see a movement away from dangerous symmetry towards still greater asymmetry, which essentially is what allows human life to take shape.

Thus, we propose that despite the fact that the typologies of animism and totemism, at least by the implication of former anthropological studies, appear to be rather unlikely bedfellows, it turns out that in Siberia the two modalities include, much as in the Chinese *taiji* (or *yin-yang*) diagram, their apparent opposites within themselves. This makes us suggest that the terms totemism and animism rather than being seen as to two opposed, coherent and explicitly articulated doctrinal ontologies, as implied by their '-isms', are rather to be understood as orientations towards the spirit world, which are so deeply co-implicated that one cannot really exist without the other.

Notes

1. The terms 'animic' and 'totemic' seem to be an invention of Descola or his translator, and are also used by Ingold. We for our part use the term 'animistic'. However, we do replace the term 'totemistic' with 'totemic', since the latter seems to have been used to refer both to specific totems and to the phenomenon of totemism at least since Needham's translation of Lévi-Strauss (Lévi-Strauss 1964), and since 'totemistic' is a bit clumsy.
2. Human soul in Eveny is *khanjan*.
3. See also Vitebsky (2005: 111–12) for the Eveny of Sebyan, and Willerslev (2007: 163) for the Yukaghir.
4. See Willerslev (2007: 164) for a similar idea among Yukaghir.
5. It is in fact impossible to provide a set of consistent and rigorous distinctions between Chukchi and Koryak, as stressed by Waldemar Bogoras (1904–1909), Waldemar Jochelson (1908) and Alex King (2002). The two groups are very similar in terms of language, culture and religious ideas.

References

Beattie, J.H.M. 1980. 'On Understanding Sacrifice', in M.F.C. Bourdillon and M. Fortes (eds), *Sacrifice*. London: Academic Press, pp. 29–44.
Bodenhorn, B. 2006. 'Calling into Being: Naming and Speaking Names in Alaska's North Slope', in G. vom Bruck and B. Bodenhorn (eds), *Anthropology of Names and Naming*. Cambridge: Cambridge University Press, pp. 139–56.
Bogoras, W. 1904–1909. *The Chukchee*, 3 vols. New York: G.E. Stechert.
Corsín Jiménez, A., and R. Willerslev. 2007. 'An Anthropological Concept of the Concept: Reversibility among the Siberian Yukaghirs', *Journal of the Royal Anthropological Institute* 13: 527–43.
Descola, P. 1996. 'Constructing Natures: Symbolic Ecology and Social Practice', in P. Descola and G. Pálsson (eds), *Nature and Society: Anthropological Perspectives*. London: Routledge, pp. 82–102.

——— 2006. 'Beyond Nature and Culture', *Proceedings of the British Academy* 139: 137–55.
Evans-Prichard, E.E. 1954. 'The Meaning of Sacrifice among the Nuer', *Journal of the Royal Anthropological Institute* 84(1/2): 21–33.
——— 1956. *Nuer Religion*. Oxford: Clarendon Press.
Gell, A. 1998. *Art and Agency: An Anthropological Theory*. Oxford: Clarendon Press.
Godelier, M. 1999. *The Enigma of the Gift*, trans. N. Scott. Cambridge: Polity Press.
Gorbacheva, V.V. 1985. 'Sovremennyj byt a čajvajamckix olennyx korjakov', in I.M. Raj (ed.), *Istoričeskaja ètnografija: Problemy arxeologii i ètnografi*. Leningrad: Izdatel'stvo Leningradskogo Universiteta, pp. 12–17.
Guemple, L. 1994. 'The Inuit Cycle of Spirits', in A. Mills and R. Slobodin (eds), *Amerindian Rebirth: Reincarnation Belief among North American Indians and Inuit*. Toronto: University of Toronto Press, pp. 107–22.
Hubert, H., and M. Mauss. 1964. *Sacrifice: Its Nature and Functions*. Chicago: University of Chicago Press.
Ingold, T. 1986. 'Hunting, Sacrifice and the Domestication of Animals', in T. Ingold, *The Appropriation of Nature: Essays on Human Ecology and Social Relations*. Manchester: Manchester University Press, pp. 243–77.
——— 2000a. 'Totemism, Animism and the Depiction of Animals', in T. Ingold, *The Perception of the Environment: Essays on Livelihood, Dwelling and Skill*. London: Routledge, pp. 111–31.
——— 2000b. 'From Trust to Domination: An Alternative History of Human–Animal Relations', in T. Ingold, *The Perception of the Environment: Essays on Livelihood, Dwelling and Skill*. London: Routledge, pp. 61–76.
Jochelson, W. 1908. *The Koryak*. New York: American Museum of Natural History.
King, A.D. 2002. 'Without Deer There Is No Culture, Nothing', *Anthropology and Humanism* 27(2): 133–64.
Leach, E. 1976. *Culture and Communication*. Cambridge: Cambridge University Press.
Lévi-Strauss, C. 1964. *Totemism*, trans. R. Needham. London: Merlin Press.
——— 1966. *The Savage Mind*. Chicago: University of Chicago Press.
Mauss, M. 1990. *The Gift: The Form and Reason for Exchange in Archaic Societies*, trans. W.D. Halls. New York: Norton.
Pedersen, M. 2001. 'Totemism, Animism and North Asian Indigenous Ontologies', *Journal of the Royal Anthropological Institute* 7(3): 411–27.
Pika, A. 1993. 'The Spatial-temporal Dynamic of Violent Death among the Native Peoples of Northern Russia', *Arctic Anthropology* 30(2): 61–76.
Plattet, P. 2005. 'Le double jeu de la chance: imitation et substitution dans les rituels chamaniques contemporains de deux populations rurales du Nord-Kamtchatka (Fédération de Russie, Extrême-Orient sibérien): les chasseurs maritimes de Lesnaia et les éleveurs de rennes d'Atchaïvaiam', Ph.D. thesis. Paris: Université de Neuchâtel and Ecole Pratique des Hautes Etudes.
Ragtytval', R.I. 1986. *Meinypil'gynskaia Kollektsiia semeinykh sviatyn: Kraevedcheskie zapiski* 14: 101–8. Magadan, Russia: Magadanskoe Knizhnoe izdatel'stvo.
Smith, B.K., and W. Doniger. 1989. 'Sacrifice and Substitution: Ritual Mystification and Mythical Demystification', *Numen* 36(2): 189–224.
Strathern, M. 1988. *The Gender of the Gift*. Berkeley: University of California Press.
Tugolukov, V.A. 1997. *Istoria i kultura evenov*. St Petersburg: Nauka.
Ulturgasheva, O. 2008. 'Ideas of the Future among Young Eveny in Northeastern Siberia', Ph.D. thesis. Cambridge: University of Cambridge.

Vitebsky, P. 2005. *Reindeer People: Living with Animals and Spirits in Siberia*. London: HarperCollins.
Viveiros de Castro, E. 1998. 'Cosmological Deixis and Amerindian Perspectivism', *Journal of the Royal Anthropological Institute* 4(3): 469–88.
Weiner, A.B. 1992. *Inalienable Possessions: The Paradox of Keeping-while-giving*. Berkeley: University of California Press.
Willerslev, R. 2007. *Soul Hunters: Hunting, Animism, and Personhood among the Siberian Yukaghirs*. Berkeley: University of California Press.
——— 2009. 'The Optimal Sacrifice: A Study of Voluntary Death among the Siberian Chukchi', *American Ethnologist* 36(4): 693–704.

Chapter 3
Animism and the Meanings of Life: Reflections from Amazonia

Laura Rival

A substantial part of my research has dealt with plant symbolism and plant knowledge.[1] More recently, I have become particularly interested in the Amerindian ethnoclassification of manioc (*Manihot esculenta*) in 'bitter' and 'sweet' types, as well as in the diverse ways of cultivating, processing, storing and consuming manioc varieties. My interest has grown from having worked with two extremely different groups of manioc cultivators, the Huaorani and the Makushi.

A domesticated species of the genus *Manihot* in the Euphorbiaceae family with hundreds of different landraces, manioc contains a powerful toxic element, hydrocyanic acid (HCN), commonly known as prussic acid. High and low acid-content varieties are distinguished according to the amount of HCN contained in the tubers. This differentiation has no real taxonomic value given that toxicity depends as much on soil conditions, age of the plant, size of the roots and method of cultivation as it does on the clone itself. However, the classification of manioc cultivars in two main types is common both among cultivators and scientists, who have basically adopted the folk classification of the early Tupi and Arawak people who first domesticated the plant (Rival and McKey 2008). Although there has been some research on the relationship between intraspecific variability, relative toxicity and ecological features associated with regional specialisation, there is no good explanation yet as to why native Amazonians have selected for bitter and sweet varieties, or why they grate and squeeze the bitter but roast or boil the sweet, to use Carneiro's (2000: 68) judicious phrasing. Why is it that some Amazonian societies predominantly cultivate bitter varieties, while others exclusively cultivate sweet varieties remains to this day a mystery.

The oddity of manioc as a poisonous crop should have interested Amazonianist anthropologists, but apart from a few exceptions (e.g., Hugh-Jones 1979; Descola 1994; Rival 2001), authors have preferred to focus their theoretical attention on animal predation, hunting and shamanism. More generally, there has been a paucity of work on plant symbolism.[2] Descola (1994) may be singled out for his systematic comparative analysis of the treatment of cultivated plants (manioc being the paradigm) and hunted animals, in terms of contrastive and complementary sets of kinship relations. 'Perspectivism' and 'ontological animism', which have been used to analyse a relatively narrow range of symbolic ecological data, mainly derived from the treatment of animals, may be renewed by refocusing the analytical lens on representations involving plants. The mental and practical separation of manioc landraces in two ethnospecies, a separation that pervades classification systems, modes of cultivation and modes of preparation, deserves further study. The bitter/sweet contrast, which is significant on both ecological and symbolic grounds, raises interesting questions about the symbolisation of the domesticatory process. One hypothesis to be tested through further ethnographic research and comparative analysis is that it is not as a living plant growing in fields that manioc is finally domesticated, but, rather, as food prepared by the hearth, the most domestic of all places. A better knowledge of the symbolism at work here would deepen our understanding of the representations of life and personhood in lowland South America. Some of the questions we need to address are: What agency is attributed to manioc? What kind of being is the manioc plant in Amerindian thought? In what ways can it be said that the manioc plant is treated as a person? What homology is drawn between the human person and the plant person, and between the manioc plant and other non-human persons? And to what extent can we say that these representations have guided or at least influenced the cultivation practices that have led to the domestication of manioc?

My goal here is not to offer answers to these questions, but, rather, to focus on three theoretical issues that require further elaboration before we can even start envisaging the ontological status of plants in Amerindian thought. The first issue deals with the propensity or capacity to communicate that seems to underlie animistic beliefs: What kinds of agency and intentions are at work in communication events between humans and non-humans? The second issue concerns the attribution of life to animated beings, and the third one, the life attributed to plants in symbolic representations and ritual actions.

What Intentionalities Are at Work within Animism?

That animism characterises most, if not all, native Amazonian philosophies of life is a view shared by many Amazonianist anthropologists today. This raises a difficult conceptual problem, that of the make up of the person in animistic thought. Philippe Descola, who renewed the anthropological interest in animism, defines animist ontology as the granting by humans to non-humans of an interiority identical to theirs, an attribution that humanises animals (and plants), for the soul they are gifted with allows them not only to behave according to human social norms and ethical principles but also to communicate with each other (Descola 2005: 183–84).[3] Whereas the body causes differentiation and individualisation, the soul, or spiritual principle, enables intersubjectivity to occur between all existing beings. By speaking of 'a disposition that humanises plants, *and above all animals*' (my emphasis), Descola signals from the outset that relations of intersubjectivity occur more 'naturally' between humans and animals than they do between humans and plants. This implicit distinction becomes clearer when the author offers an interpretation of Leenhardt's ethnographic encounter with Kanak thought. For the Kanak, it is their shared internal substance, conceptualised as essentially human, which makes humans identical to plants. By contrast, the organic form, which determines the mode of existence, differentiates humans from plants. The Kanak agree that humans do not develop, behave, feed or reproduce in the same way as plants do (ibid.: 185). Existing beings are thus made up of two parts, an interiority (or soul), a source of identity, and an exteriority (or body), a source of differentiation and individualisation. In other words, a person as conceived in animistic thought combines bodily discontinuity and substantial continuity, or, in Descola's own terms, 'substantial community' (ibid.: 184–85).

In a special issue of *Ethnos* on the relationship between animism and the meaning of life, Ingold (2006), Hornborg (2006), Bird-David (2006) and Scott (2006) discuss animism as a relational ontology founded on a core principle, the human need – or desire – to communicate. Their approach, like Descola's, gives precedence to the function of enabling communication across species boundaries. Their focus, however, is slightly different, as they reflect on the properties of animation in relation to life. The central point of discussion concerns the manifestations of animation, and whether they are equivalent or not. Ingold, Hornborg, Bird- David and Scott all seem to agree that where there is communication, there is intentionality; where there is intentionality, there is consciousness; where there is consciousness, there is life; and where there is life, there is movement. They seem to apprehend the soul as the place where one forms a consciousness of one's own existence as well as of that of others, a consciousness which becomes the source of a desire to communicate, in the sense that for communication to take place successfully and in all openness, one must treat others as subjects identical to oneself. In other words, it is my desire to communicate and establish a relationship which constitutes the tree, the plant, the hammock, the pot, the peccary or the stone as active subjects constituted by the same desire to relate back to me and to communicate with me.[4] I see here a good example of the hazardous slippage between animacy, agency and intentionality that has occurred with increased frequency in recent anthropological discussions. What do anthropologists writing about animism mean when they speak of intentions?

The central place accorded to intentionality in discussions on animism may be traced back to the seminal work of Alfred Gell on art (Gell 1998), a work of great originality left unfinished by the author's premature death, and published posthumously. Inspired by his initial encounter with cognitive psychology, Gell develops his theory of art as a theory of communication calling for a new conceptualisation of intentionality. Many of the examples of 'enchantment technologies' given in *Art and Agency* deal with animistic beliefs, although the author avoids the terms animism and animation, for which he prefers to substitute those of social agency and animacy. He explains that 'in ascribing social agent status, it does not matter what a thing or a person is in itself, what matters is where it stands in a network of social relations ... because agency implies the possession of a mind which intends actions prior to performing them' (ibid.: 123). With reference to idolatry, Gell further notes that 'the idol may not be biologically a living thing, but if it has intentional psychology attributed to it, then it has something like a spirit, a soul, an ego lodged within it' (ibid.: 129).

Gell completely renews anthropological approaches to religious art in his novel discussion of the role of religious images in South Asia, in particular of the eye that sees and in which one sees oneself while at the same time seeing beyond, straight into the spirit of the divinity (whether a statue, a painted image, or a virgin little girl), hence forming the illusory feeling of getting access to the divinity's intentional consciousness – that is, of communicating with her. In so doing, he wryly notes the limits of Boyer's cognitive theory of religion (Boyer 1994). If Boyer was right, then representations of divinities would always be as counter-intuitive as possible, as this would render them more remarkable and easier to remember. They would all be aniconic objects like, for example, the beautiful black stone, perfectly spherical and polished, with which the Daitas of Orissa represent the world as a seed.[5] However, such representations are in fact very rare. It is much more common to find anthropomorphic representations that are so anthropomorphic that they create a seamless continuity between the live, embodied personification of the divinity and its image. 'The more materially realistic the image, at least in certain key respects, the more spiritually it is seen' concludes Gell (1998: 132). Furthermore, if inanimate objects can be anthropomorphised, humans can be dehumanised and treated as beings devoid of intentionality, and this, for Gell, is another reason why Boyer's thesis is problematic. As the dividing line between the intentionality of human beings and that of anthropomorphic objects is hard to establish, it is preferable to speak of distributed persons, and deal with the conceptual difficulty by focusing on the agentive capacities of objects and of their properties, while accepting that art and magic partake of the same powers of seduction.

Bloch's discussion of Gell's theory of art as the attribution of intentionality and power to representational objects (Bloch 1999) highlights the fact that to speak in terms of the intentionality of the distributed person will not solve the conceptual difficulty at work here. On the one hand, Bloch enthusiastically praises Gell's work as an anthropological approach to art that is entirely consistent with cognitive anthropology, and in direct line with Tylor's view of animism. Art as analysed by Gell implies a mode of knowing the world that depends on the human capacity to read minds in very much the same way as animistic beliefs derive from the human propensity to treat non-humans as if they were partly human – that is, as if they possessed a spirit or soul and were capable of intentions. The innate human capacity to grasp the intentionalities of other minds means that humans can attribute beliefs and desires to others, as well as understand the messages that others wish to transmit, whether these are linguistic or not. For the cognitive anthropologist, 'what is of significance in the notion of intentionality is not so much the capacity of human beings to organise their behaviour in relation to their own beliefs and desires, but their ability to understand and control the beliefs and desires of others, in order to adopt the right conduct towards them' (ibid.: 122, my translation). Bloch readily accepts Gell's view that 'art objects are always in some way objects of idolatry', given that 'idolatry, like anthropomorphism, relates to the attribution of a quasi-human will to objects', and, like fetishism, 'depends on the attribution of human traits to species or objects *which are not human*' (ibid.: 123–25)., my translation).

The notions of distributed person and social agency put forward by Gell do not, however, receive the same enthusiastic approval from Bloch. Bloch indicates that he would have preferred Gell to use the term 'intention' rather than 'intentionality'. If the term intentionality 'highlights the fact that art objects are best thought in terms of the imagined or real intentionalities that meet in them' (ibid.: 130, my translation), speaking of 'intention' would have made it clearer that what is at stake is 'the representation of the relation between beliefs and wishes of others, and, to a certain extent, the way in which we represent to ourselves what makes us act' (ibid.: 131, my translation). Gell did not have the time to clarify his thoughts on the ontological status of the art object, and the same ambiguity characterises Bloch's appreciation. If Bloch treats art objects as 'material relays between persons within social networks' (ibid.: 124) in one section of the review, he speaks, in another one, of 'social actors in their own right,' (ibid.: 125), and appears to be much more comfortable with the latter view, which allows him to treat art objects as a technology of communication, very much as writing is.

Far from being a digression, this discussion allows us to appreciate in all its complexity Descola's proposition that the soul is what unites all communicating beings. This question is not trivial, as it takes us beyond animism straight into the heart of the nature/culture debate, a debate which is fundamentally about the ideal and the real (Godelier 1986), or, in the post-humanist terminology used by Barad (2007), agential realism. If intentions and the desire to communicate are so central to animism, the issue then becomes one of establishing whether intentionality and sign exchange is exclusively a human property, or not.

Is Life Intentional?

The redefinition of animism in terms of intentional relatedness offered by authors as different as Bird-David, Ingold, Hornborg, Descola, Gell and Bloch raises the question of anthropocentrism. Is not the desire to communicate with and relate to not only other humans but also the world a profoundly human characteristic? Regardless of their philosophical or epistemological starting point, these authors offer explanations that converge on the fact that beings standing in a relation of communication vis-à-vis humans, whether they are perceived, experienced or cognised by humans to be so, loose their status of mere objects and become subjects.

For Ingold, wherever there is relationality and communication, there is a beginning of life: 'indigenous peoples to whom the label of animism has classically been applied ... are united not in their beliefs but in a way of being that is alive and open to a world of continuous birth. In this ... ontology, beings ... issue forth through a world-in-formation, along the lines of their relationships' (Ingold 2006: 11). Life does not come about within an already existing world, peopled with objects and organisms; rather, life is part of the process through which the world gets continuously renewed. Life is immanent in the 'coming-into-being' of the world. Ingold thus rejects the view that animism is a belief system aimed at attributing life and spirituality to inert objects. Animism should be understood as a way of being-in-the-world, more, as a condition of:

> being alive to the world, characterised by a heightened sensitivity and responsiveness, in perception and action, to an environment that is always in flux, never the same from one moment to the next ... The animacy of the lifeworld ... is not the result of an infusion of spirit into substance, or of agency into materiality, but is rather ontologically prior to their differentiation. (ibid.:10)

Bird-David, who argues that 'animistic epistemology is relational rather than objectivist' (Bird-David 2006: 44) agrees with Ingold that dialogical animacy, rather than animism, is the defining character of indigenous relational epistemology. Unlike Ingold, however, she specifies that even among the Nayaka animistic epistemology is not the only way of knowing the world, and that, therefore, ways of knowing are intentionally selected. When the Nayaka use animism to describe and understand what happens between them and other beings, and by so doing perceive the latter as animated, *they purposefully choose to do so*.

After having praised the scientific animism of von Uexküll and Bateson, Alf Hornborg (2006) opts for a clear-cut differentiation between the living and the non-living world, or at least, for keeping machines and machine-made objects separate from the rest of the world. Animism should be kept distinct from fetishism as two very different ways of knowing or, rather, not knowing the world. Unlike Ingold, Hornborg does not think that all animations have the same significance. Animations should be categorised according to their political and economic history. Primarily concerned with the power imbalances that structure contemporary interconnectedness, Hornborg upholds the claim that: 'we more than ever need to retain our capacity to distinguish between those aspects of technology that derive from Nature and those aspects that derive from Society. The Laws of Thermodynamics and the political economy of oil prices require completely different analytical tools' (ibid.: 30). Anthropologists, he concludes, must theorise animism and animation in historically informed terms, and establish the impact of modernisation on the cognition of subject–object relations.

Speaking of animation, rather than animacy, Scott (2006) remarks that to be alive is to have agentive powers. There is in Cree culture, as in many other cultures, a category corresponding to the concept of 'animation', as well as a one for 'death', but none for the state of non-animation. Bloch (1998: 48) has similarly noted that whereas the Zafimaniry word for living (*velona*) applies not only to all living beings, but also to some objects and things (such as clouds, quartz stones and motor engines), the word for dead (*maty*) 'applies to almost anything that does not work or is broken', adding that the word for corpse (*faty*, literally 'that which has died'), which is derived from the same root as *maty*, only applies to humans and to a few animals. Scott sees it as very significant that for many people the state of 'non-animation' does not receive conceptual or categorical elaboration. There is much ethnographic evidence to show that people do not always agree on what life is about or means, and even when they seem to agree they may do so for entirely different reasons. Furthermore, there seems to be no universal distinction between what is alive and what is not (Bloch 1998; Ingold 2006). Rather, what is striking about the conceptualisation of life is its 'more or less' character (Bloch 1998: 53). Theorising within the ritual context the enigmatic commonality that connects humans and other species that share life, Bloch stresses that 'the recognition of intentionality in other animate beings' is a central feature of 'the content of the cognition of "life"' (ibid.: 50).

Scott (1996, 2006), on the other hand, pays careful attention to animal behaviour, and to the ways in which native Americans get to know geese or bears as sentient and communicative beings well aware of humans as hunters. Animals learn through interaction, and communicate what they learn to other members of their species. Scott's detailed and suggestive descriptions of interactions between animals and humans not only illustrate how the Cree grant human-like intentions to animals, but also how animals actively communicate with humans, although their actual intentions are, of course, always perceived through human interpretations. He thus gives readers a real sense for what shared life means in practice where and when humans interact with animal species. Kohn's exploration of the Runa treatment of their hunting dogs (Kohn 2007) similarly stresses the embodied, historical and emergent nature of animal–human interactions, but in a very different cultural context, although both Cree and Runa may be said to have the same broad conception of shared human subjectivity, and thus to accept the possibility of trans-specific communication. Whereas Scott discusses communication events between human hunters and game animals, Kohn analyses the way in which human hunters interact with their hunting dogs through feeding practices, rites and interpretations of their pets' mental states. Kohn argues that 'in their mutual attempts to live together and make sense of each other, dogs and people increasingly come to partake in a shared constellation of attributes and dispositions' (ibid.: 7).

Kohn convincingly shows how Amazonian perspectivism works in the Runa context to render dogs wilder and less domesticated than they actually are biologically and ethologically. He also successfully conveys the fraught and ambivalent nature of this historically and culturally constructed dog–human relationship, in which dogs get entangled in the relations of domination that have structured their masters' lives since colonial times. What makes his ethnography so poignant, however, is the revelation of the gulf that exists between the dogs' natural disposition to serve, obey and anticipate human wishes on the one hand, and, on the other, the Runas' determination to treat their dogs as unattached, ambivalent forest beings not fully controllable and not fully deserving the tender and loving care that humans normally grant to those who live with them. However, as in Scott's examples, we inevitably get to know much more about human intentions and representations of dogs' mental states than we do about the dogs' representations of their masters. It follows that Kohn's generalisations about semiotic interaction between and within phenomenal worlds (ibid.: 4) do not fully engage 'the place of cognition within the historical process' (Bloch 2005: 1). In any case, he is certainly right in trying to develop a theory of the 'ecology of selves' and an 'anthropology of life' on the basis of ethnographic studies of the domesticatory process, for it is in domestication that the lives of humans and other species get the most entangled, either intentionally or not (Rival 2006, 2007).

Are Plants Alive?

In his contribution to a book I edited some years ago, Bloch (1998) argues that the attribution of life, which derives from the human disposition to interpret animation as a sign of intentionality,[6] is necessarily graded. This is why animals are generally considered to be more alive than plants. He thus concludes that recurrences in plant symbolism and religious use noted in so many ethnographies can be partly explained by the fact that the presence or absence of not just intentionality but *life itself* is uncertain in plants. Bloch's inclination to link so closely the attribution of life and the attribution of intentionality may be due to the influence of Malagasy and African religious use of natural symbols. It is possible that there is in this part of the world a cultural tendency, as in Western thought, to contrast conscious life with vegetative life, and to restrict the former to humans and animals. This may in turn explain why Bloch favours Carey's 'claim that young children's conceptions of the biological world are anthropocentric' (Atran and Medin 2008: 121) over Atran's thesis that an 'initial assumption of an underlying essence for biological kinds ... may be universal' (ibid.: 136).

Atran's approach to folkbiology through ecological reasoning gives much importance to conditions of learning – that is, to whether children are in intimate contact with nature, and whether their understanding of biology has been modified by schooling. It also gives full significance to the cultural system in which children are socialised. The Itzaj Maya's knowledge of their forest environment is structured by their systematic search for causal ecological explanations. In their 'ecology on a human scale', 'to infer how the forest can stay alive is to imagine how they can survive' (ibid.: 174). Environmental knowledge is not just a matter of perception but also of commitment to 'the spirited Maya landscape' (ibid.: 168–69). Perception is combined 'with affective value that sustains reciprocity, respect and fitness and goes beyond mere observation and consideration of the entities involved' (ibid.: 169). It is clear that the Itzaj Maya and the Zafimaniry inhabit different animistic worlds.

The disagreement between Atran and Bloch on the nature of living kinds may also be related to the fact that their interest in cognitive constraints on plant knowledge arise from slightly different concerns. Whereas Atran's interest stems from his theoretical concern with the continuities and discontinuities existing between folk and scientific knowledge, Bloch's interest relates primarily to his work on the nature of ritual communication. As discussed earlier, for Bloch, the ritual manipulation of plant symbolism plays on the similarities and differences between human life and life in non-humans, the latter being constructed as far more uncertain and graded than the former. Moreover, as I have already indicated, the close link that Bloch establishes between human life and social intelligence – that is, the capacity to attribute mental states and intentions to others, and to read the minds of others, as well as their readings of our own minds – leads him to interpret ethnographic data in terms of a radical difference between human beings and other ontological species, which then gets played out in ritual substitution. This method of analysis, in my view, does not consider with sufficient attention the possible status differential between living beings (a plant, an animal, or a child), and inert objects (a stone, a wood carving, a bamboo flute, or an aeroplane).

The significance of the difference between something alive and something lifeless that I am trying to get at here is well captured in Gell's discussion of the aesthetic qualities of yams in the Sepik. In a brief paragraph, which to my knowledge has never been commented upon before, Gell mentions art objects whose artistic value is 'self-made':

> Long yams are displayed at annual festivals by the Abelam of the Sepik district, New Guinea, as cult objects. They are in fact decorated (painted and provided with masks) but the object on display is the yam itself, rather than the mask. Yams grow themselves. It is true that yam growers can assist yams to grow, technically, by hollowing out the earth around the growing tuber, and socially, by refraining from sexual intercourse, which is deleterious (or, more precisely, offensive, to yams). The yam must be magically protected, but the magic of yam-growing does not cause tuberous growth. The powers of growth inherent in yams is precisely why they are cultivated ceremonially and exhibited ... [Y]ams are alive and social agents, just like people, [they] provide a suitable example of indexes which exert agency with respect to themselves ... [A]ll living things are agents with respect to themselves in that their growth and form may be attributed to their own agency. (Gell 1998: 41)

It is as biological organisms with the inherent power to grow that these yams become valued art objects. It is their power to grow themselves and be alive which causes admiration and makes them into social agents 'just like people'. The intentions of the yam cultivator or of the mask maker are not projected onto the yams, or at least their ritual efficacy does not seem to derive from such intentionality. Humans recognise qualities they value in the yams' vitality and will to live; in fact, they partake of these shared qualities, hence the sexual prohibitions. However, the will to live is not human-centred or intentional; it is located in the body rather than in the mind. Gell again refers to the extraordinary power of living things to grow in a later section of his book dedicated to sorcery (ibid.: 96-101). Like plants, human bodies have parts that grow continuously – hair, nails, and skin – which disperse around us, and may become the targets of witch attacks.

This acknowledgement by Gell of a 'vegetal' property shared by all living beings – but especially salient in plants – is particularly significant, as well as his distinction between the kind of intentionality that arises in socially constructed forms of communication and in organic growth. Of course, we will never know how Gell would have reconciled the power of self-creation with his theory of animation, or with his proposition of multiple intentionality in agents. However, Gell clearly stressed the symbolic significance of the fact that a stone, even when endowed with a spirit, will never be alive, grow, reproduce or die.

Gell's appreciation of organic life is echoed by Hornborg (2001, 2006) and Kohn (2007), who stress that communication between humans constitutes only a small part of a much wider flux of communicating signs within nature. Both urge anthropologists to engage with a renewed, generalised and emergent semiotics, which alone will allow for the correct interpretation of animistic cultures. With his call for a 'materially grounded semiosis' which would look at interactions between humans and 'other kinds of living selves', Kohn boldly states that 'sign production and use are internal to biological dynamics' (Kohn 2007: 18). Like Barad (2007), he is wary of anthropocentric understandings of the life and communicative acts of non-humans. Although Barad is, like Kohn, interested in renewing the nature/culture debate by offering new ways of conceptualising the real and the material, she has no interest in the biotic, organic world, or in ecological relations per se. Her semiotic reflection involves the world of quantum physics. The material reality she is concerned with reconfigures matter/discourse entanglements of 'space/world/body' and 'matter/space/time' (ibid.: 185). To apprehend the dynamism and vitalism of matter, Barad aims to overcome what she sees as the anthropocentric representationalism that lies at the core of Judith Butler's theory of performativity.[7] When Barad speaks of the 'agentivity of matter' she refers to the dynamism of matter, which needs to be kept distinct from human agentivity (ibid.: 445, n.43) but in a way that accommodates the need to abolish the distinction between 'internal' and 'external' (ibid.: 136). How, then, should we theorise the agentivity of non-humans? Is it possible to theorise agency or agentivity without any reference to human intentionality? And, more importantly, is it what Amerindians do in their own epistemologies? Is there a place in Amerindian thought for a conception of biological life autonomous from social intelligence and its socially determined intentions?

By paying careful attention to the role that plants play in the 'materially grounded semiosis' envisaged by Kohn, we will further our understanding of the agentivity of non-humans in Amerindian thought, which is characterised, as many authors have stressed, by a recurring obsession with the body as 'ontological operator' (Descola 2005). I have offered my critical reflection on the state of current debates regarding animistic beliefs as a first and necessary step towards the worthy project of examining, to use Kohn's terminology, the interactions between humans and other kinds of living selves in a variety of cultural contexts. I have shown the dangers of rethinking animism in terms that reconceptualise material facts as the products of human intentionality, or as effects of human agency, for there is more to materiality and to life as they are apprehended by the human mind, in Amazonia and elsewhere. One of the issues at stake, as I hope to have made clear, is what is actually meant by 'living' in 'living selves' and by 'ecology' in 'ecology of selves'.

On the basis of this renewed discussion of animism, I would like to propose the hypothesis, to be examined through further field research, that culturally significant plants such as manioc may be thought by native Amazonians as living a double life. Preliminary field research among the Huaorani and the Makushi suggests that two distinct life forces may be at work, one characterising the intentionality of the master spirit or soul of the plant, the other relating to its biological condition. These two life forces must be distinguished, for they refer to two different kinds of will: the will to communicate, and the will to live. In researching plant symbolism, we should be careful not to assume from the outset that the soul in the plant relates and communicates as if it were in any other kind of body, or that the plant-person is a self like any other self, be it human, animal or spirit. Furthermore, we should examine very carefully the ways in which native Amazonians reason about ecological relations, and use this thinking to inform the extraordinarily diverse and dynamic system management that has given rise to the domesticated landscapes of lowland South America.

Notes

1. On plant symbolism, see Rival (1993, 1997, 1998b, 1999, 2001); on plant knowledge, Rival (1998a, 2009), Rival and McKey (2008) and Clement, Rival and Cole (2009).
2. Notable exceptions are Chaumeil and Chaumeil (1992), Hugh Jones (1993), Barbira Friedman (2002) and Lenaerts (2004).
3. The original passage reads, 'Cette disposition humanise les plantes, et surtout les animaux, puisque l'âme dont ils sont dotés leur permet non seulement de se comporter selon les normes sociales et les préceptes éthiques des humains, mais aussi d'établir avec ces derniers et entre eux des relations de communication'.
4. Compare with Bloch's remark: 'The naïve psychology involved [here] is the ability to interpret animation as the sign of intentionality, or, in other words, the imaginative attribution of a mind to other beings' (Bloch 1998: 49).
5. See Gell (1998: 132, and 146, fig.7.12/1).
6. See note 4, above.
7. 'It seems that at every turn lately every "thing" (even materiality) is turned into a matter of language or some other form of cultural representation' (Barad 2007: 132).

References

Atran, S. 1999. 'Itzaj Maya Folkbiological Taxonomy: Cognitive Universals and Cultural Particulars', in D. Medlin and S. Atran (eds), *Folkbiology*. Cambridge, MA: MIT Press, pp. 119–204.

——— 2001. 'The Vanishing Landscape of the Petén Maya Lowlands: People, Plants, Animals, Places, Words, and Spirits', in L. Maffi (ed.), *On Biological Diversity: Linking Language, Knowledge, and the Environment*. Washington, DC: Smithsonian Institution Press, pp. 157–74.
Atran, S., and D. Medin. 2008. *The Native Mind and the Cultural Construction of Nature*. Cambridge, MA: MIT Press.
Barad, K. 2007. *Meeting the Universe Halfway: Quantum Physics and the Entanglement of Matter and Meaning*. Durham, NC: Duke University Press.
Barbira Friedman, F. 2002. 'Tobacco and Curing Agency in Western Amazonian Shamanism', in P.A. Baker and G. Carr (eds), *Practitioners, Practices and Patients: New Approaches to Medical Archaeology and Anthropology*. Oxford: Oxbow Books, pp. 136–60.
Bird-David, N. 2006. 'Animistic Epistemology: Why do Some Hunter-gatherers Not Depict Animals?' *Ethnos* 71(1): 33–50.
Bloch, M. 1998. 'Why Trees, Too, are Good to Think with: Towards an Anthropology of the Meaning of Life', in L. Rival (ed.), *The Social Life of Trees:Anthropological Perspectives on Tree Symbolism*. Oxford: Berg, pp. 39–56.
——— 1999. 'Une nouvelle théorie de l'art', *Terrain* 32: 119–28.
——— 2005. *Essays on Cultural Transmission*. Oxford: Berg.
Boyer, P. 1994. *The Naturalness of Religious Ideas: A Cognitive Theory of Religion*. Cambridge: Cambridge University Press.
Carneiro, R.L. 2000. 'The Evolution of the Tipití', in G.M. Feinman and L. Manzanilla (eds), *Cultural Evolution: Contemporary Viewpoints*. New York: Kluwer Academic/Plenum Publishers, pp. 61–93.
Chaumeil, B., and J.P. Chaumeil. 1992. 'L'oncle et le neveu: la parenté du vivant chez les Yaguas (Amazonie péruvienne)', *Journal de la Société des Américanistes* 78(2): 25–37.
Clement, C., L. Rival and D. Cole. 2009. 'Domestication of Peach Palm (Bactris Gasipaes Kunth): The Roles of Human Mobility and Migration', in M. Alexiades (ed.), *The Ethnobiology of Mobility, Displacement and Migration in Indigenous Lowland South America*. Oxford: Berghahn, pp. 117–40.
Descola, P. 1994. *In the Society of Nature: A Native Ecology in Amazonia*. Cambridge: Cambridge University Press.
——— 2005. *Par delà nature et culture*. Paris: Gallimard.
Gell, A. 1998. *Art and Agency: An Anthropological Theory*. Oxford: Clarendon Press.
Godelier, M. 1986. *The Mental and the Material: Thought, Economy and Society*. London: Verso.
Hornborg, A. 2001. *The Power of the Machine: Global Inequalities of Economy, Technology, and Environment*. Walnut Creek, CA: AltaMira Press.
——— 2006. 'Animism, Fetishism, and Objectivism as Strategies for Knowing (or Not Knowing) the World', *Ethnos* 71(1): 21–32.
Hugh Jones, C. 1979. *From the Milk River: Spatial and Temporal Processes in Northwest Amazonia*. Cambridge: Cambridge University Press.
Hugh Jones, S., and C. Hugh Jones. 1993. '"Foods" and "Drugs" in Northwest Amazonia', in C.M. Hladik, A. Hladik, O.F. Linares, H. Pagezy, A. Semple and M. Hadley (eds), *Tropical Forests, People and Food: Biocultural Interactions and Applications to Development*. Paris: UNESCO/Parthenon, pp. 533–48.
Ingold, T. 2006. 'Rethinking the Animate, Re-animating Thought', *Ethnos* 71(1): 9–20.
Kohn, E. 2007. 'How Dogs Dream: Amazonian Natures and the Politics of Transspecies Engagement, *American Ethnologist* 34(1): 3–24.

Lenaerts, M. 2004. *Anthropologie des indiens Asheninka d'Amazonie: nos soeurs Manioc et l'étranger Jaguar*. Paris: L'Harmattan.

Rival, L. 1993. 'The Growth of Family Trees: Huaorani Conceptualization of Nature and Society', *Man* 28(4): 635–52.

——— 1997. 'The Huaorani and their Trees: Managing and Imagining the Ecuadorian Rain Forest', in K. Seeland (ed.), *Nature is Culture: Indigenous Knowledge and Socio-cultural Aspects of Trees and Forests in Non-European Cultures*. London: Intermediate Technology Publications, pp. 67–68.

——— 1998a. 'Domestication as a Historical and Symbolic Process: Wild Gardens and Cultivated Forests in the Ecuadorian Amazon', in W. Balée (ed.), *Principles of Historical Ecology*. New York: Columbia University Press, pp. 232–50.

——— 1998b. 'Trees: From Symbols of Life and Regeneration to Political Artefacts', in L. Rival (ed.), *The Social Life of Trees: Anthropological Perspectives on Tree Symbolism*. Oxford: Berg, pp. 1–36.

——— 1999. 'Trees and the Symbolism of Life in Indigenous Cosmologies', in D. Posey (ed.), *Cultural and Spiritual Values of Biodiversity*. Nairobi: UNEP, pp. 358-63.

——— 2001. 'Seed and Clone: A Preliminary Note on Manioc Domestication, and its Implication for Symbolic and Social Analysis', in L. Rival (ed.), *Beyond the Visible and the Material: The Amerindianization of Society in the Work of Peter Rivière*. Oxford: Oxford University Press, pp. 57–80.

——— 2006. 'Amazonian Historical Ecologies', *Journal of the Royal Anthropological Institute*, special issue 12S: 97–116.

——— 2007. 'Domesticating the Landscape, Producing Crops, and Reproducing Society in Amazonia', in D. Parkin and S. Ulijaszek (eds), *Convergence and Emergence: Towards a New Holistic Anthropology?* Oxford: Berghahn, pp. 72–90.

——— 2009. 'Huaorani Ways of Naming Trees', in M. Alexiades (ed.), *The Ethnobiology of Mobility, Displacement and Migration in Indigenous Lowland South America*. Oxford: Berghahn, pp. 47–68.

Rival, L., and D. McKey. 2008. 'Domestication and Diversity in Manioc (*Manihot esculenta* Crantz ssp. *esculenta*, Euphorbiaceae)', *Current Anthropology* 49(6): 1119–28.

Scott, C. 1996. 'Science for the West, Myth for the Rest? The Case of James Bay Cree Knowledge Production', in L. Nader (ed.), *Naked Science: Anthropological Inquiry into Boundaries, Power and Knowledge*. New York: Routledge, pp. 69–86.

——— 2006. 'Spirit and Practical Knowledge in the Person of the Bear among Wemındji Cree Hunters', *Ethnos* 71(1): 51–66.

CHAPTER 4

Stories about Evenki People and their Dogs: Communication through Sharing Contexts

Tatiana Safonova and István Sántha

The Evenki people have inspired a number of anthropologists to reflect on the problem of communication between them and neighbouring people. In 1935 Shirokogoroff introduced the Evenki word *shaman* into scientific discourse, shamanism later becoming an independent anthropological category (see Shirokogoroff 1999). He devoted much of his writing to the description of social structures and kinship terms that the Evenki obtained from neighbours, such as Buryats or Yakuts (Shirokogoroff 1929). He also wrote a chapter on Evenki character, in which he described the way Evenki were attentive observers and learners, and how they tricked strangers. Lindgren (1936) analysed *andaki* relationships (business contacts) established between Russians and Evenki in Manchuria. Her account illuminates the intense and coordinated long-term collaboration between people with quite different social positions. More recently, Ssorin-Chaikov also addressed the problem of intercultural communication and the place of the Evenki in Soviet state institutions and organisations such as *kolkhozes* (Ssorin-Chaikov 2003). He described how the state (represented mainly by Russians) was constructing a special role (the so-called 'Last Evenki') by stigmatising one person from the Evenki community as a 'child of nature', and supported the emancipation of Evenki women. These tendencies were observed in different parts of Siberia, and even in the Far East, where Kwon (1993) conducted his doctoral research. Kwon worked among the Oroch people, who share the Manchu-Tungus origin of the Evenki people. According to Kwon, women were much more educated and suffered from the inability to find appropriate marriage partners among Oroch men, most of whom they considered uncivilised.

Both pre-Soviet colonisation policy and Soviet intrusion led to the problematic position of Evenki as an independent cultural group in relation to Russians, Buryats and Yakuts. But local ethnographic accounts demonstrate that, despite institutionally supported pressure, Evenki people from different local groups managed to safeguard their egalitarian ethos – one of the most recognisable characteristics of hunter-gatherers all over the world (Lee and Daly 1999).

Willerslev (2004) has made an attempt to introduce materials about Siberian hunter-gatherers into the debate about egalitarian epistemology. He studied the relationships between Yukaghir hunters (a group whose lifestyle resembles that of the Evenki), animals and spirits, and demonstrated that these can be described in terms of perspectivism, a theory based on data about Amazonian people. Strathern describes perspectivism as pointing to 'spiritual or intellectual unity and corporal diversity … perspectives are different according to the body one has' (Strathern 2005: 140). Willerslev stated that for Yukaghirs hunting is a process of seduction and play with the boundary between people and animals. The hunter needs to feel distance between themselves and their prey in order to communicate with it and at the same time not become too involved and forget the real distinction between themselves and the animal.

In the case of Kurumkan Evenki, we doubt that such an interpretation of hunting is relevant because we see the need to avoid interpretations in terms of subordination and domination. For Evenki, prey is more like a competitive partner who is not in any sense weaker or stronger. Evenki are not trying to seduce or cheat their prey, but rather prefer to come across it accidently and then compete with it regarding speed of reactions. Hunting is emotionally appealing and interesting to Evenki only if this view is realised. This is also the basis for their critical attitude towards poaching, which they nonetheless practise without ascribing any verbal interpretation to it. Poaching becomes emotionally involving when other people, such as nature-reserve rangers, are involved as competing and equal partners.

Evenki social organisation can be interpreted as based on animistic epistemology as described by Bird-David (1991) and Ingold (2000: 111–31). In her attempt to revise animism, Bird-David turned to the concept of the 'dividual' person formulated by Strathern (1988) on the basis of the latter's study of Melanesian ethnographic materials. The dividual person expresses itself and exists in the relationships it establishes with others. These relationships are pre-existing in the person, not in the form of accumulated norms and knowledge about social dispositions but as distinctions that anticipate the relationships (ibid.). This thesis is also true for Evenki people, for whom verbal knowledge is secondary in comparison to the skill and ability to conduct relationships with others.

The Kurumkan Evenki can help us study the intra-cultural communication process. First, in their everyday life they present most of the patterns associated with egalitarian social organisation. While Kurumkan Evenki avoid any trait of hierarchy in face-to-face interactions (remaining silent if it prevents the development and demonstration of someone's authoritative position), their neighbours the Buryats (who are frequently the only possible marriage partners or colleagues at work) insist on a patriarchal structure and verbal displays of subordination or dominance. Which cultural device helps the Evenki cope with Buryats while retaining their feeling of autonomy from hierarchical structures imposed by Buryats?

Secondly, Evenki spiritual life shares common features with animism and perspectivism, but does not absolutely fit the proposed theoretical schemes. If the Amazonian version of perspectivism is based on the idea that people, animals and spirits are equal, but that a hierarchy is created by the perspective from which every creature sees the others (every creature sees itself as human, and the others as either superior spirits or subordinated animals), Evenki see interaction between people, animals and spirits as a competition in which all participants are equal. For example, Evenki dogs are equal partners in hunting and they have their own hunting luck, *talan*. On one occasion we observed how, during a ritual devoted to the celebration of the spirit of rain and river, the Evenki tried to compete with the celebrated force, and even risked death to cross the river in full flood. They did not show any trait of subordination to natural forces (such as full flood or bad weather), and instead of asking for something from nature they wanted to take up the challenge. Evenki avoid hierarchies in their relationships with other species and spirits, but have to collaborate with non-Evenki people in terms of hierarchical principles. How do they manage to do so without breaking the consistency of their egalitarian selves? We found the answer to these questions with help from Evenki dogs.

Secrets, Stories and Communication

The relationship between Evenki people and their dogs is an intricate problem, not only for scientists but also for their neighbours, the Buryats. One Buryat shaman said he never understood how Evenki hunters could communicate with their dogs during hunting. To him, it seemed that dog and hunter do not communicate at all but work independently. He never heard the hunter give orders, but at the same time watched as man and dog succeeded in coordinating their actions with amazing synchronicity and harmony. He had the impression that an unseen thread existed between the hunter and their dog. This was an incomprehensible Evenki secret for Buryats. However, this secret lies not in spiritual ties between a dog and a hunter, but in the whole social organisation of the Evenki community, and the basic skill of situated communication.

This chapter is devoted to the problem of the form communication between humans and non-humans takes in different contexts of social organisation. That means the possibility of mutual understanding, or coordination of mutual actions depending on skills, that in turn is embedded in and predetermined by social organisation. At the same time, the experience of successful interaction between humans and non-humans and coordination shapes the idea of self. The absence of strict boundaries between species in the communicative sphere is an important part of animistic epistemology (Bird-David 1991).

The ecological environment which shapes Evenki lifestyle is important if we are interested in depicting a total picture of the communicative process. Things like rhythm of life, emotional involvement and experiencing emergencies and risks constitute crucial contexts and frames without which the communicative process is impossible. This is why we are interested in the distinction presented by Pedersen (2001) between taiga and steppe modes of thought. If thought is seen as a process, then it exists primarily in communication. This distinction also describes the difference between two regimes of communication. A Buryat shaman understands this difference as a secret. We will return to the problem of secrets in culture contacts later, when we expand our theory of communication to situations of cultural contacts.

To explain how communication should occur is a complex task which requires a reflexive attitude towards logical typing,[1] which Bateson thought to be an 'inevitable ingredient in the relationship between any describer and any system to be described' (Bateson 1958: 294). Here we refer to the notion of metacommunication introduced by Bateson (1979). To understand communicative processes is to reveal those metamessages incorporated in the communicative process itself. To understand each other, we need to communicate not only the contents of our messages but also messages about how this content should be interpreted – information about the frame of interpretation is the metamessage.

The transmission of culture happens not only through the transfer of knowledge from one generation to the other (which can happen in forms of storytelling), but also through acquiring storytelling skills. Only the successful transmission of these skills guarantees understanding (Sacks 1992). Storytelling and understanding stories are reversible processes founded in experiencing stories. By presenting stories, in this chapter we hope their content will not fail to transmit important metamessages and skills of communication that we learned from Evenki people during fieldwork.

We conducted fieldwork in the spring of 2006, when we spent two months with an Evenki family at a remote farm called Camp Jirga. We lived with the shaman, Orochon, and his wife, Grandmother Masha, and did everything we could to help their son Stepan and his wife Olya with the household and cattle. Three of Stepan and Olya's children also lived there: Kolya, a boy of 7; Luba, a girl of 6; and Tamara, a girl of 3.

Cattle breeding is not a new occupation for Evenki in this region. This particular group is called Murchen, which means 'people who breed horses'. This specialisation differentiates them from the neighbouring Evenki group, the Orochony, reindeer herders, whose name Grandfather Orochon received when he was born, because at that moment some Orochony were living nearby. Even before the October revolution of 1917, local Evenki bred cattle, like the neighbouring Buryats. In 1990, after most of the surrounding forest was designated as a nature reserve, Evenki were denied hunting as a legal occupation. But, as we have shown elsewhere (Safonova and Sántha 2007), they maintained their social organisation by preserving balances between everyday involvement in cattle breeding and culturally preferable emotional states. These states are associated with hunting, aggression and risky behaviour during heavy drinking and inappropriate (from a Western perspective) risks in travelling. Sympathy and aggression are so closely related in this community that you never find one without a touch of the other. The attitude towards dogs is no exception.

Palma: A Russian Dog from the TV Tower

The first story is about a dog from the TV tower. We once went with Orochon to the TV tower across from his former hunting territories. The trip there took a day, and we stayed overnight. The aim was to ask people from the tower for petrol, which they had previously promised (petrol is like gold in this part of Siberia, a precious and rare substance). We were not very successful. The people at the TV tower told us that the tower would soon be closed, and, as a result, they would have no chance to transport petrol for us. When we left the tower, the guard dog living there followed us. She was a fine, nice dog called Palma. We felt she somehow knew the tower would be destroyed, and was trying to find a new home. She proved herself a very good companion in the forest, quiet and independent; we saw her from time to time searching around the area. Orochon said she behaved like a very good hunting dog, but she was not raised among Evenki. We did not understand why her socialisation was so important. When we stopped for tea on our way home, Orochon shared bread and butter with Palma. When we approached the camp the other dogs aggressively tried to drive her out. Orochon didn't stop them, but continued talking to Palma in a calm manner as he had done all the way. He said things like: 'We are going together', 'Run, run with us'. He repeated these phrases without paying any attention to the dog. It seemed to us that Orochon was glad, because his own dog had died recently and he said he could not imagine spending the summer at the camp alone with Grandmother (Stepan and his family migrate to the summer camp in the summer, leaving the old couple alone). But when we awoke the next day, the dog was gone. Grandmother told us that Stepan had banished her early in the morning. He said the dog was dangerous for children. Palma was not aggressive, and Stepan's explanation could only be understood in the context of Orochon's doubts about her socialisation.

According to Bargai, the Buryat shaman, Evenki previously stole dogs from their neighbours, but only puppies. Bargai thought the reason why Evenki paid so little attention to the heredity of a dog, which was the most important thing in Buryat opinion, but were so concerned about the dog's socialisation, was a secret. We should be clear that by socialisation we do not mean the process of education or direct teaching. During our fieldwork we witnessed three little puppies living at the camp and the neighbouring cordon of the nature reserve (the home of one of Orochon's younger daughters) to whom nobody taught anything. There was no place for mistakes in Evenki society – you could feel the important frames of interaction, or be excluded from them. For example, Evenki would not excuse the little puppy for attempting to catch and kill a chicken or a sheep. They believe a dog that tastes the blood of domestic animals will repeat its attempts. Evenki do not teach by punishment. If the dog makes such a mistake, confusing hunting in the forest with life at the camp, they kill the dog. Socialisation is a process not of correction but of survival of the most flexible and intelligent individuals. There is only one way to become an Evenki dog: to grow up with Evenki children. And likewise, to become an Evenki person, you must grow up with Evenki dogs.

Children playing with dogs and puppies were sometimes very cruel. Nobody stopped them; it was a way to give children their autonomy, and at the same time to give them an opportunity to learn to be aggressive. Aggression is a social feeling which children have to learn, and for which they need space for practice (Harrison 1989). Dogs are partners in this mutual socialisation process. At the same time, dogs learn to bear this aggression and not withdraw from interaction. Evenki dogs, like Evenki themselves, never interpret violence as punishment, because their earliest experiences of aggression are not attempts to improve their behaviour but an ordinary and quite neutral expression of relation. Biting or kicking does not send a message of correction.

This frame is important for teaching Evenki people and their dogs to be autonomous from each other. The dog from the TV tower was different because she would never understand this relation, and would either obey or resist aggression. She was dangerous for children because she could teach them to fear aggression (either by biting them or by showing her own fear) and this posed a very big threat for the Evenki. It was not the fangs of the dog that were dangerous but her patterns of interaction learned in Russian society that could introduce foreign frames for Evenki children.

It was interesting that Evenki never worried about our influence on their children. We spent a lot of time with them but never became as close to them as they became with their dogs. The border between Evenki and their dogs was much thinner, one might say, than the border between Evenki and us. Our presence among the Evenki was similar to that of a strange dog, occasionally no more than a good companion for a trip.

Sveta and the Puppies

The next story explores an episode between one of the younger daughters of the shaman and her dogs. Sveta worked as a ranger at the local nature reserve and lived in the cordon that was two kilometers from the farm of her family. Sveta's house was the last one in the taiga and she spent most of her time in the forest. Though she had cows, her household was not strongly dependent on cattle breeding. She had a very nice dog, the mother of two puppies. The four were always together, separating only when Sveta went to the village. Sveta always drank in the village and came home late at night unable to speak or interact sanely.

To get to the village we had to cross several rivers, the first of which was rather unpredictable. It was called the Sukhaja, meaning 'dry' in Russian, because it was usually possible to cross in high rubber boots. But in spring there were unpredictable changes people called 'high water' (*Bol'shaja voda*). Everything depended on the sun, which melted ice in the mountains, turning Sukhaja into a big, dangerously strong river. It was not only the sun; rain and other meteorological influences led to the same result. So we never knew when it would be possible or safe to cross the Sukhaja, especially as there was no bridge.

One day, all the members of the Evenki family went to the village for roentgen analysis, an obligatory medical examination that is done to prevent tuberculosis. Quite often locals use this matter as an excuse to leave their households. At the same time, Buryats were conducting a ritual to pray for Evenki ancestors who had inhabited the land before. The ritual was called 'high water', and happened on a day when the Sukhaja was in flood. The Evenki were returning to camp with a case of vodka they had received from the Buryats, but they were stopped by the river. On the other bank of the river, Sveta's dogs were waiting for her. They had left the house and travelled several kilometers to meet her, but could not cross the river. Sveta was already drunk and cried when she saw them. They were very happy to see each other, but could not be together. Then Sveta started to cry about her cows, abandoned at home because of the river. She said she would cross the river, which seemed like suicide. Everybody tried to calm her down. But the only way to do so was to conduct a ritual involving more vodka. It was two days before we managed to cross the Sukhaja. We wondered how the dogs knew where and when to meet Sveta. That was a mystery for us, just as the way an Evenki hunter and his dog could coordinate their actions without seeing or hearing each other was a secret for Bargai.

This story presents an opportunity to think about the form of communication Evenki use with their dogs. We suppose they communicate not by sharing messages but by sharing contexts, or 'frames' to use Gregory Bateson's term (Bateson 1972: 177–93). When Evenki travel with their dogs they never call them or give orders. For example, when we went with Sveta to look at the damage caused by a forest fire, we saw how she walked with her puppies. The puppies tried to imitate their mother and go ahead of Sveta, but they frequently took the wrong path. Sveta never called them and never showed any sign of anxiety. The puppies had to learn to control their curiosity and to watch Sveta at all times. They learned to share the context of travelling together. When we saw Sveta walk with her grown-up dog we were amazed at how the dog managed to remain ahead of us and on the right path. It seemed that their mutual experience of sharing the context of travelling was so complete that they could feel each other's rhythms and knew by slight movements and expressions where to go.

The type of communication we are describing is very close to ostensive communication (Bateson 1979: 120–21). According to Bateson, this communication is essential for humans in language learning; all children must use ostensive communication before they can use words. Together, pointing and speaking constitute a process of learning contexts, and a process of learning words as speech acts in contexts. Ostensive communication, with words or without them, consists of explication of common and shared situational contexts.

When Sveta did not react to her puppies' mistakes, but continued along the correct path, she pointed to the important context of action; she introduced the correct path as a frame for common action. Her puppies learned not to follow Sveta, but to develop common contexts. When they were correct and chose the right way, it was they who chose the road, and it was their decision that determined the way. Walking, for Evenki and dogs, is a process of creation and sharing common contexts in which both parties are equally active. Some day, the decisions of these puppies will become crucial in hunting.

The socialisation of dogs among Evenki is an interesting process. They do not try to train the dog or punish it for mistakes, or even teach it to be in a hierarchical relation with people. On the contrary, they need an independent creature that can be a partner and can make decisions. At the same time, sharing contexts, and feeling that an understanding exists based on these common experiences and mutual orientation to the behaviour of one another, creates a very strong relationship between Evenki and their dogs. This relationship comes from a very deep understanding of body language.

The Death of Orochon's Dog Durak

The dogs from camp spent every night outside and we frequently heard them running and barking. Grandmother Masha told us dogs become independent at night and they resolve all of their problems by themselves. On several occasions we awoke to find little wounds on the dogs, a sign of night-time hunting. The dogs frequently tried to catch the badger living on the neighbouring hill, without success. Sveta somehow knew what happened at night with the dogs, and told us that on one particular night the dogs were trying to catch a wild boar. She laughed about the puppies' attempts to catch it. The nightlife of dogs was full of real risk and they enjoyed it.

Once, after listening to the barking all night, we failed to find Orochon's old dog Durak. For several days we did not see him, and then Orochon found him lying in the bushes. He was unable to stand. Orochon did not try to bring him home, but left him there. The next day, Durak somehow managed to move to the centre of camp, and lay down near the pathway that crossed it. He died several hours later. There was no attempt to heal him. Orochon said we should let him die. The news that Durak had died was accepted without regret. It was just a fact. Orochon took us and his grandson, Kolya, to burn Durak. He said: 'What burns won't rot'. That was his act of sympathy towards old Durak – not to let his body rot and become food for other animals. Orochon made a loop out of wire and tied it around Durak's neck. Then he made a handle out of a stick and we dragged Durak's body to the place for the fire. We collected a lot of firewood to burn everything, including the wire with which we dragged him. We were not gloomy, but even a little playful. Orochon told us about Durak's life, how he was good at hunting squirrels early in his life, and how he was once knocked down by a tractor that left him lame. Durak's body was under the firewood and we couldn't see it burn. We left the place while there was still a big fire. Only the two of us (without Orochon) returned to look at Durak's body. Everything was burnt except his skeleton. We saw the broken ribs which were probably the cause of his death. After that, nobody seemed to remember him. The first story, of Orochon's attempt to get a new dog, is a continuation of this one.

The life of a dog is shorter than the life of a man. Durak was not the first or last dog for Orochon. But for the time they were together, they were partners. They shared roads and food together. Durak was very strong, and, despite being lame, was not in any way subordinate to other dogs at camp. At the same time, he was not a leader, just as his owner, the oldest man at the camp, was not an authoritative figure. The life of dogs was rather free at the camp. Pirate, the dog of Yekhe Bair, Orochon's son-in-law living in the village, came to the camp for the summer. It was his own decision and nobody invited him; he just came and was not refused. Masha and Orochon fed all the dogs once a day, collecting their food in a special bucket. The dogs were never tied. They lived parallel with people at the camp. All the dogs were interested in hunting, and though they rarely went with people, they enjoyed it on their own at night. The night was a risky time for dogs, but it was the time of real freedom. During the day they were sleepy and very calm, tolerating the aggression of children without as much as a growl. But at night, they took their revenge and showed themselves as real hunting dogs, courageous and aggressive. This risky nightlife served as a substitute for hunting with people. These risks help Evenki dogs continue to act like hunters even in times when they cannot hunt. Evenki people also need such spheres: drinking and travelling. The risk that led to Durak's death was also important for people, who took risks by drinking and travelling. Durak died in a situation structurally similar to the second story, about Sveta's potential death.

Once there were risky activities common to people and their dogs, but now they are separated. Dogs survive night-time accidents with wild animals alone, without people. And people survive aggressive and drunken clashes with each other while travelling without their dogs. These are the adaptation strategies of Evenki and their dogs to a world without hunting. And the price of this adaptation is their occasional separation.

The Hunting Luck of Buryat and Evenki Dogs

If we accept the distinction made by Pedersen (2001) between totemistic and animistic societies of North Asia, we could associate Buryats with the former and Evenki with the latter, according to the attention paid to vertical and horizontal relations in these neighbouring societies. This distinction is too sharp, and at the end of the chapter we touch on the more interesting problem of the interconnectedness of totemism and animism in the context of culture contact. But here this distinction is appropriate for thinking about epistemologies (different in different cultures) that determine the place of dogs in society. The dog's character is a result of socialisation, which is, in turn, shaped by the epistemological concerns of a society. Totemism could probably be studied, as animism was by Bird-David (1991), as a pattern of relationships significant to a culture. This 'pattern which connects', to use Bateson's phrase (Bateson 1979: 12), is a generic epistemological principle that grasps skills and practices in a system of inter-balanced circuits. This means that, knowing basic harmonies of concrete epistemology, we can predict some of its practical accomplishments. The dog, being part of the system, becomes adjusted to it and to some extent reveals the patterns of the system. Based on the analysis presented by Willerslev (2004) and Bird-David (1991), we can suppose that in frames of animistic epistemology the borderline between human and non-human is weakest; the more intensive interaction takes place between creatures. Thus, if a dog and a man share situational contexts, they cannot be seen as species of a different kind, and the characterisation of their interaction as one between human and non-human is no longer relevant in animism. On the contrary, totemic epistemology proposes that the origin of a creature is most important, and no common or shared circumstances can obliterate its domination. The only way to organise communication between species of different origins is to construct relations between the origins of species, but not between the species themselves. Hierarchical structures would predominate here. If we compare the place of a dog in Evenki and Buryat communities, we see how perfectly they fit the models sketched above.

Buryats say that the good qualities of a dog are inherited from its mother, and a dog's reputation is based, at least in narrative, on the qualities associated with its mother's nest. Luck in hunting depends on a number of complex conditions, which it is possible to understand in hindsight. The dog doesn't play a crucial role in this process. If it does not do well in the forest, though it has a reputation as a good dog due to its heredity, a Buryat would not blame the dog but would try to find an explanation in past mistakes. For example, they would rather suppose they met someone on the way to the forest, or ignored some other signs of misfortune. The same thing occurs when the hunter is lucky in hunting; it is never directly associated with the work of the dog. However, in practice, the efficacy of the dog is estimated, and the decision to keep or get rid of a dog is made on the basis of these reflections. In narratives, a dog is always judged not by its behaviour but by its heredity. For example, a Buryat would prefer to sell an unsuccessful dog but always claim it has a very good reputation and good inheritance. A really successful dog will never be praised but kept silently. A dog is never fully trusted among Buryats, and there are even cases when hunters lead their dogs on a rope to the forest and free them only when it seems they have noticed something. The hunting dog is like an instrument helping the hunter, who is himself a professional among non-hunters in doing his job. There are other types of dogs, such as guard dogs, that have nothing to do with hunting. Buryats prefer to control their dogs and provide all of their food, without giving them the freedom to look for food in other places. They care for their dogs a great deal, and may even let their dogs in the house, especially in winter. This attitude lies within a frame where dogs are subordinated, obey commands, and are thoroughly dependent, acting more like the property of the hunter than their partner.

Among Evenki, dogs play quite a different role. Evenki dogs never get such care from their owners, and this lack of attention helps them maintain their autonomy. They run free at night and are never allowed inside the house. They are never fed enough and need to hunt wild animals at night for nourishment.

We frequently saw spots of blood on their fur in the morning – signs of their luck in hunting. Being so independent, the dogs share their luck hunting with people. If we recall the socialisation of dogs among the Evenki, which is aimed at raising a partner that can make an important decision in the forest, we see the luck of the hunt is shared by man and dog, just like the road, risks and food.

Evenki dogs are not respected, but people cannot imagine life without them. A dog, being a partner for life, is needed as an extension of the man. We can recall how Orochon needed a new dog after the death of his old one. Having a dog does not mean owning property but means luck in hunting, even if people do not utilise this potential. Luck in hunting is very important for Evenki, allowing them to feel comfortable in life. Luck means captured prey, but it is also the absence of prey. There is a principle of circularity that Evenki use in their everyday life predictions and management. The absence of prey is a sign of future good luck, as if luck is a circuit that needs a fall to reach its peak. In contrast to Buryats, Evenki luck in hunting is about something that happens and not about something that does not happen. For Buryats, luck is important when they do not have it, and when they think they have not done something important to have it. For Evenki, hunting luck is a process of everyday practices, such as ordinary raids through hunting territories in order to watch and clear paths. The fact that they do not capture prey during these trips is not a sign of misfortune but, on the contrary, important grounds for future luck. From this point of view, the immediate efficacy of a dog is also not so important. Any Evenki dog that grew up with them could be neither good nor bad, and nobody would get rid of it unless the dog caused some kind of harm. The dog would not survive without hunting skills, so its fortune is in its own paws, so to speak. Evenki are interested in dogs not as assistants or instruments for successful hunting but as attentive travelling companions.

Conclusion

The recent debate on perspectivism in Siberia (see this volume) demonstrates the need to pay attention to the process of interaction between different modes of thought. Because perspectivism itself originated as a theoretical construction describing the epistemology shared by different peoples in Amazonia, the question of culture contact lies at the core of the phenomenon. And, without making this fact explicit, it is quite problematic to transpose it to the anthropology of other regions and develop it into a concept at a theoretical level.

Culture contact, as a schismogenetic process (Bateson 1972), has a very strong tendency to reach collapse of either a complementary or a symmetrical nature. This means that culture contacts are processes of mutual adjustments to a situation of coexistence, which can lead both to rivalry and to assimilation. If we find stable interactions between two cultures, we always need to look at the circuits that help keep them in balance. Evenki and Buryats have lived near each other for quite a long time and have exchanged many things and skills. For example, western Buryats obtained the skill of hunting from Evenki, and Evenki from the Kurumkan region learned cattle breeding and the Buryat language. How did they manage to do so without escalating complementary or symmetrical schismogenesis?

Secrets are the self-corrective mechanisms helping people maintain the balance between Evenki and Buryat cultures. The process of generating a secret is circular, as we will illustrate with the example of the secret about Evenki dogs. Through the example of two shamans, living more than one thousand kilometers from each other, we will show that secrets come from mutual efforts, even if there is no direct communication between presenters of cultures in contact.

Bargai, an Ekhirit Buryat shaman who spent a lot of time hunting with Evenki people in the taiga, told us about an Evenki secret. As an expert in relations with Evenki people, he was experienced enough to determine the limits of his knowledge. He said he never could understand how Evenki communicated with their dogs, and how they coordinated their actions during hunting. What Bargai described was an absence of context, without which he could not attain meaning or gain knowledge. He had hunted frequently with Evenki from his childhood, but had never lived with Evenki day by day. Bargai could not understand the process from his Buryat perspective, because Buryats train their dogs in a different manner. Bargai tried to solve the problem, not through the investigation of contexts but by assuming that Evenki have some secret knowledge about dogs that they do not reveal to Buryats. Bargai tried to interpret the episodes of Evenki hunting in frames of Buryat totemistic epistemology by constructing a relationship not between concrete creatures, such as Evenki hunters and their dogs, but between more abstract and prototypical ones, like Evenki as spirit masters and dogs as spirits. Bargai said that he had the impression that a magical link exists between the dog and the hunter, and that the hunter somehow communicates with the dog in an unknown way. These assumptions were the first step in generating a secret.

Orochon, the Evenki shaman, living in the Kurumkan region, did not pretend to have any special secrets about dogs. When his dog died he invited us to help him cremate it, and did not perform any kind of special esoteric ritual devoted to the celebration of the dog's soul. When we asked if there was any special knowledge about dogs, he was uncertain what we meant. What was clear was that there was no special esoteric knowledge about this actual dog. When we asked Orochon about hunting luck and how it was connected with a dog, he presented us with elaborate terminology, which was practically a translation of Buryat terminology into the Evenki language. The Buryat term *talan* for Evenki means either the prey or the routine tasks to obtain luck. Hence, the information we received looked like a chaotic mass of Buryat and Evenki motives. When we asked about the role of dogs as guardians, meaning how dogs save their masters from bad spirits, Orochon's wife, Masha, told us that man is the worst spirit. It seemed that Evenki took most of the allegoric expressions we used to obtain secret knowledge about spiritual life as direct, practical questions. Their interest in concrete experiences and indifference towards sophisticated reflections were also present in their everyday communication. They were never interested in abstract questions and avoided them by saying that the time had not yet come to talk about it. This was tricky, because they never directly denied that they had some specific knowledge but avoided situations when we might have expected them to reveal what we had asked them about.

This technique was not an attempt to manipulate but a way not to reject and exclude us from communication. Orochon was thoroughly aware that among Buryats (the referential environment of his shamanic activity) the shaman is expected to bear a special, secret knowledge, such as genealogies or prayers. And Orochon had to deal with these expectations without destroying our relationship. If he said he had no such knowledge at all, we (and probably Buryats as well) would not believe him, and would think he was keeping it secret and did not want to share it. For Evenki, sharing is very important, especially for men, who are expected to share everything they have with each other as a basis for successful companionship in hunting. In order not to spoil our companionship Orochon did not destroy our expectations but tried his hardest to prevent direct communication on the matter. As a result of his efforts, we felt even more strongly that he was keeping secrets.

Secrets are forms without special content, which presenters of contact cultures can fill as they wish without the risk of destroying the communicative situation. The secret about Evenki dogs was generated in the course of culture contact in hunting, when Buryats tried to assimilate the skill of Evenki hunting without the context of the socialisation of dogs. Evenki people did not deny the existence of this secret, as it was an effective mechanism in maintaining interaction, even if there was no complete understanding between the two parties. The same expressions about spirits and the relationship between owners and dogs can be either allegorical in the Buryat totemistic context, or quite concrete in Evenki animistic epistemology. This duality of secrets helps to bridge cultures and provides an important illusion of understanding, or the possibility of it. In frames of Buryat culture it is quite understandable why Evenki do not reveal their secrets, and as a result it is an appropriate behaviour. For Evenki people, sharing situational contexts is crucial. And, by pretending to know something, they integrate other people into their practices.

Notes

1. *Logical typing* is the term introduced by Bertrand Russell, which he used to describe the hierarchic structure of thought (Bateson 1979: 20).

References

Bateson, G. 1958. *Naven: A Survey of the Problems Suggested by a Composite Picture of the Culture of a New Guinea Tribe Drawn from Three Points of View*. Stanford, CA: Stanford University Press.

―――― 1972. *Steps to an Ecology of Mind: Collected Essays in Anthropology, Psychiatry, Evolution, and Epistemology*. San Francisco: Chandler.

―――― 1979. *Mind and Nature: A Necessary Unity*. New York: E.P. Dutton.

Bird-David, N. 1991. 'Animism Revisited: Personhood, Environment, and Relational Epistemology', *Current Anthropology* 40: 67–91.

Harrison, S. 1989. 'The Symbolic Construction of Aggression and War in a Sepik River Society', *Man* 24: 583–99.

Ingold, T. 2000. *The Perception of the Environment: Essays on Livelihood, Dwelling and Skill*. London: Routledge.

Kwon, H. 1993. 'Maps and Actions: Nomadic and Sedentary Space in a Siberian Reindeer Farm', Ph.D. thesis. Cambridge: University of Cambridge.

Lee, R.B., and R.H. Daly (eds). 1999. *The Cambridge Encyclopedia of Hunters and Gatherers*. Cambridge: Cambridge University Press.

Lindgren, E. 1936. 'Notes on the Reindeer Tungus of Manchuria: Their Names, Groups, Administration and Shamans', Ph.D. thesis. Cambridge: University of Cambridge.

Pedersen, M.A. 2001. 'Totemism, Animism and North Asian Indigenous Ontologies', *Journal of the Royal Anthropological Institute* 7(3): 411–27.

Sacks, H. 1992. *Lectures on Conversation*. Oxford: Blackwell.

Safonova, T., and I. Sántha. 2007. 'Companionship among the Evenki of Eastern Buryatia: A Study of Flexible and Stable Cultural Elements', *Max Planck Institute for Social Anthropology Working Papers, No. 99*. Retrieved 10 November 2009 from: www.eth.mpg.de/pubs/wps/pdf/mpi-eth-working-paper-0099.pdf.

Shirokogoroff, S.M. 1929. *Social Organization of the Northern Tungus*. Shanghai: Commercial Press.

―――― 1999[1935]. *Psychomental Complex of the Tungus*. Berlin: Reinhold Schletzer Verlag.

Ssorin-Chaikov, N.V. 2003. *The Social Life of the State in Subarctic Siberia*. Stanford, CA: Stanford University Press.

Strathern, M. 1988. *The Gender of the Gift*. Berkeley: University of California Press.

―――― 2005. *Kinship, Law and the Unexpected: Relatives Are Always a Surprise*. Cambridge: Cambridge University Press.

Willerslev, R. 2004. 'Not Animal, Not Not-animal: Hunting, Imitation and Empathetic Knowledge among the Siberian Yukaghirs', *Journal of the Royal Anthropological Institute* 10: 629–52.

Chapter 5
Making Animals into Food among the Kanamari of Western Amazonia

Luiz Costa

This chapter will analyse the ways in which the Kanamari, a Katukina-speaking people of western Amazonia, ensure that the animal flesh that they eat is rendered as food.[1] As is probably universal in Amazonia, the Kanamari claim that, in certain contexts, animals are persons, occupying the position of subjects in their relationships with humans.[2] My aim is to investigate how, given this condition, the Kanamari make animal subjects into food that, when shared out among co-residents, cooked and eaten together, serves to create or reinforce kinship ties.

Although my investigation will be limited to the Kanamari, I intend it to be an ethnographic example of a more general feature of Amazonian 'animist ontologies' (Viveiros de Castro 1998: 472–74). Throughout the region, as various authors have noted, 'intentionality and reflexive consciousness are not exclusive attributes of humanity but potentially available to all beings of the cosmos' (Fausto 2007: 497). This fact makes animals into agents, who must thus be treated as 'proper persons' (Descola 1992: 114) or who are persons to themselves, possessing, in their own eyes, human bodily form and human culture (Viveiros de Castro 1998: 477). If animals can be persons or are equivalent to persons, then the hunting of animals and the consumption of animal flesh emerge as dangerous enterprises that always run the risk of drifting into warfare and cannibalism. Yet the sharing of animal meat and its consumption is one of the principle vectors for the production of kinship: eating the same food together is not only an index of kinship relations, it actually makes people who eat together into kin (Gow 1991; Vilaça 2002). The question, then, is: How are animals that are persons made into food that can serve as a vector for the creation of kinship ties?

As Fausto has recently argued, the Amazonian solution to the problem posed by so-called animist systems is that the consumption of meat in order to create kinship ties requires that the animal-person be de-subjectified, thereby distinguishing the eating of animals from cannibalism: 'in daily meals the animal-as-subject must be absent for identification to occur between humans'

(Fausto 2007: 504). This Amazonian approach to hunting makes the societies of the region different from others that are also categorised as 'animist', such as the Siberian Yukaghirs, for whom there is 'no absolute solution to the moral dilemma posed by killing and eating prey' (Willerslev 2007: 78). The process of de-subjectivisation, however, is not uniform throughout Amazonia. In some cases, such as the Piaroa, shamans are capable of reducing animal-subjects to vegetable foods (Overing 1975: 39); in others, it is culinary fire that finally neutralises all traces of animals' subjectivity (Fausto 2007: 504); and in others still, notably the societies of the Upper Xingu, the consumption of game is mostly prohibited, and only less person-like fish are consumed (Gregor 1985: 75). As for the Yukaghirs, Amazonian methods for making animals into food are never absolute and always run the risk of failing and thereby projecting cannibalism onto commensal relations (Hugh-Jones 1996; Fausto 2007: 513).

In what follows I investigate some of the ways that the Kanamari reduce animals to food through the analysis of a series of apparently simple procedures carried out on the carcass. These occur alongside terminological reclassifications and behavioural dispositions that help to ensure that game subjects are made into objects that serve to channel kinship relations. More specifically, Kanamari hunting techniques converge upon changes to certain body parts and substances of game animals, particularly blood and skin. I will show that blood is associated with the soul while the skin is the seat of bodily form, and that both are opposed to the unspecificity of the flesh from which they must be separated in order for the animal to become food. By ensuring that blood and skin are dealt with in a certain manner, the Kanamari are able to conduct the animal through a series of states that are intermediate between the person-like qualities of a wild animal in the forest and the object-like qualities of cooked pieces of meat. Kanamari consumption of meat depends on their ability to ensure a progression through a sequence in which animals are first made inert and lifeless and then made into flesh that can be butchered, redistributed and cooked.

It would be wrong, however, to analyse the production and consumption of meat as if they could be extirpated from a range of relationships within which they are implicated. As the ethnography of Amazonia attests, the hunting of animals is one facet of 'a sociocosmic system in which the direction of predation and the production of kinship are in dispute' (Fausto 2007: 500). If humans prey on animals to satisfy their hunger and make kinship, animals, spirits and enemies prey on humans to the same end (Viveiros 2002).[3] I will therefore carry out an analysis of hunting through a comparison between processes that the Kanamari execute on the body of animals and those that occur on their own bodies. My comparison will not focus on the specific ways that non-human others make themselves into kin through preying on humans, but rather on how humans experience and try to prevent animal predation, which will serve as a counterpoint to how they make animals into food. If the hunting of animals and the proper treatment of meat thus emerge as active engagements and necessary preconditions for the creation of kinship ties among humans, the destruction of human bodies is an event which, from a Kanamari perspective, severs kinship ties.

Kanamari Hunting

The Kanamari number some 1,600 people spread out over a vast part of Brazilian western Amazonia. Their origin is in the Juruá river basin and most still inhabit the tributaries of its middle course. Although the Kanamari worked in rubber extraction and in logging during the first half of the twentieth century, today most are engaged in a mixed subsistence economy based on swidden horticulture, the gathering of wild or semi-domesticated fruits, fishing and hunting. Regardless of the relative nutritional weight of any of these food sources in their diet, the Kanamari are typical Amazonian 'predator-gardeners' who value hunting over food-production (Descola 1992: 115). No Kanamari meal is considered complete without either game or fish.[4] Their diet is remarkably comprehensive and includes most animals that are consumed by Amerindian peoples. To my knowledge, the only species that are consumed by the Kanamari's neighbours but prohibited among them are animals of the Pilosa order, namely sloths and anteaters.[5]

The Kanamari word that comes closest to our 'animal', *bara*, includes all land-dwelling species, most birds and some insects, but excludes fish. The word can take on the more specific meaning of 'prey' or 'game animal', such as in the Kanamari word for 'hunting', *bara-man* (literally, 'to get prey'). However, it is only in reference to hunting activity that *bara* comes to mean prey, since in other instances the term cuts across the broad distinction between game animals and those that are not consumed through a series of qualifications that partition the category *bara* into sub-sets whose basic criteria for inclusion are ethology and distinguishing physical traits. *Bara-potyam*, for example, refers to 'winged animals', which generally means birds but also bats and some insects; *bara-paohnim* refers to arboreal species, mainly monkeys but also sloths and squirrels. These sub-sets are far from rigidly defined, and there is much disagreement concerning their composition. While some animals are unambiguously considered to be of one set or the other, less prototypical instances tend to be classified differentially.

As far as I know, there is no sub-set that unequivocally covers large, land-dwelling mammals, which tend to be simply called *bara*. This includes white-lipped peccaries, collared peccaries, tapirs, pacas and deer. Along with certain species of monkey, these are the preferred game of the Kanamari. When a hunter proclaims that he will hunt, he usually means that he will try to kill individuals of these species unless he is unable to find any and must settle for less desirable prey. In the past, these animals were always hunted with bows, but today the Kanamari tend to use shotguns.

The analysis that follows is only concerned with the hunting of these paradigmatic examples of *bara*. Although I believe that, with some adjustments, what I have to say is applicable to the hunting of all animals (and, in some cases, to fishing as well), there are three reasons why I limit myself to large land-dwelling mammals. The first is that it is these animals that are most often referred to as being 'persons' (*tukuna*) because both humans and *bara* have a soul whose origin, if not trajectory, is the same. This common origin is expressed in the generic way for referring to the soul: since the word for soul, *-ikonanin*, must be preceded by a noun or pronoun, the most unspecific way of referring to the soul, be it the soul of humans or of animals, is *tukuna-ikonanin*, 'person-soul'. When a soul of a dead human or animal haunts a village, for example, and before it is known what the soul's former body was like, it is simply called 'person-soul' until its former identity can be shamanically ascertained and the name of the species or of the individual replaces the generic label *tukuna* in Kanamari discourse (Costa 2007: 294). In other words, humans and *bara* have bodies that are produced differently out of the same soul, which is why both are (or can be) 'persons' (see Viveiros de Castro 1998: 471). For this reason, large mammals are the object of greater attention and care during the hunt than other prey. Second, the technique for hunting these animals requires that they be killed with a projectile that results in bloodshed. Traditionally, some animals, such as monkeys, were hunted with blowguns and were therefore killed by the poison that was rubbed onto a dart rather than from bleeding resulting from perforation (see Erikson 1984; Rival 1996). Since bleeding is an important part of the sequence that I describe, I will limit myself to those instances in which it is a constitutive aspect of the hunt. Third, the only part of the integumentary system of large mammals that has to be removed in the butchering process is the skin. Whereas birds have their feathers plucked and monkeys have their fur burnt off, large mammals need only be skinned before being cut up into pieces of meat. Plucking feathers and burning fur function, in many ways, as analogues of skinning, but since one of my aims is to juxtapose the hunt with processes that occur on the bodies of humans, I will limit myself to animals whose anatomy, in this sense, is similar to that of humans.

What follows is an ethnography of the interval between an animal being shot and its flesh being cooked. Although more could be said on the important role of cooking fire in neutralising subjectivity, my concern is with hunting and butchering as technologies for de-subjectivising game animals and I will therefore describe the hunt in relation to how the Kanamari negotiate their way through the different stages that an animal crosses from being alive and in the wild to becoming food.

Blood and Soul

The Kanamari word that refers to the living body of humans, animals and some plants is *-warah*.[6] This word is always relational and always implies a form that is indexed by a noun that qualifies it. There is no generic, unspecific way of designating a body and *-warah* must always refer back to a form, which can be that of a species or of an individual within a species. To refer to the body of 'deer', *bahtyi* in Kanamari, and to ensure that the listener knows that the deer in question are alive and in the wild, the speaker will refer to *bahtyi-warah*, 'deer-body/bodies'.

Before a hunter sets out he may declare that he intends to hunt a certain type of game, peccary for instance, by saying either 'I will kill peccary' or 'today peccary will die'. The Kanamari verb that comes closest to the English 'to kill' is *-ti* and that for 'to die' is *tyuku*, but *-ti* refers to any act carried out with the intent to cause harm, while *tyuku* refers to any state of illness or loss of consciousness. If a man strikes another, for example, it may be said that he 'killed' him, even though the latter has not lost his life; similarly, a man who was ill may say that he 'died', even though he made a full recovery.[7] 'To kill' is to harm another through violent means, possibly leading to 'death', which is a potentially reversible state – a process more than an event – involving a loss of volition, of movement and vital principles, but which need not be permanent. This is not unique to the Kanamari but is rather a common feature of Amazonian etiologies. As Viveiros de Castro has said of the Araweté, 'an actual death is simply a more violent instance … among the many deaths and resurrections that a person suffers' (Viveiros de Castro 1992: 196; see also Taylor 1996).

Just as death is no guarantee that a life has been permanently lost, neither is it equivalent to a change in condition from body to corpse, *boroh*. This is true of humans as much as of animals, and it poses a problem for hunters since the success of the hunt depends on the existence of an animal corpse where before there was a body. Once a hunter's prey has been hit, he has tracked it until the place where it collapses and he stand before it, he has no unambiguous method for ascertaining whether what lies before him is a body, a corpse or something in-between. There are, nonetheless, certain indications that suggest to him that a change may be taking place. His initial reaction is to check the animal that he has wounded for signs of vitality. If the animal ceases to move, 'does not breathe' (*huh'am tu*) and 'its heart does not beat' (*diwahkom biktunim*), the hunter will know that the animal has died. But these aspects, on their own, are no guarantee that its living body has subsided once and for all. The most precise method that he can rely on for confirming that a body is passing away into corpse is to attend to certain other signs, notably to changes in characteristics of the animal's blood and particularly to the cessation of its flow.

For the Kanamari, blood (*mimi*) is the sensible aspect of the soul (*-ikonanin*), the visible counterpart to a mostly invisible principle. The two are not reducible to one another, and we will see that the meaning of soul extrapolates the qualities of blood, but the latter is nonetheless all that is normally available for reaching conclusions concerning the former. Even though there are unrelated words for the two, both are instances of movement, which the Kanamari consider to be a default condition of animacy. If the soul is the common denominator of species, movement is their primitive quality. In its original and originary state, movement is erratic, irregular, uncoordinated and external to bodies. Although antithetical to bodies, uncoordinated movement is the condition from which bodies are made through intentional acts of kinship that serve to coordinate it. Coordination of movement is achieved in acts of care, through feeding and commensality, and the moulding of bodies by massage and the manipulation of its parts, all of which are coterminous with making the disordered movement of soul and blood into the intentional motion of bodies.

This process is already evident at the moment of birth. For the Kanamari, the bleeding that accompanies birth is a manifestation of the infant's blood, and not the mother's. Infants are said to have 'unripe' (*parah tu*) bodies that are barely able to contain blood, which therefore seeps from them into their mother whilst they are in the womb, and then out of her as lochia and post-partum haemorrhaging. In this way, the circulation of blood within the body is framed by an initial moment of 'bleeding' (*mimiok*), which occurs first inside the womb and then at birth. This bleeding antecedes the ordered circulation of blood in the same way that erratic and uncoordinated movement is anterior to coordinated movement: phylogenetically, the generic movement of the soul is prior to the coordinated movement of a body, just as, ontogenetically, bleeding is prior to the circulation of blood. By getting rid of the blood that is exterior to bodies and caring for infants that have blood flowing within them, each species fabricates individuals whose mobile patterns are coordinated in a certain way. The circulation of blood thereby becomes movement contained in opposition to unbounded movement in the body's exterior.[8]

In this sense, it is blood flow rather than blood that is analogous to the soul. While it is the body that ensures that the movement of soul and blood remains confined to its limits, it is also the soul and the circulation of blood that makes bodies move. The fact that features of the body are contingent on the previous movement of a soul which is manifest in bodily substance highlights the well-known difficulty in positing 'any absolute rupture between material body and immaterial soul' in Amazonia (Fausto 2007: 504). It also brings to the foreground the relationship between soul and blood, which is widespread in the region. It receives its most salient expression in the link between the blood and the soul/spirit of an enemy killed in warfare (Albert 1985; Viveiros de Castro 1996; Conklin 2001b). But blood is more generally associated with many of the same capacities as the soul, being conceived of as a vehicle for an animating force (Crocker 1985: 41), as the source of strength and health (Conklin 2001a: 139–40), or as the seat of heat and energy that is necessary for vitality (Surrallés 2003: 55). For the Kanamari, blood is an aspect of basic, primordial movement which bodies should be made to contain and order through a regular intravenous flow. So long as it is contained within the body and remains, as the Kanamari say, 'in our veins' (*tyo-tyinpru naki*), blood has a positive effect, akin to a vital principle that is responsible for the body's activity.

What then of the hunter standing before the animal he has shot, checking for changes in the characteristics of its blood? Post-mortem lividity and coagulation indicate to him that blood flow has ceased and, consequently, that the body no longer contains the soul. The process is identical for both humans and animals: when the body falls dead, the soul is said to 'stand up' (*dadyahian*) and leave it, as is evidenced by the gradual decrease in blood flow, changes in its colour and the last palpitations and dying twitches of the body. The hunter's arrow or his shot have had an evident effect on the capacity of the body to contain blood. Bleeding, which had been a precondition for the fabrication of the animal's living body, now gradually makes all of its movements stop and, in time, blood will also cease to flow from the wound. Does this mean that the animal, now devoid of movement, is a corpse?

'Becoming-corpse' and Producing Flesh

If the animal bleeds for some time and then this bleeding stops, if blood becomes darker as a result, and all of the animal's movements come to a halt, then the hunter can conclude that the animal *boroh-pa*.[9] As we have seen, *boroh* means 'corpse' and *-pa* is a verbaliser that evinces transformation; *-pa* indicates a present continuous aspect, a process of transforming into or becoming the noun to which it refers, and not the result or conclusion of the becoming. In this way, *boroh-pa* cannot be translated as 'to become a corpse', but must be glossed as a hypothetical verbalisation of 'corpse', such as 'to corpsify' or, perhaps more accurately, as 'becoming-corpse'. Moreover, *boroh-pa* always has an object, in the sense that one can say 'the peccary is becoming-corpse' (*boroh-pa wiri*), but it has no unambiguous subject. A Kanamari hunter may say 'I killed the peccary', 'I shot the peccary', or some variation thereof, but he does not say *i-boroh-pa wiri (*'I have "corpsified" the peccary'). Neither is *boroh-pa* reflexive: it is not the peccary that makes itself (in whatever manner) become corpse. The term *boroh-pa* is thus a verb with a null-subject that denotes an ongoing process of transformation from a body into a corpse.[10]

The relationship between 'becoming-corpse' and the action that triggers it is complex, and I limit myself to two observations. First, to recognise that an animal has ceased to bleed, and that its blood no longer circulates, and to conclude, based on these observations, that 'the animal is becoming-corpse', is not to say that the animal, which a short while ago was a living body, has already become a corpse. Instead, it is to admit one or both of the following conditions: that changes in blood flow have placed a process in motion and the animal is on its way to becoming a corpse; that the available evidence is insufficient for the Kanamari to unambiguously determine that this transformation has taken place. Either way, the hunter stands before an animal that cannot be classified as a corpse with any certainty. Second, the null-subject indicates that although an animal may die because of the actions of a hunter, the process of 'becoming-corpse' escapes the intentions of a subject: while a wound caused by a projectile shot by a hunter can put this process in motion, the process itself lies beyond the scope of the hunter's volition.

Even if, at this stage, the hunter could know for sure that the animal had become a corpse, this would be insufficient, since it is the flesh, and not the corpse, that he and his kin crave. Flesh is not immediately available to the Kanamari and it requires that further work be carried out on the carcass. More specifically, it requires that the animal be butchered, a process that the Kanamari call *hai-bu*, derived from *hai*, 'flesh' or 'meat', and *bu*, 'to produce'. The term literally means 'to produce flesh' and it refers explicitly to the cutting up of the corpse. Furthermore, it refers to the process as carried out in the household to which the hunter will take the animal that he has killed. Although hunters often disarticulate parts of the animal after a kill, in order to fit them into carrying baskets that facilitate transport, this is not considered to be 'producing meat' because no matter how much a hunter cuts up the carcass he will not skin it completely before arriving in the village. *Dak-puni*, literally 'skin-remove', is carried out by men other than the hunter in the house to which the hunter takes the carcass. Skinning is the first step in meat production and the butchering of the carcass into pieces that can be shared out and cooked follows from it.

One of the reasons that the animal needs to be skinned in villages rather than in the forest is so that those who will eat it can identify it as a specific former body. The arrival of the hunter always results in a flurry of activity that is triggered by the shouts of the first woman or child who sees the hunter coming along a path towards the village. These shouts always specify the species of the animal killed by proclaiming, for example, that 'peccary has died' or 'peccary is becoming-corpse'. The animal is thereby recognised as an edible species.

As the hunter walks through the village towards the house to which he will take the carcass, most people gather around him, and children often circle the hunter in a playful frenzy, poking at the carcass and stating the parts of the animal that they want to eat. This activity is in stark contrast to the apprehension of adults and especially to the silence of the hunter. He will drag the carcass across the house floor, dropping it next to a hearth. He then normally sits down and ignores the attention that his kill has drawn. His participation in the proceedings is over. For a while, people inspect the carcass, commenting on its sex, the amount of fat and any other feature worthy of observation, without actually beginning treatment. A man other than the hunter will then take the initiative by saying to the others 'let us produce its meat' (*a-hai-bu adik tyo*) or 'let us skin it' (*a-dak-puni adik tyo*). Regardless of what is said, what is meant is the process of removing the skin, and the interchangeability between the affirmations confirms that skin-removal is the first stage in meat production. Once this is done, and unless something out of the ordinary has been observed, the men step back and allow the women to begin butchering the flesh. The remaining process – from butchering, through the distribution of raw pieces of meat among the various households, to cooking – is now no longer a male affair and is entirely the business of women.[11]

Meat production is the pivot of the hunt, a necessary hinge between predatory and kinship-producing activities. After the skin has been removed, people will refer to the carcass as being the flesh of the hunted animal. Occasionally, the species of the animal is suppressed at this stage, and it is simply called *bara-hai*, 'animal-flesh'. This effacement of the animal's identity through a process of skinning is possible because the skin is the extent of the animal's form and one of the principal sites upon which the production of specific bodies rests. Its removal is therefore tantamount to the subtraction of a distinguishing trait of a body. As Viveiros de Castro notes, in Amazonia 'we are dealing with societies which inscribe efficacious meaning onto the skin [which is] their distinctive equipment, endowed with the affects and capacities which define each animal' (Viveiros de Castro 1998: 482). This is equally true of humans, except that 'humans possess a sort of blank skin which can be decorated, dressed, or even changed by the appropriation of designs, patterns, feathers and animal pelts' (Fausto 2007: 512). The skin is an integral aspect of the faculties and bodily form of animals and humans, and while a change or embellishment of the skin can transform a human body into another, the removal of an animal's skin so as to reveal the underlying flesh is an act of de-subjectivisation that cancels the distinguishing characteristics of the species. For this reason, the Kanamari discard the skin of the animals that they are making into meat, thereby removing their form and the spectre of transformation from the space of kinship relations.[12]

Skinning is a part of meat production, a process that is marked by the verb *bu*. Unlike the verbaliser *-pa*, which expresses a continuous aspect and lacks a clear-cut subject, *bu* indicates a fully intentional act that is carried out by those doing the producing and over which they have control. *Bu* has a wide semantic range and it designates activities that we would loosely translate as 'work'. In fact, the concept receives its most indeterminate form in the idea of *ta'anyan-bu*, 'to do things', 'to work'. *Bu* can be suffixed to almost anything in order to refer to the process of its making, usually specifying the production of an artefact out of raw materials, such as baskets produced from vines or ceramics produced from clay. It also forms verbs such as 'to paint' or 'to write' (*akanaro-bu*) and 'to clear a garden' (*baohnim-bu*). It should not be assumed, however, that *bu* refers only, or even preferentially, to production in the sphere of material goods, since it also applies to the intentional production of human persons. 'To impregnate' a woman – to make a foetus grow in her womb through repeated acts of intercourse – is said to be *ityaro-mi-bu*, 'to produce the woman's womb'. *Bu* also describes intentional acts of moulding the human body, of purposefully massaging it so that it acquires or maintains a human semblance.

Production is a social act in which people or things are made within relationships in order to create social ties, or things are made to be shared within kinship relations or exchanged beyond them. Food is produced by the hunter who kills the animal, the men who skin it and the women who butcher it so that it can feed the village and, through commensality, favour the establishment of kinship. These intentional activities of human kinship are dependent on a previous process that is articulated to hunting, but which, unlike productive action, remains partially outside the scope of human control: the 'becoming-corpse' of the game animal.

Preying on Humans

In order to understand why a specific sequence in the treatment of game must be followed, it is necessary to compare hunting with processes that the bodies of humans undergo. This comparison is not meant to reveal a contrast at the level of physiology. Although bodies define different ways of being, the Kanamari, like many Amerindians, do not make physiological differences between species into a system of classification, recognising instead that most species have bodies that are anatomically comparable (Viveiros de Castro 1998: 478; Surrallès 2003: 37–38). In other words, bodies differ in important ways, but they are also analogous and many of the processes that apply to the destruction of game animals also apply to humans and vice versa. Instead, the contrast concerns changes in the direction of predation, in the orientation of human action, and also in the way that blood and skin impinge upon corpse and flesh.

Blood and skin are component parts of living bodies and they must be removed sequentially in order to make the body become corpse and to produce flesh during the hunting process. The logic of the hunt keeps the states of an animal separate and seeks to prevent their overlap: by managing blood flow, the body of the animal is first set on a process of 'becoming-corpse' before the removal of the skin makes it flesh completely. However, the Kanamari know, from their own bodies, that this is not only a matter of adhering to a formula. They know this because a healthy living body is not only constituted by blood and skin, it also subsumes both corpse and the flesh within it, and these are prone to emerge during moments of affliction. More specifically, corpses emerge in parts of the body that grow morbid due to reduced blood flow, while the flesh appears in accidents that scrape the skin. Although it is once again changes in blood flow that result in a corpse and removal of the skin that exposes the flesh, the ways in which blood and skin articulate with the living body makes evident the need to observe a sequence in hunting. Before discussing these differences, it is necessary to explain how corpse and flesh come to appear in a body.

While *boroh* can denote a state, it also refers to a general condition of sluggishness, morbidity and inactivity which can affect only parts of a person's body. A person's excessively fat belly, for example, is called *boroh nak*, 'big corpse', with some Kanamari contemptuously saying of obese people that their bellies are full of maggots. Similarly, the word for 'swelling' is *borohtyok'am*, which literally means 'corpse has come out'. One of the principle causes of swelling is the presence in one's body of the shamanic darts of enemy sorcerers or spirits, which results in a tumour that exudes pus, and which must be removed by a shaman lest it lead to death. The distension and dilation of body parts is thus equivalent to the emergence of a corpse where there should be a body. What makes parts of the body into 'corpse' is precisely the disturbance of circulation through them, as indicated by the salience of pus or the presence of maggots. A corpse, in sum, is either a whole body with no blood flow, or a part of it that cuts, diverts or otherwise reduces the flow of blood.

We have seen that the flesh of an animal during the hunt is revealed through skinning, the first step in meat production. For this to occur there must first be sufficient evidence based on the animal's blood flow to allow the Kanamari to conclude that the animal is, at the very least, 'becoming-corpse'. No one would butcher an animal that bleeds incessantly and they would immediately stop butchering if, at this stage, their incisions into the carcass drew out fresh blood.

This would be a sign that the animal is not 'becoming-corpse'; indeed, it would suggest to the Kanamari that the animal is somehow still a living body and that they are exposing its flesh. This is similar to processes that can occur with their own bodies. Although wounds are called *ohon*, a wound that removes the skin in a specific body part may receive the name of that body part followed by the term for flesh, *hai*. Thus an injury to one's toe, for example, may be referred to as 'my toe's flesh' (*i-ih-kom-hai*). The Kanamari's main definition of a wound is that it bleeds and exposes the flesh of a body, and not of a corpse or a body on its way to becoming one.[13]

Pathologies that affect living bodies differ from actions intentionally done to game animals during hunting and butchering in two important respects. First, in hunting what the Kanamari stress is the ordered, consecutive and (within possibility) intentional transformation of the whole body (and not just parts) of the game animal into states that exclude each other. Game must first be put into a process of 'becoming-corpse' entirely so that all of it can be made into meat in a successive and coordinated subtraction of aspects of the former living animal. Since corpse and flesh are possible aspects of living bodies, recognising their appearance in a part of the body is not in itself enough evidence for the transformation of subjects into objects. To ensure their success in a hunt, the Kanamari must guarantee that a specific order is observed and that, in respecting this order, the whole animal shifts between states that follow from and exclude each other.

Second, the sequence through which animals are first made into corpse and then into flesh inverts the way that blood and skin affect living bodies in pathologies. In hunting, blood is managed in a way that seeks to order a sequence of transformations, whereas in pathologies that affect body parts this order is avoided. In the former, the entire body of the animal undergoes a process of 'becoming-corpse' through an injury caused by an arrow or a shell that perforates the skin and causes bleeding, and it is the end of this bleeding that indicates to the hunter that the animal is 'becoming-corpse'. In the latter, conversely, a part of the body becomes a corpse not through perforation but because of a stretching or deformation of the skin that reduces blood flow without bleeding. The equivalent inversion applies to the different ways that flesh can be made to appear. While an animal is made meat through the complete removal of the skin with a cutting implement that results in little or no bloodshed – since, hopefully being a corpse, the animal no longer has any blood flowing through its body – in parts of living bodies, on the contrary, the flesh appears when the skin is perforated and a wound bleeds. In sum, body parts reveal the corpse in the absence of bleeding but expose the flesh through a wound that bleeds; while the whole body becomes-corpse through bleeding and has its flesh exposed without significant bloodshed.

These are not substantive features of different processes, but rather human – that is, Kanamari – perspectives of the same process as it occurs to the animals that they hunt or to their own bodies. Pathologies that affect the living bodies of humans are moments when others (humans or non-humans) prey on Kanamari bodies, and which they have to counter in order to prevent their bodies from being subjected to the same process to which they subject the bodies of animals. The order of the hunt is thereby not only avoided, it is also resisted: injuries heal, shamans remove projectiles, and swelling is abated. The ordered process of making animals into meat, on the other hand, ensures that the states that emerge are complete and irreversible by cancelling the possibility of their regeneration and guaranteeing that what could be an injury to a part of the body comes to have an effect on all of it. Although the 'becoming-corpse' of the animal is ambivalent, if blood ceases to flow the Kanamari can be confident enough that its carcass can be produced as flesh. In the absence of bleeding, the production of flesh then results in portions that can be redistributed, cooked and eaten. By getting rid of blood and the skin, conduits of vitality and form, the Kanamari promote the successive loss of mobility, form and appearance, as the animal gradually shifts into corpse and then into meat. By preventing the sequence from operating on their own bodies, the Kanamari are able to remain healthy enough to make animals into food and, in so doing, to continue to make themselves into human kin.

Corpse, flesh, blood and skin must thus relate to each other in a specific way for subjects to be made objects, while these relations must be resisted in order to prevent the same process from occurring. Concurrently, many of the dangers that may result from the consumption of game animals are caused by a glitch in the hunting sequence. Animals that, when perforated, bleed little, or that continue to shed blood long after sustaining injuries, are those that are probably unfit for consumption. Similarly, those corpses that bleed when skinned are dangerous to eat. In other words, it is because the process of hunting somehow failed to adequately make the animal subject into an object by obliterating all traces of its intentionality that its consumption, instead of establishing kin ties among humans through commensality, would unmake them through illness.

Conclusion

Although this explains why a specific sequence is observed in hunting, it still does not account for the ambivalence of the 'becoming-corpse' of the animal in opposition to the relative certainty of the production of flesh. It is not enough to say that the latter is intentional and under human control, because while this is true it is nonetheless dependent on the former, which escapes intentional human action. If the consumption of animal meat requires that a sequence be followed and that no stage of it be bypassed, then intentional human action can only be effective if a prior transformation has taken place.

The Kanamari must deduce the 'becoming-corpse' of an animal from the evidence of changes in blood, which always remains indeterminate. I suspect that these deductions are insufficient for reaching a definite conclusion – one, for example, that would allow them to claim, during the hunt, that the animal is a 'corpse' – because blood flow is only one aspect of axiomatic movement, the other being manifest in its counterpart, the soul, a principle that, under normal conditions, is invisible to the naked eye. Although the two are versions of each other in that they are manifestations of primordial movement, the cessation of blood flow can only be an imperfect clue as to the complete termination of movement. In other words, although blood is the sensible quality of the soul and the only method that the Kanamari have for diagnosing a 'becoming-corpse', movement eludes the visible signs of blood. Even if blood coagulates, the soul may linger, moving still in the vicinity of the animal that is 'becoming-corpse'.

Sometimes the Kanamari, particularly children, are afflicted by an illness that is caused by the soul of the animals that they consume. As I mentioned above, these afflictions can be avoided if there are physical signs that the animal is not a corpse and it is therefore discarded. In other moments, disease follows the consumption of an animal which was not a corpse although it appeared to be one. This lack of fit between the appearance of the animal and its actual state can result from some unforeseen mishap in the smooth functioning of the hunting sequence or because the coagulation of blood did not make the animal's soul depart and it therefore preys on the living, particularly on children whose bodies are 'unripe'. An adult man must then drink a tree-bark infusion known as *omamdak* that allows him to see the soul of the aggressive animal and to blow it away, so that it ceases to harm the living.

If, however, meat is consumed and nothing negative happens; if food abates hunger and makes people content, then – and only then – can it be known for sure that the hunter was successful in making the living body of his prey become a corpse. When the Kanamari later narrate the events of this specific hunt they will claim, with no ambivalence, that the hunter brought an animal's corpse into the village and that it was then partitioned, cooked and eaten by those present. This certainty can only ever emerge after the fact since, during the hunt, people are limited by what their eyes can see.[14]

The disjunction between what the hunter and his kin are able to see and the transformations which an animal undergoes during the hunt brings us back to the problem of the relationship between 'becoming-corpse' and producing meat, which is an ethnographically specific example of the articulation of an animist ontology with the creation of kin ties through commensality. The establishment of a hinge between predatory and kinship-producing activities is a recurring feature of animism, although attitudes concerning the possibility of doing so or its effectiveness vary. The Siberian Yukaghirs, we saw above, have no absolute means of distinguishing commensal relations from cannibalism, but they nonetheless make kinship through the ways that meat is shared: first hunters divide their kill during expeditions, they then share once more when they return to village and again after meat is cooked; these moments of sharing serve to draw boundaries of closeness and distance across an undifferentiated number of kin (Willerslev 2007: 39–41). Sharing, however, does not cancel the potential cannibalism that underlies the consumption of animals-as-persons, and some people may even refuse their share of meat if they deem that the animal has been killed in improper ways, such as through shamanic means (ibid.: 78).

Unlike the Yukaghirs, many Amazonians differentiate between two processes of transformation that stem from the consumption of meat – one which, in the words of Fausto, 'results from eating someone (cannibalism) and the other from eating *like* and *with* someone (commensality)' (Fausto 2007: 500). As Fausto (ibid.: 513) stresses, however, there is no complete rupture between these processes and Amazonians remain unable to fully extricate kinship relations from the predatory relations which underpin them. This is not only because humans and animals are immersed in a cosmic schema in which the direction of predation is in dispute, or because actual predation is a necessary precondition for the production of real food. For the Kanamari, at least, the productive activity that enables kinship through commensality also depends upon the observance of a sequence in which producing meat is conditioned by a prior process of 'becoming-corpse' that is precarious, partially imperceptible and mostly independent of human intention.

Notes

1. This chapter greatly benefited from comments during the conference 'Humans, Animals, Plants and Things: Personhood in Amazonia and Siberia', and I would like to thank Marc Brightman, Vanessa Grotti and Olga Ulturgasheva for inviting me to participate and for their suggestions. I would also like to thank Carlos Fausto and Joana Miller for their comments on earlier drafts of this chapter. I am especially grateful to Hilton Nascimento, Leonardo Patrício Resende and Marco Aurélio Tosta for cross-checking some of my data with the Kanamari. Any mistakes are, of course, my own.
2. On the contextual 'personitude' or humanity of animals in Amazonia, see Descola (1992) and Viveiros de Castro (1998, 2002: 132–37). For similar Siberian concepts, see Kwon (1998) and Pedersen (2001).
3. For a Siberian perspective on this, see Kwon (1998: 119).
4. The fact that throughout Amazonia meals tend to be considered complete only when meat or fish is available should not be understood as a devaluation of garden products. Unlike certain Siberian peoples who refuse to eat vegetables (e.g., Willerslev 2007: 78), some Amerindians consider garden products more important in the definition of proper meals than meat (e.g., Rivière 1969: 42). As Hugh-Jones (1996) has shown, much of the logic behind the ambivalence of meat – which is both admired and feared – stems from the dangers inherent in its consumption for people who do not deny human intentionality to animals, which is precisely what this chapter will investigate.
5. The Kanamari diet evidently excludes those animals that are never (or almost never) consumed as food by Amazonian peoples: large predators, such as the jaguar, the anaconda and the black caiman; those that are excessively aggressive, such as snakes and bush dogs; or scavengers, such as vultures. The Kanamari also avoid bats and opossums and, traditionally, the capybara was not eaten, although today it is on certain occasions.
6. The word *-warah* has a much wider semantic scope than 'living body', since it also means, simultaneously, 'owner' or 'master', through which it also comes to mean 'chief'. Indeed, I have elsewhere translated *-warah* as 'body-owner' and analysed its role in Kanamari socio-cosmology, focusing on the ways in which the *-warah* is scaled-up from living bodies, to village chiefs, to the chiefs of river basins and beyond the realm of kinship (Costa 2007, 2010). For the sake of economy, I will here gloss *-warah* as 'body' or 'living

body', since it is this aspect of the word that is relevant to my present discussion. In many ways, this chapter investigates the flipside, as it were, of my former study of how the *-warah* is constituted through progressively more inclusive intervals by focusing on how the concept is dismantled, making living bodies into flesh.

7. In some cases, 'to die' can be nuanced with verbal modifiers that make it clear that the person in question only 'sort of died' (*otyuku*) or 'almost died' (*tyuku niwuti*). The Kanamari use a different verb, *tyohni*, for people who died a long time ago and who are therefore no longer mourned.

8. The body as a container of movement has important resonances with the widespread Amazonian theme of the body as a container-transformer of energy. Indeed, in this sense the body is analogous to tubes in which air, blood and food flow in a particular manner (Hugh-Jones 2001). For a discussion of the body in relation to its ability to contain or release certain flows in myth, see Lévi-Strauss (1985). For a recent discussion of the relationship between aerophones and bodies as transformers of flows, see Brightman (2011).

9. An alternative to the phrase *boroh-pa* is *bokoh-pa*. The two phrases are interchangeable and seem to reflect certain dialectal variations in the Kanamari language. Among the Kanamari of the Itaquaí river, where I carried out most of my fieldwork, the second expression is more common, but I will show that it is the meaning conveyed in the first that is always intended.

10. This conclusion is based on my interpretation of the Kanamari language and relies on my fieldnotes and a study of a number of instances in which *boroh-pa* or *bokoh-pa* appear in recordings that I made. It is not based on any native explanation of the use of *boroh-pa* and it is possible that, linguistically, *boroh-pa* can in fact take a subject (although one would still have to explain why the use of *boroh-pa* during the hunt seems to always drop the subject). All that I can say is that, based on those instances that I investigated, *boroh-pa* appears to be an impersonal verb. I should stress that if my interpretation is correct, it does not denote a constant feature of verbs created through *-pa*, since some, such as *-tanei-pa*, 'to dream' (i.e. 'to become-dream'), must necessarily take a subject.

11. The Kanamari in fact sub-divide *hai-bu*, 'to produce flesh', into two moments, split across gender lines: *dak-puni*, 'to skin', is the first stage carried out by men; *hai-pik*, 'to butcher', is the second stage, carried out by women.

12. Many internal organs can be consumed, including, on some occasions, the entrails, which are cleaned out and made into a stew. Those organs that are not eaten are unceremoniously discarded, or else fed to dogs. Bones are not consumed, but bone marrow is an admired delicacy. Hooves and antlers are disarticulated early on in the butchering process and may be discarded, but there is no need to remove them from the area of food preparation. The skin is therefore the only part of the animal that must always be discarded or, at least, removed from the space where flesh will be butchered.

13. Injuries that bleed and expose the flesh may appear accidental, but this is not how the Kanamari interpret them. Accidents are caused by a generalised state of misfortune that the Kanamari term *miori*, resulting from a failure to behave in an ethical manner, including a disregard for the proper treatment of game animals during hunting. Misfortune is not necessarily a reflexive affair and any co-resident of the hunter can become *miori*. In this sense, 'accidents' can also result from the predation of human bodies by others.

14. In these conversations it is possible to verbally express this certainty and to say that the animal in question became a corpse through the process of hunting. The Kanamari add the suffix *-nim* to *boroh-pa* in order to stress the conclusion of a process which, at the moment of its apprehension, had been ongoing and ambivalent. *Boroh-pa-nim wiri*,

for example, means 'the peccary became a corpse', and it is only said of a peccary that, showing no signs of anomaly, is consumed and no illness ensues.

References

Albert, B. 1985. 'Temps du sang, temps des cendres: représentation de la maladie, système rituel et espace politique chez les Yanomami du Sud-Est (Amazonie brésilienne)', Ph.D. thesis. Nanterre: University of Paris.

Brightman, M. 2011. 'Archetypal Agents of Affinity: "Sacred" Musical Instruments in the Guianas?' in J.-P. Chaumeil and J. Hill (eds), *Burst of Breath: New Research on Indigenous Ritual Flutes in Lowland South America*. Lincoln: University of Nebraska Press, pp. 201–18.

Conklin, B. 2001a. *Consuming Grief: Compassionate Cannibalism in an Amazonian Society*. Austin: University of Texas Press.

——— 2001b. 'Women's Blood, Warrior's Blood, and the Conquest of Vitality in Amazonia', in T. Gregor and D. Tuzin (eds), *Gender in Amazonia and Melanesia: An Exploration of the Comparative Method*. Berkeley: University of California Press, pp. 141–74.

Costa, L. 2007. 'As faces do jaguar: parentesco, história e mitologia entre os Kanamari da Amazônia Ocidental', Ph.D. thesis. Rio de Janeiro: Museu Nacional.

——— 2010. 'The Kanamari Body-owner: Predation and Feeding in Western Amazonia', *Journal de la Société des Américanistes* 96(1): 169–92.

Crocker, J. 1985. *Vital Souls: Bororo Cosmology, Natural Symbolism and Shamanism*. Tucson: University of Arizona Press.

Descola, P. 1992. 'Societies of Nature and the Nature of Society', in A. Kuper (ed.), *Conceptualizing Society*. London: Routledge, pp. 107–26.

Erikson, P. 1984. 'De l'apprivoisement à l'approvisionnement: chasse, alliance et familiarization en Amazonie amérindienne', *Technique et Cultures* 9: 105–40.

Fausto, C. 2007. 'Feasting on People: Eating Animals and Humans in Amazonia', *Current Anthropology* 48(4): 497–530.

Gow, P. 1991. *Of Mixed Blood: Kinship and History in Peruvian Amazonia*. Oxford: Oxford University Press.

Gregor, T. 1985. *Anxious Pleasures: The Sexual Lives of an Amazonian People*. Chicago: University of Chicago Press.

Hugh-Jones, S. 1996. 'Bonnes raisons ou mauvaise conscience? De l'ambivalence de certains Amazoniens envers la consommation de viande', *Terrains* 26: 123–48.

——— 2001. 'The Gender of Some Amazonian Gifts: An Experiment with an Experiment', in T. Gregor and D.Tuzin (eds), *Gender in Amazonia and Melanesia: An Exploration of the Comparative Method*. Berkley: University of California Press, pp. 245–78.

Kwon, H. 1998. 'The Saddle and the Sledge: Hunting as Comparative Narrative in Siberia and Beyond', *Journal of the Royal Anthropological Institute* 4: 115–27.

Lévi-Strauss, C. 1985. *La Potière jalouse*. Paris: Maspero.

Overing [Kaplan], J. 1975. *The Piaroa: A People of the Orinoco Basin*. Oxford: Clarendon Press.

Pedersen, M. 2001. 'Totemism, Animism and North Asian Indigenous Ontologies', *Journal of the Royal Anthropological Institute* 7: 411–27.

Rival, L. 1996. 'Blowpipes and Spears: The Social Significance of Huaorani Technological Choices', in P. Descola and G. Pálsson (eds), *Nature and Society: Anthropological Perspectives*. London: Routledge, pp. 145–64.

Rivière, P. 1969. *Marriage Among the Trio: A Principle of Social Organization*. Oxford: Clarendon Press.
Surrallès, A. 2003. *Au cœur du sens: perception, affectivité, action chez les Candoshi*. Paris: CNRS Editions.
Taylor, A.-C. 1996. 'The Soul's Body and its States: An Amazonian Perspective on the Nature of Being Human', *Journal of the Royal Anthropological Institute* 2: 201–15.
Vilaça, A. 2002. 'Making Kin out of Others in Amazonia', *Journal of the Royal Anthropological Institute* 8: 347–56.
Viveiros de Castro, E. 1992. *From the Enemy's Point of View: Humanity and Divinity in an Amazonian Society*. Chicago: University of Chicago Press.
——— 1996. 'Le meurtrier et son double chez les Araweté (Brésil): un exemple de fusion rituelle', *Systèmes de Pensée en Afrique Noire* 14: 77–104.
——— 1998. 'Cosmological Deixis and Amerindian Perspectivism', *Journal of the Royal Anthropological Institute* 4: 469–88.
——— 2002. 'O nativo relativo', *Mana* 8(1): 113–48.
Willerslev, R. 2007. *Soul Hunters: Hunting, Animism and Personhood among the Siberian Yukaghirs*. Berkeley: University of California Press.

Chapter 6
'Spirit-charged' Animals in Siberia

Alexandra Lavrillier

The purpose of this chapter is to analyse the concept of 'spirit charge' which the Evenki reindeer herders and hunters of Siberia apply to all humans and to some animals they consider ritually powerful. The analysis will show that this concept implies individual differentiation among animals and the attribution of intentionality to certain animals. It will also contribute to fostering the comparative perspective adopted in this book, insofar as there seems to be no concept with the same Evenki specific understanding of 'spirit charge' in Amazonia. In addition, it will feed, on the basis of recent Siberian ethnographic materials, the debates about some notions especially highlighted in Amazonian anthropology, such as 'intentionality' and 'agentivity' (Descola 2005; see also Gell 1998). Moreover, it will question the applicability to the Siberian domain of the model of homology of applied to humans and animals. It will also specify the complexity of the distinction between humans and non-humans by showing in which important ways non-humans are differentiated.

The analysis presented here is research built on eight years of fieldwork among the Evenki of southern Yakutia and the Amour region in Russia, mostly among the nomadic reindeer herders and hunters.[1] As I have shown elsewhere, the Evenki attribute a 'spirit charge' or *onnir* – a source of ritual power – to humans, shamans and ordinary people (Lavrillier 2005: 267–71, 492–523). Recently I decided to extend my analysis of the nomads' discourse about ritual actions attributed to some wild and domestic animals. Based on this analysis, in this chapter I differentiate indigenous kinds of ritual actions or agency. To this end, the expressions 'invisible acts' or 'to act in an invisible way' will designate ritual acts without gestures (by thinking and so on), 'ritual gestures' or 'rituals' will refer to the ritual acts with gestures or ceremonial, and 'ritual actions' will designate both 'invisible acts' and 'ritual gestures'. This analysis will show that ritual actions are not always attributed intentionality.

For this research, I started to analyse a set of ritual actions attributed to animals. I also studied the numerous prohibitions and proscriptions linked with animals. My analysis of indigenous taxonomy shows that animals are not only classified into several categories, but also that those categories – which have specific interrelationships - are thought to be organised into diverse worlds of socialisation. After a short presentation of the group of Evenki I worked among, I will first propose a detailed study of the categories of beings, then I will attempt to analyse their alleged ritual interactions. Finally, I will detail the constituents which are attributed to humans and animals. Instead of 'soul(s)' and 'body', I will use 'constituents' to designate immaterial and material elements of individuals (see below). Regarding the specificities of this Evenki concept, I will not use the term 'personhood' but rather 'individual'. Even if there is individual differentiation among animals, it does not mean that they are considered here to be strictly human-like beings. Likewise, the notion of 'person' (originally meaning 'mask' or 'social role') is strictly attached to humans and/or to the possession of a proper name in Mauss's studies (Mauss 1991: 303–62). Even Descola relies more frequently on the term 'individual' than 'person' or 'personhood' when referring to an animal (Descola 2005). According to the ethnographic data I am working with, I prefer to use 'person' concerning animals only when they are given a proper name by humans. Then, indeed, they become 'personified' in a human-like way whilst differing slightly from other individuals of their own species. Among the Evenki, this is the case for the most valued reindeers and for dogs. This fits with Lévi-Strauss's view according to which one of the three functions of a proper name is to classify an individual within a specific social realm (Lévi-Strauss 1962).

It is important to be aware of the lack of explanatory indigenous discourse about rituals, spirits or cosmogony in Siberia. Specialists who have this kind of knowledge, the shamans, are extremely rare nowadays. After seventy years of Communist 'militant atheism', an implicit view of the world I have noticed in my fieldwork seems to be present in the minds of nomads, but mostly at an unconscious level. Only a handful of people are able to explain beliefs and cosmogony as a coherent system.

The Evenki (previously called Tungus) are spread in small diversified groups over a vast area that stretches from western to eastern Siberia and into northern Manchuria. According to censuses, in 2000 there were 35,000 in China, and in 2002 in Russia there were 35,000.[2] They all live by hunting different kinds of game. Most of these groups are reindeer breeders, though some breed horses or other livestock. Partly settled by Communist Party policy, only a few of them still lead a truly nomadic lifestyle. The others now live in villages and towns. However, even for villagers and townspeople, the figure of 'nature' has a central place in their ideology.

The Evenki of southern Yakutia and the Amour region have a dual economy and a dual logic of subsistence, between hunting and reindeer herding, with seasonal interplay between the two. This dual economy seems to influence different spheres of their society, their social organisation (based on both a hunter's and a herder's worldview), their understanding of beings and spirits, and their conception of space. The main subsistence activity is mobile hunting and fishing. People keep small herds of reindeer for transport purposes, but also to have a 'stock of meat' in case of a shortage of food game. Each species of fur game or food game is hunted following a rigid seasonal calendar and diverse strategies. Thus, hunting is carefully planned so that every species can breed successfully. During the winter period, hunting keeps people occupied, whereas during late spring and summer more attention is paid to reindeer herding. Consequently, the size of the nomadic community also varies according to the seasons. While herding needs numerous human resources, the Evenki's way of hunting is best conducted in small, mobile family groups (Lavrillier 2005: 170–207; 2011).

According to the Evenki, humans and animals (both wild and domestic) may have a ritual action but with variable capacities. Thus, human beings 'act' upon their own group, as well as upon domestic and wild animals. Also, certain individual wild or domestic animals have the power to 'act' positively or negatively on the human group, on their relations with humans in terms of gifting and counter-gifting, and on natural elements.

'Spirit-charged' Humans

The concept of *onnir*, or 'spirit charge', is omnipresent in the background of everyday life among Evenki, whether they be nomads, villagers or townspeople. Such a concept appears through the many proscriptions, prohibitions and all kinds of rituals.

Onnir designates a specific capacity that every human has in themselves, with which they have to 'play' (sing, dance, shamanise, draw, and so on) in order to perform ritual actions.[3] The shaman differs from ordinary people only by the fact that 'he "plays" better than the others'. The partner of the 'ritual games' 'played' with or without shamans is *Buga*, an entity conceptualising the natural environment and the spirits that inhabit it. While 'traditional' shamans are disappearing, Evenki people each 'play' in their own way; or they turn to other ritual specialists such as elders, healers, imitators of shamans or 'shamans-to-be'. These ritual specialists are acknowledged as having a 'heavy spirit charge' that makes them ritually powerful and able to perform rituals. To designate the persons with a 'heavy spirit charge', people use the expression 'there are different kinds of individuals'.

The 'spirit charge' varies in strength from one individual to another. It also accumulates in the course of a lifetime through several processes: the acquisition of skills and forms of knowledge; successful breeding; social relations with humans and non-humans; taking part in, or performing, rituals with or without shamans. It should be noted that a 'spirit charge' being 'heavy' or 'light' does not correspond to 'positive' or 'negative'. For example, a fertile woman, a craftsperson skilled in the art of sewing, an old or sick person, or a murderer are all considered to have a 'heavy spirit charge', but all for different reasons. Their 'charge' will have different effects, either beneficial or harmful. An individual's 'spirit charge' leaves a positive or negative 'imprint' on all the objects and beings they touch and on all their actions. This 'imprint' can be 'active' even after their death.

Thus, humans are thought to leave their 'imprint' on hunting and herding tools, on the land they walk on, on the clothes they wear, on the meat they take when hunting, on the skins they tan, on the items they sew, on the reindeer they herd, ride or treat for illness and so forth, and on all the ritual gestures they perform. Depending on individuals, the meat will taste good or bad, the gun will fire accurately at its target or not, the domestic reindeer will reproduce or will grow thin and die. With some people, wounds become infected, clothes fall to pieces, the ritual does not have the expected effect, people or domestic animals die. Besides these 'direct' actions on things or beings, the *onnir* of humans can also have 'indirect actions' – that is, through objects. For example, one should not wear the clothes or shoes, nor sit on the bed of old or ill people, as they are considered to have a 'heavy' and dangerous 'spirit charge'; the latter is able to make younger people fall ill or die. Likewise, among the Eveny (another Tungus people) of northern Yakutia, one should not sit on the larch trunk fixed to the floor of the tent, at the edge of the sleeping area. This particularly concerns young people, because, as informants told me, 'different kinds of individuals cross this trunk, leaving on it "something from themselves", either beneficial or negative. This beneficial or negative 'imprint' will enter the body of people sitting on this trunk. Old people do not risk a lot, but young people are not able to fight against that'.[4]

The 'imprints' left by ordinary people are sometimes thought to be so powerful that shamans, for the most difficult rituals, have to enter the tent by crawling in through the back. Indeed, the door is said to be laden with the 'imprints' of the different individuals walking through the door. These 'imprints' might disturb the shaman in his ritual performance.

Onnir means as much the 'spirit charge' as its 'imprint' or the effect of its 'imprint'. The meaning of the root *o-* is 'to stand', 'to perform', 'to do'. Even though *onnir* is omnipresent as an implicit concept, only a few people know the word. During my fieldwork, I observed the same meaning among the Eveny of northern Yakutia.

Such 'imprints' left by individuals with a heavy 'spirit charge' are thought to be able to 'act' even after their death either directly or through objects. This is why people avoid walking over dead people's camps or using their guns or knives. For the same reasons, it is strictly prohibited to touch or use a dead shaman's items. The Evenki fumigate objects and living beings with plants such as Labrador tea or juniper in order to get rid of these negative 'imprints'.

This 'spirit charge' is supposed to make humans able to perform all ritual actions. Some individuals are thought to provoke events or cause sickness or injuries to other people just by 'thinking about it'. For example, an elder (a shaman's son) said that he has an undesired ability, with which he had to be very careful. When he is angry with somebody, if he thinks of a punishment, such as 'let his leg be broken', it automatically happens. Everybody knows about his skill and tries not to make him angry. A 'spirit charge' is thought to be transmittable through inheritance. Thus, many people said to have a 'heavy spirit charge' are descendants of shamans.

One informant, a shaman's daughter, gave me a more complete explanation of 'spirit charge'. She said:

> All Evenki have *onnir*, it is made up of spirits inside them. Spirits can enter the body, or leave it for a while. For example, if someone breaches a prohibition, the spirit of a dead person can enter his or her body, and thus his or her 'spirit charge' gets heavier. In this case, he or she will become sick and 'act' negatively on all beings and things he or she touches. The shaman's *onnir* has more spirits than ordinary people's. He is able to 'win' over spirits, because he 'plays' better than other people. The *onnir* consists of different kinds of spirits, some of which can be good to people. Each individual has at least one beneficial spirit, which manifests itself by a special skill for something: singing, dancing, decorating, drawing, telling stories, writing, hunting, herding, curing reindeer, playing an instrument, performing rituals and so on. Everyone has spirits but has to learn how to 'make good use' of them. The shaman is able to control all the spirits of his *onnir* and to put them to good use. This is why he is a 'master' in all skills and knows or sees many things which ordinary people do not see. The specificity of the *onnir* depends on the quantity and quality of the spirits and also depends on the manner in which the individual 'uses' his or her spirits and controls them. Thus, as he or she gets older, a person accumulates experience, learns more skills; the number of his or her spirits increases and his or her *onnir* becomes more powerful. Consequently most elders can perform rituals. However, if they do not learn how to put the spirits to good use, the spirits of the *onnir* will 'win' them over and 'eat' them, so they will suffer or die. For this purpose, they should 'play' (sing, dance, decorate, perform rituals) because 'playing' is the best means to make one's *onnir* richer and more powerful. That is why the shaman 'plays' periodically even if he is not asked to carry out a ritual for fear of losing control of his 'spirit charge'.

In discourses attributing ritual actions to some animals, the Evenki use the same recurrent sentence as they do for humans with a heavy 'spirit charge'. Informants say: 'Among domestic and wild animals, fur game and so on, there are different kinds of individuals'. Apparently, both wild and domestic animals can be said to have an *onnir*, a 'spirit charge'. But is an animal's *onnir* similar to a human being's in the Evenki conception of this notion? Are the spirits of an animal's *onnir* similar to those of a human's *onnir*?

'Spirit-charged' Animals

Just as shamans are considered to have a 'spirit charge' which is heavier than that of other humans, so certain individual reindeer, dogs or sables are considered to have a heavier 'spirit charge' than other individuals of their species.

The 'spirit charge' is not one and the same thing as the recyclable vital entity *omi* which is reincarnated from one generation to another within the same species or line. It also differs from the collective representation according to which the bodies of humans and certain animals can be the temporary seat of an *omi* which is alien and usually independent. For example, the *omi* of a dead human may take up residence for some time in the body of a bear in order to take revenge on that human's descendants. This alien *omi* will force the bear to devour their herd of reindeer in order to fulfil its desire for revenge, and will then leave the bear's body. The *omi* of a dead shaman may also be said to inhabit a wild animal briefly, appearing to humans in the forest without any special aim.[5]

The Taxonomy

There is a common conception of 'beings' to which humans, wild and domestic animals, trees and rivers belong called *iinekir*. Nevertheless, the diversity of terms shows an ideological differentiation between different kinds of 'beings'. All terms are based on roots linked to diverse variants of the notion of 'life'. For instance, animals and humans are called *bideril* (the living), while spirits are *ichil* (with life) (see Fig. 6.1). While the root *i-* (of terms *iinekir* and *ichil*) means 'to live, living', 'to be alive', the root *bide-* means 'to lead a life', 'to live somewhere'. All the 'beings' constituting the taiga (with the exception of the earth, stones and mountains) are supposed to be able to 'communicate' (speak or sing in Evenki) with humans. Such differentiation between beings and spirits contrasts with the works of Bird-David and Århem about the general homology of beings in Amazonia (see Descola 2005: 186). It seems to confirm the position of Hamayon explaining the importance of the differentiation between beings for relations of exchange (Hamayon 1990, 2001). The fact that one criteria of differentiation between humans, animals and spirits is 'to live somewhere' echoes the case of the Trío and other native Amazonians (Grotti and Brightman, this volume).

Evenki taxonomy, which derives from my fieldwork investigations, is composed of three main categories of animals (see Figs. 6.1 and 6.2). Here is a short presentation:

1. The category of domestic animals includes domestic reindeer and dogs. The Evenki term for designating this category seems to have disappeared. However, there is a significant differentiation in terminology as well as ideology

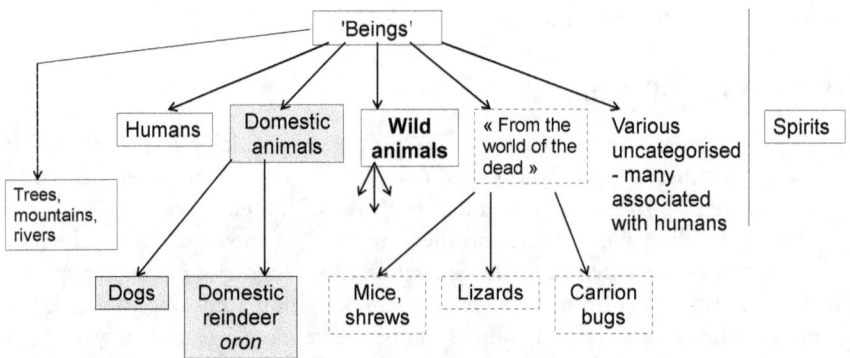

Figure 6.1: Evenki taxonomy. © Y. Doremieux and A. Lavrillier.

between the wild reindeer *beyun* and the domestic reindeer *oron*. Vitebsky has noticed the same linguistic distinction among the Eveny, and among many other reindeer peoples, which labels wild and domestic reindeer as 'different kinds of creatures' (Vitebsky 2005: 27). Another sign of the ideological differentiation between indigenous understandings of notions of 'wild' and 'domestic' is the existence of different verbs meaning 'to kill'. One is *vada* for wild animals; the other is *tepulida* for domestic animals (reindeer and dogs). The semantic difference concerns ways of killing (during hunting or near to the home).
2. One category stands apart and is composed of animals said to come 'from the world of the dead': mice, shrews, lizards and carrion bugs (see below).
3. The third main category, *beyngal*, is constituted by wild animals and divided into five sub-categories. The sub-category of food game (*beyur*) includes wild reindeer, red deer, roe deer, moose, grouse, bears, mouse deer and others. The giant wood wasp – *beyutkan*, or 'little black blood game' (*Urocerus gigas* L.) – is also part of this category, and is thought to be the 'soul' of big game (reindeer or moose) (see below). Fur game also constitutes a sub-category for which I did not record a specific term except for a word of Mongolian origin meaning the 'economic allochthonous partner' (*andahil*). Sable hunting is the most important commercial activity.[6] Other sub-categories are constituted by migrating birds (geese, swans, cranes, ducks); by small birds, which are supposed to be a seat for the human recyclable vital entities of future babies; and by fish (salmon, char, eelpout, pike). The sub-category of fish is considered and treated distinctly from game; the terminology used is not the same as for other hunted animals. The verb 'to kill' used for fish means 'to catch'. The way the remains of fish are dealt with compared to other animals hunted by humans is also different to those in other categories.

On the other hand, there are various uncategorised insects, many of which are associated with humans. There is no generic 'insect' category. Some of them are treated as a kind of pet, such as the big beetle (*Cerambix cedro* L.), or the birch-tree rhynchite (*Byctiscus betulae* L.). Others, like spiders, are thought of as ancestor protectors of the home.

The Relationships between Beings of Different Categories

The Evenki have economic relations or contacts (through hunting or herding in particular) with some of these animals and conceptualise different kinds of relationships with them. The social organisation or behaviour of some animals is seen as an ideal for humans. For instance, species such as bears and ground squirrels have developed relationships of mutual aid which are highly regarded. Some kinship relations with humans are believed to exist (for example, with bears), as well as between different species (like between bears, wolverine, sable and ground

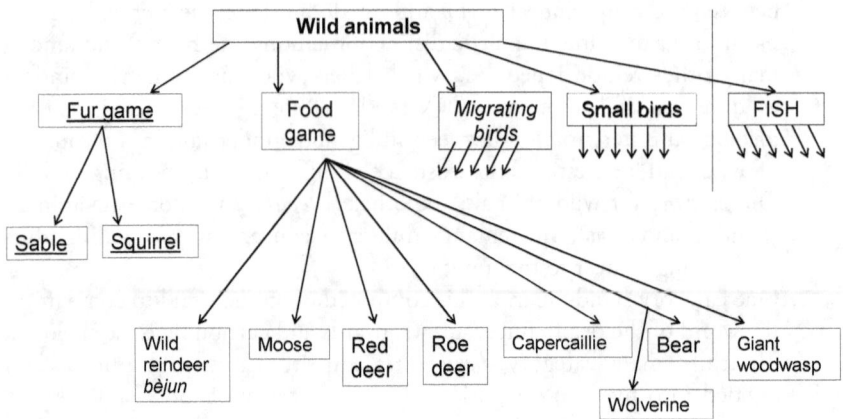

Figure 6.2: The category of wild animals in the taxonomy. © Y. Doremieux and A. Lavrillier

squirrels). The discourses regarding the strategic abilities of various animals in a predatory relation with other animals or when they are hunted by humans are especially detailed. But the most attention is paid to ritual interactions between animals and humans.

Discourses relating to ritual relationships between humans and domestic and wild animals provide the subject for a great deal of discussion during the night palavers of Evenki nomads. Let me make an overview of ritual interactions between humans and animals as seen by the Evenki (see Fig. 6.3). The Evenki attribute to wild animals some ritual actions which affect humans. Wild animals are supposed either to offer themselves (during hunting, by 'putting their tracks in the path of humans', according to their own will or the will of their master-spirit) or to avoid humans (by not being seen during hunting). They are also supposed to reinflict the wounds inflicted on them when being cut up by a hunter on to the hunter or his lineage for one or several generations, or to cause directly or indirectly the death of someone who killed too many members of a species. They are thought to be able to make their fur disagreeable to the one who wears it.

Wild animals are also supposed to 'act' ritually upon domestic animals, often to take revenge on a human who acted wrongly towards them. For example, bears and wolves will devour the herds of a person who has destroyed a den or taken a bit of their prey from the forest. Regarding this kind of relationship, we could say that this example is a form of 'indirect' reciprocity between humans and wild animals (through domestic animals). It could mean that the Evenki consider their reindeers as extensions of themselves and the concept of 'dividual' (Strathern 1988: 268–70) could then be applied here. But can we consider it as a ritual action?

Wild animals are also supposed to 'act' upon their own species. Some individuals are considered as especially ritually powerful. Some males and some females

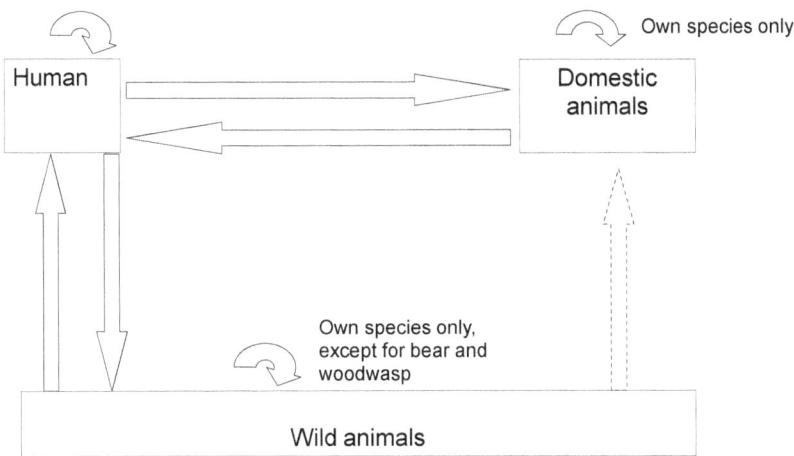

Figure 6.3: Direction of the ritual gestures and invisible acts of the main categories of the taxonomy. © Y. Doremieux and A. Lavrillier

are believed to guarantee exceptional reproduction and protection against misfortune for their own group. Others, like the white sable and albino or physically abnormal *cervidae*, are considered very powerful and are supposed to attract all the members of their own species towards them. They will also attract all their fellow creatures towards the hunter who killed them. Very few discourses I have noted among Evenki concern alleged ritual actions between different species of wild animals. Nevertheless, there is the example of the giant wood wasp, which is considered a game insect, like a 'soul' of a *cervidae*. It is supposed to come of its own volition to the camp to offer itself (as game) to humans. If humans throw it into the fire, it will bring *cervidae* game to the hunters of the encampment very soon. Another example is a bear killed during the winter hunt; it is considered to bring all kinds of game to humans in the following year.

The Evenki think that domestic animals can 'act' upon humans and even perform some ritual gestures, which may affect them. As well as wild animals, domestic ones are supposed to 'act' by reinflicting (during their life or after death) on humans the wounds that were inflicted upon them by humans during their life or after death. For example, as with wild animals, they will reinflict the wounds inflicted upon them during their butchering either directly on to the human inflicting the wounds or to their lineage. They can also provoke the tragic death of those who slaughtered (killed) too many of their species. In terms of ritual capacity, the Evenki make a difference between dogs and reindeer. When dogs die because of old age, the Evenki attribute to dogs the capacity to attract their master toward them in the world of the dead. Like humans, they are allegedly able 'to envy' their master, and through that they are supposed to bring about their impoverishment. Dogs are some of those rare animals that are supposed to have ritual gestures. When they repeatedly rub their hindquarters on the ground or when they dig several holes around a tent, people say that they want to provoke the death of a member of the encampment. Thus people interpret the dog's behaviour as a ritual gestures. To try to cancel the effectiveness of the ritual act, the dog is then shot by a person external to the encampment and without a family, for fear of retaliation by the dog.

Domestic reindeer, especially the best and older working reindeer, are supposed to be able to predict the future using human language once in their life. The old saddle reindeer are taken far away into the forest when their death is imminent to prevent them from attracting their owner toward them.[7] Certain individual domestic reindeer are thought to be able to cause trouble for a reindeer breeder who has made many reindeer suffer: they are supposed to make their descendants hunchbacked. In such a case, a certain ritual intentionality is assigned to animals, due to the desire for revenge. According to informants, a reindeer who takes revenge has a particularly heavy 'spirit charge' and is not always the reindeer that suffered from the actions of the herder. In addition, like the human's 'spirit charge', that of domestic animals is also thought to be transmissible from one generation to the next. In contrast, it is not the case of wild animals' 'spirit charge'.

Two ritual gestures are also attributed to reindeer, which are supposed to have consequences for their own group. When they turn around anti-clockwise inside the enclosure, they are supposed 'to want to disappear' – their herders will not find them for several days and the herd will lose a number of head to predators. Certain individual domestic reindeer are supposed to have the ritual capacity to protect their herd (males) or to guarantee a high reproduction rate within their herd (females). Usually, the shaman or some elders have to perform ritual gestures with the aim of strengthening this animal capacity; for example, to make a sacred reindeer protector of the herd.

At first sight, it seems that the Evenki do not imagine 'direct' – that is, where the human is absent – interactions by domestic animals on wild animals, by wild animals on domestic animals, and between different species of domestic animals. Moreover, ritual interactions most often involve only two categories of the taxonomy (including humans) at any one time, though sometimes when there are interactions in an indirect way, this involves a third category, illustrated by the fact, discussed above, that wild animals can devour domestic reindeer to take revenge on humans. These are relations of positive or negative reciprocity (see Fig. 6.4). Sometimes, this reciprocity skips a generation. Some individual animals can continue to be ritually powerful even after death.

It seems that, unlike the 'spirit charge', which is attributed to individual domestic as well as wild animals, ritual gestures are attributed only to domestic animals. Other invisible acts are supposed to be performed by means of thought or will. Domestic animals are those to which the largest variety of ritual actions are attributed. They are thought to be able to predict the future (often bad) and to talk in human language. They have the alleged power to attract a member of their species or their master towards the world of the dead.

Some nomads also mentioned invisible acts attributed to some other animals. Regarding these, nomads did not use the phrase 'there are different kinds of individuals'. Therefore, I assume that they do not attribute 'spirit charge' to these animals.

Non 'Spirit-charged' Animals

Among the non 'spirit-charged' animals, some species such as the cuckoo (called 'shaman-birds'), the ladybird (called 'little shaman') and the swan, are attributed with some capacity to act ritually, as it appears in the first stages of analysis (for some of them at least), in a certain intentional manner. In contrast to species that have 'spirit-charged' animals, the non 'spirit-charged' animals' power is attributed to these species as follows: all individuals in one species have the same strength and the same power. Their alleged intentional ritual efficacy is not expressed in terms of 'spirit charge'. Thus, the cuckoo is said to be able to influence the weather, announce the rebirth of nature in spring and predict people's future; certain plants are also thought to be its clothes, lasso, hat, and so forth. With the ladybird, in order to become lucky, one has to 'play the shaman' – that is, give it a little piece of wood that it will beat 'like a drum'. Among the 'species' 'from the world of the dead' (see Fig. 6.1), mice, shrews and lizards are supposed to be able to attract people to the world of the dead, and Evenki are quite frightened of them. Among the 'species' 'migrating birds' (see Fig. 6.2), swans are supposed to provoke famine or worse for the family that does not keep all containers outside the tent full of water during their and other birds' migration: nomads often say, 'migratory birds may need to drink water during their trip. If they cannot find it, they can drink your blood!' Pike are seen as 'frightening fish' and one of the more dangerous spirits of the shaman. Here, it seems that the notion of individual is not relevant.

Finally, the other species of non 'spirit-charged' animals are not attributed any agency. It seems that most birds, most fish and most insects are considered neither to have power to act ritually and intentionally, nor to have a 'spirit charge'. At the same time, plants and trees are not attributed any agency as such. Some trees and stones with abnormal forms are thought to be the seats of diverse spirits to which humans offer gifts.

The Constituents of Humans and Animals

The individual specific capacity (*onnir*) attributed to all humans and to some animals seems to be one of the constituents of human and animal individuals. Let us have a look at the constituents of humans and animals which we know. Representations of the constituents of beings can be very different among the Evenki, from one regional group to another. In order to present a global overview I will draw on Shirokogoroff (1935, 1966) and Vasilevich (1969) as well as my own field materials (see Fig. 6.4).

Beings in the categories of humans, wild and domestic animals are attributed, in equal quantity, to an entity that can be reincarnated within one's line of descent, called *omi*, a shadow (*hanyan*) in the literal sense, some vital force (*musun*) and a set of 'meat-bones-skin-guts' (*beyen*). We have no information about the constituents of other categories of beings. Although the representations of these constituents of humans are relatively well studied ethnographically, there is only scant information about animals' constituents.[8]

What varies from one individual to another is the 'spirit charge'. Among 'spirit-charged' categories of beings, just as the shaman is thought to have a 'heavier' 'spirit charge' than other humans, so sacred reindeer, 'herdmothers' of domestic herds or albino sable, albino moose or wild 'herd mothers' are considered to have more ritual power than others of their species.

We have seen that the Evenki consider animals not as a uniform whole, but that they make several levels of differentiation within the animal realm. The differentiation between wild and domestic animals seems to be very significant in terms of ritual action. Obviously, familiarisation is one of the reasons why Evenki attribute so many ritual abilities to domestic animals (see also Safonova and Sántha, this volume). It also seems that the distinction between humans and non-humans is important but not fully representative of the Evenki system of representation. The realm of the non-human is divided into several complex levels (sub-categories of non-humans) and is organised into several worlds of socialisation.

My ethnography indicates that domestic animals, food and fur game are also attributed a 'shadow', as humans are. If this is so, in contrast with other categories, the members of the world of socialisation comprised of humans, domestic animals, and food and fur game are attributed the same kind of constituents.

Worlds of Socialisation

On the basis of the foregoing, it is possible to distinguish a number of different worlds of socialisation, into which different beings are divided. The first of these worlds is constituted by the Evenki and the beings with which they engage in relations of positive or negative reciprocity: animals hunted for fur and food, and domestic animals. In this world, beings are characterised by the possession of a 'spirit charge' (varying from one individual to another within the same species), as well as by an alleged intentionality and capacity to 'act' ritually as an individual.

Other worlds of socialisation are constituted by stricter taxonomic categories of fish, small birds, migratory birds and ordinary insects. Within each of these categories, one species is considered more powerful than others. For example, within the world of socialisation of small birds, the cuckoo is supposed to have different capacities, and so on for each species (see Figs. 6.5 and 6.6). So, the notion of an individual being ritually more powerful than others of its group is applied here also. It means that, in the worlds of non 'spirit-charged' animals, the notion of individual in terms of ritual capacity is not perceived at the level of the individual (within the same species) – as it is in the world of 'spirit-charged' humans and animals – but at the level of the whole species (inside one taxonomic category).

		Human	Domestic animals	Food and fur game	Other categories
Vital entity recyclable within one's line	Vital **Identical**	Always	Always	Always	
Shadow		Always	Always ?	Always ?	?
Life force	**Common**	Always	Always	Always	
Meat – bones – skin – guts	Defined by the category	Always	Always	Always	
'Spirit charge'	**Variable quantity – individuating**	Always	Always	Always	?
Heavy 'spirit charge'		Shaman	Sacred reindeer, Herdmother	Albino sable Albino moose 'Herdmother'	

Figure 6.4: The constituents of humans and animals. © Y. Doremieux and A. Lavrillier

Conclusion

The attribution of ritual agency to certain animals raises a number of questions: What can this 'spirit charge' tell us about Evenki notions about the constituents of human and animal beings? The notion of 'spirit charge' partly reminds us of the Melanesian concept of *mana* analysed by Mauss (1991: 101–15). We can also find some of the specificities of the Evenki concept in other similar notions, such as the *naualaku* studied by Boas among the Kwakiutl (ibid.: 340–45) and the *tonalli* of the Nahuas of Mexico (Descola 2005: 290–91). Amazonian peoples attribute souls, intentionality, agency and so on to some animals, plants and things, whereas others do not (Descola 1986: 120; 2005; see also Fausto, this volume; Grotti and Brightman, this volume), and this could be interpreted in global terms of 'spirit charge', but I did not find the same Evenki specific understanding of 'spirit charge' among Amazonian societies, such as the Achuar, Candoshi or Makuna as discussed by Descola (2005). In contrast with other cultures' conceptions of a constituent of human and animal beings – a source of ritual power which implies individual differentiation – the *onnir* is not determined by day of birth or an astrological event (as it is among the Nahuas and the Tzotzil of Mexico), by a proper name (as among the Kwakiutl and Tlingit), by social position or class (as with *mana*, *naualaku* or the concept of *kamo* among the Kanak of New Caledonia), by moral qualities or personality (as among the peoples of Ancient Greece and Rome, and some people in India), or by the kinship identity of the individual (such as among the Kwakiutl, and the Samo of Burkina Faso).[9] One of the exceptional aspects of the Evenki concept is the idea of an active 'imprint'. Thus, *onnir* seems to identify the individual as a ritual agent among humans and animals, but not to identify the 'person' as such – that is, corresponding to the moral quality, the temperament and the social position of the individual.

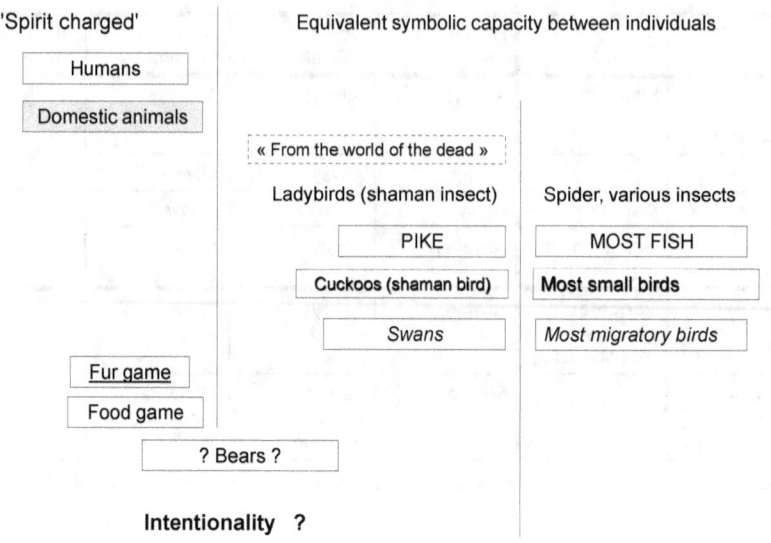

Figure 6.5: Worlds of socialization of 'spirit-charged' and other categories of beings.
© Y. Doremieux and A. Lavrillier.

'Spirit charge' seems to be linked with the hunter's logic of the relationship with nature, based on the 'gifting and counter-gifting' of vital force between humans and game (Hamayon 1990: 548–71, 592). The 'acts' of 'charged' animals are mostly thought of in relations of reciprocity (gift and counter-gift, revenge, and so on). Does this system of representation attribute 'spirit charge' only to humans, domestic animals and fur and food game because of their close economic relationship? Humans also exploit trees, rivers and mountains yet do not attribute them *onnir*. It is interrelated with the close ritual relationship – for example, when the shaman tries to obtain a blessing for reindeer herding and hunting. Indeed, they foster a relationship of exchange organised and sealed by a shaman or by elders. In contrast, the idea of reciprocity is absent of the conception of the relation between humans and non 'spirit-charged' animals: humans are not thought to be able to act ritually upon non 'spirit-charged' animals. Also, the Evenki do not imagine ritual action from cuckoos, swans or pike on their own group, nor upon other wild or domestic animals.

What are the similarities and differences between the ritual abilities attributed to humans and animals? One of the more obvious specificities of the ritual action attributed to animals is that they can mostly be ritually powerful without ritual gestures, in contrast to humans, for whom the main way to 'act' is to perform ritual gestures, which imply making codified gestures and using specific items. For example, there is no mention in discourses I have studied of offerings made by animals to spirits. In addition, animals are attributed fewer forms of 'playing' than humans. Animals are considered to 'play' when they are rutting, singing or dancing on the ice, or when they imitate human ritual as when the ladybird beats its 'shaman drum' (see above). 'Nature' is also supposed to 'play' through rock paintings in order to predict the future to humans by showing different drawings every year. Another difference is that, while the notion of an 'active imprint' is essential among humans, the discourses rarely mention an alleged effect from an animal's 'active imprint'. Moreover, they are not thought to 'act' through things, but thought to ritually 'act' mostly 'directly'. In addition, one ritual 'act' seems never to be attributed to any animals: bringing back to the world of the living a vital entity that had been stolen by spirits.

In discourse about the ritual action of domestic animals and those concerning all ritual 'revenges' (wild and domestic), their intentionality is clearly voiced. In most other discourse, the Evenki do not stress this aspect of the ritual actions of animals; it is presented like a kind of 'automatic action', which is not really dependant on an animal's will – for example, referring to the cuckoo's prediction of the future.

This concept, which implies individual differentiation between animals, could seem contradictory to the generic understanding of animals. This notion, spread throughout Siberia, considers domestic or wild animals as simultaneously one individual 'being' and a generic representative of their species. For example, in discourses on hunting, herding or rituals, the words used for animal species use the indefinite accusative case, 'a bit of': when making offerings to the fire, one says, 'Give me "a bit of" wild reindeer'. Moreover, the spirits are supposed to be unique and multiple. For example, the fire spirit is considered to be single for the whole of creation and yet specific in each camp. It is probably significant that the indefinite accusative case is not used in Evenki with terms meaning 'human'.

In contrast with Amazonians' conceptions of agency (see, e.g., Fausto, this volume), the Evenki concept of *onnir* is not so much linked to ownership. Another specificity of Evenki animism in contrast with the Amazonian Achuar is that they do not imitate behaviours of kinship relationship with animals (e.g., Descola 2005: 178). They just rarely express some vague and very distant ancestral relation with the bear, for instance. Another contrast with Amazonia (ibid.: 68) is the small importance of nurturing practices, besides some exceptions such as the temporary upbringing of a baby moose, whose mother has been killed by hunters, and the special case of dogs (see Safonova and Sántha, this volume).

To what extent can the concept of *onnir* confirm or invalidate the existence of the idea of a general homology of beings in the Siberian domain? Evenki society could be classified as having an animistic ontology, which sees humans and non-humans having the same 'interiority', but with different 'exteriorities' (see Descola 2005). However, we have seen here that they do not perceive the same 'interiority' for all beings.

Also, the existence of the world of socialisation of non 'spirit-charged' animals – with different 'exteriorities' and 'interiorities' than those of 'spirit-charged' creatures – invalidates the theory of the existence of a general homology of beings among the Evenki. In addition, within the Evenki system, while the *omi* of a dead human can enter the body of an animal for some time to take revenge on other humans, no *omi* of a dead animal can enter a human body. The *omi* of dead humans are thought only to enter wild animals and not domestic ones. Moreover, the notion of the transformation of humans into animals or of animals into humans, presented as a constant of animistic ontology by Descola (ibid.: 299–301), is absent in the world-view of the Evenki. In contrast with Amazonian societies, and seemingly like most other Siberian societies, the Evenki imagine that an individual's vital entity can be reincarnated only within its own species – that is, on the basis of the good relationship of the exchange of life force between humans and animals (Hamayon 2001).[10]

Notes

1. This chapter is based on field research funded by the Fonds d'aide à l'Anthropologie Sociale Louis Dumont, the Institute Paul-Emile Victor and the Fyssen Foundation. I would like to thank Y. Doremieux for designing the figures and the Magic Circle of the Scott Polar Institute at Cambridge for inviting me to discuss this paper.
2. *Census of the Russian Federation 2002: Nationalities*. Available from: <http://www.perepis2002.ru/index.html?id=17> [29 January 2010]; *Census of Chinese Republic 2000: Nationalities*. Available from <http://www.chinadataonline.org> [29 January 2010].
3. The ritual importance of 'play' (gaming, singing, dancing, jumping, and so on) as a way of performing rituals among Siberian societies was first highlighted by Hamayon (1990, 1999/2000).
4. The remark was made during fieldwork in Topolinoye in 2009, conducted with financial support from the Volkswagen Foundation as part of the Dobes project 'Documentation of Dialectal and Cultural Diversity among Evens in Siberia'.
5. This point draws on my fieldwork data; see also Hamayon (1990: 389, 770).
6. Before Russian colonisation these animals were rarely hunted, and if so only for ritual purposes (offerings to the spirits, the clothing of spirit representations and the ornamentation of clothes).
7. Regarding similar ritual capacities of domestic reindeer among Eveny, see also Vitebsky (2005: 280–81).
8. Though it was never expressed as a coherent theory by the Evenki, and all regional groups vary, Evenki understandings of life and death can be basically summarised as follows: The set made up of 'meat-bones-skin-guts' and the shadow both disappear after death. After a person dies their *omi* leaves the physical body and goes down from the middle world (the world of the living) into the lower world (the world of the dead) where it lives a similar life to its life in the middle world. Then, the recyclable vital entity joins the upper world, where it stays with the other 'entities to be born'. When a young couple first get together, the *omi* of their future child comes down through the smoke hole of the tent and settles in the womb of the future mother. During the first year its life, the *omi* is considered to be poorly attached to the child's body.
9. The materials referred to here are as follows: on Nahua and Tzotzil, see Descola (2005: 298); on Kwakiutl and Tlingit naming, see Mauss (1991: 340, 344); on the relation between social position or class and *mana* and *naualaku*, see Mauss (ibid.: 102, 340–45), and on the Kanak concept of *kamo*, see Leenhardt (1947); on moral qualities and personality in Ancient Greece and Rome and India, see Mauss (1991: 348–55); and on

kinship identity, see Mauss (ibid.: 345) for the Kwakiutl, and Heritier (1977) for the Samo. See also Descola (2005: 168, 175).
10. Hamayon (1990) analyses the individual vital entity currently called 'soul' as a 'unit of life' destined to be reincarnated in a new individual of the same animal species or human line, stating that it is to be distinguished from the 'vital force' that circulates between animals and humans and that may also be called soul (as in the term 'soulless'). It is this point which lies behind the title of her book: *La chasse à l'âme*, 'soul hunting'.

References

Descola, P. 2005. *Par-delà nature et culture*. Paris: Gallimard.
———1986. *La Nature domestique. Symbolisme et praxis dans l'écologie des Achuar*. Paris: Edition de la Maison des sciences de l'homme.
Gell, A. 1998. *Art and Agency: An Anthropological Theory*. Oxford: Clarendon Press.
Hamayon, R.N. 1990. *La chasse à l'âme: esquisse d'une théorie du chamanisme sibérien*. Nanterre: Société d'Ethnologie.
——— 1999/2000. 'Des usages du "jeu" dans le vocabulaire du monde altaïque', *Études mongoles et sibériennes* 30/31: 11–45.
——— 2001. 'Tricks of the Trade or How Siberian Hunters Play the Game of Life-giving Exchange', in C. Gerschlager (ed.), *Expanding the Economic Concept of Exchange: Deceptions, Self-Deceptions and Illusions*. Boston: Kluwer, pp.133–48.
Héritier, F. 1977. 'L'identité Samo', in C. Lévi-Strauss (ed.), *L'identité. Séminaire dirigé par Claude Lévi-Strauss*. Paris: Grasset, pp. 51-80.
Ingold, T. 2000. *The Perception of the Environment: Essays in Livelihood, Dwelling and Skill*. London: Routledge.
Mauss, M. 1991. *Sociologie et anthropologie*. Paris: Presses Universitaires de France.
Lavrillier, A. 2005. 'Nomadisme et adaptations sédentaires chez les Evenks de Sibérie postsoviétique : "jouer" pour vivre avec et sans chamane', Ph.D. thesis. Paris: Ecole Pratique des Hautes Etudes en Sciences Sociales.
——— 2011. 'The Creation and Persistence of Cultural Landscapes among the Siberian Evenkis: Two Conceptions of "Sacred" Space', in P. Jordan (ed.), *Landscape and Culture in Northern Eurasia*. Walnut Creek, CA: Left Coast Press, pp. 215–31.
Leenhardt, M. 1947. *Do kamo: la personne et le mythe dans le monde mélanésien*. Paris: Gallimard.
Lévi-Strauss, C. 1962. *La pensée sauvage*. Paris: Plon.
Shirokogoroff, S.M. 1935. *Psychomental Complex of the Tungus*. London: Kegan Paul.
——— 1966. *Social Organization of the Northern Tungus*. Osterhout: Anthropological Publications.
Strathern, M. 1988. *The Gender of the Gift: Problems with Women and Problems with Society in Melanesia*. Berkeley: University of California Press.
Vasilevič, G.M. 1969. *Èvenki: Istoriko-ètnografičeskie očerki (XVIII-načalo XX v.)*. Leningrad: Nauka.
Vitebsky, P. 2005. *Reindeer People: Living with Animals and Spirits in Siberia*. London: Harper Collins.

Chapter 7
Shamans, Animals and Enemies: Human and Non-human Agency in an Amazonian Cosmos of Alterity

Casey High

For many indigenous peoples of Amazonia and Siberia, the intentions and capacities of non-humans are an important part of mythology, ritual symbolism and everyday subsistence practices. In both of these regions indigenous understandings of interactions between humans and animals can be seen in shamanic practices oriented specifically toward relations of alterity, transformation and domestication. In the Waorani communities of Amazonian Ecuador, shamanic engagement with non-human agencies is central not only to healing illnesses and ensuring successful hunting, but also to assault sorcery. Waorani elders explain that in the past revenge killings were often carried out in response to shamans who engaged with animal spirits for the purpose of witchcraft. When commenting on the violence of past times, when many people are to said to have died from witchcraft and spear killings, they warn that people should be careful not to speak to a shaman at night when his body is inhabited by his adopted 'jaguar-spirit' (*meñi*). This is because communication between humans and the jaguar-spirit may lead the latter to attack and kill the people they name. Even after a shaman dies, his orphaned jaguar-spirit continues to live and kill people out of sadness and anger for its adopted father.

Accounts like these draw attention to Waorani interests in animals and the consequences of relations between humans and non-humans more generally. Their detailed attention to the behaviour and perspectives of animals is characteristic of the animistic and perspectivist cosmologies described by anthropologists in Amazonia (Descola 1992; Århem 1996; Viveiros de Castro 1998) and Siberia (Kwon 1999; Willerslev 2007; Willerslev and Ulturgasheva, this volume). My Waorani hosts' fascination with animals extends to their pets, the animals they hunt and those that they do not eat or domesticate – particularly jaguars. According to indigenous understandings of shamanism, the jaguar is a quintessential predator – a subject position that I suggest has important parallels with Waorani moral evaluations of human 'enemies'. As such, jaguars are, to use Carlos Fausto's terminology, at the top of the 'agentive' hierarchy (Fausto 2007: 503). However, despite the apparent continuities between human and non-human perspectives in Amazonian cosmologies, Waorani people also emphasise important differences between the subjectivities of jaguars and people. In this chapter I argue that these differences raise seldom-explored questions of how agency is understood in Amazonia. For my Waorani hosts, human personhood is understood in explicit contrast to the highly agential predatory subject position of jaguars. This leads me to draw on recent work that views Amerindian perspectivism not just as an abstract cosmology but instead as a culturally specific form of moral evaluation that engages human and non-human perspectives.

An important issue that emerges in Waorani discussions of non-human agencies is the inherent danger associated with shamanism, in which people interact with non-human beings, such as jaguar-spirits. For the Waorani, like many other Amazonian people, shamanism is dangerous precisely because the act of adopting (or being overtaken by) the perspectives of spirits and animals is a transformational process also associated with witchcraft. As several scholars have suggested, in Amazonia shamanism and witchcraft are not understood as separate or independent processes (Hugh-Jones 1994; Fausto 2004; Whitehead and Wright 2004). In some contexts they might be better viewed as different perspectives on the same process. This chapter describes how the dangers of interacting with non-human 'others' helps to explain the recent decline of Waorani shamanism and the increasing reliance on human enemies (rather than jaguar-spirits) for shamanic curing. Specifically, I examine how Kichwa-speaking people, referred to by the Waorani as 'outsiders' or 'enemies' (*cohuori*), have become both the ideal source of shamanic services and a primary target of witchcraft accusations.

Understanding this process requires paying attention to Waorani notions of predation, agency and a specific ideal of peaceful conviviality in the aftermath of several decades of intense violence. More generally, I point to the ways in which indigenous Amazonian ideas about non-human beings are central to understanding broader socio-political relations in the region. In order to better understand Waorani concerns about animals, shamans and enemies, the chapter draws on recent theorisations of agency in the anthropology of religion that aim to decouple this concept from the liberal humanist and Christian theological traditions from which it emerged (Mahmood 2005; Keane 2007). The central question is how Amazonian cosmology, sociality and history suggest forms of agency that depart from Western understandings of individual self-realisation.

Agency and the Perspectivist Subject

In recent years anthropologists have increasingly interpreted Amazonian ideas about humans and non-humans through the lens of Viveiros de Castro's formulation of perspectivism and ontological predation. In perspectivist cosmologies, humans, animals and other beings share a universal 'culture' or 'spiritual unity' insofar as all beings see themselves as persons in the same way that human beings do (Viveiros de Castro 1998: 470). One's perspective is thus determined by the body rather than by cultural differences, leading Viveiros de Castro to contrast Western notions of 'multiculturalism' to Amerindian 'multinaturalism'. While animals and spirits are attributed the consciousness and intentionality of human subjects, perspectivism is also predicated on a relation of predation by which beings struggle to assert their own perspective upon others. While perspectivism goes a long way in challenging Western notions of 'nature' and 'culture', Viveiros de Castro's interpretation relies heavily on a familiar opposition between subject and object (Course 2010). In Viveiros de Castro's model, the predatory struggle of perspectivism involves attempts to assert one's humanity as a perceiving subject ('predator') rather than an object of perception ('prey'). Within this cosmic battle for perspective, people are at risk of being tricked or overpowered by non-human subjectivities that transform them into a prey-object (Viveiros de Castro 1998: 483; Lima 1999). While this formulation of Amerindian perspectivism appears to resonate strongly in much of Siberia (Pedersen 2001; Willerslev 2004, 2007; Pedersen, Empson and Humphrey 2007) and Melanesia (Kirsch 2006), it fails to take into account the multiple ways in which indigenous Amazonian people themselves envision and evaluate everyday social practice (Londoño Sulkin 2005).

Only recently have anthropologists working in Lowland South America challenged this strict subject/object dichotomy and looked more closely at the different kinds and degrees of subjectivity in Amerindian cosmology and social practice beyond the positions of 'predator' and 'prey' (Londoño Sulkin 2005; Rival 2005; Bonilla 2007; Walker 2009; Course 2010). In this chapter I look to build on work in this direction by raising questions about the different kinds of agency Waorani people attribute to humans and non-humans, and how they are related in shamanic practices and inter-ethnic relations.[1] In contrast to writings on perspectivism that describe the 'predator' perspective as denoting a universally human perspective, in everyday life Waorani people often identify themselves as 'prey' to outside aggressors – whether in the form of jaguars, spirits or human enemies (Rival 2002; High 2009a). Rather than emphasising a struggle to assert one's perspective (as subject), I suggest that Waorani people struggle to reconcile the moral implications of different forms of agency and intentionality that transcend 'human' and 'animal' kinds.

Traditionally, anthropological writings have adopted a view of agency consistent with liberal humanist and Christian theological preoccupations with the moral value of individual consciousness, freedom and self-realisation (Keane 2007). This can be seen, for example, in anthropological debates about structure and agency, studies of resistance in subaltern studies and critical feminist approaches in anthropology (Mahmood 2005). Webb Keane makes clear that this conceptualisation of agency has been central to what he calls a 'moral narrative of modernity' in which the 'emancipated subject' is liberated from false beliefs (Keane 2007: 4–5). He suggests that this philosophical move, which insists on the conceptual division of body and soul, model and reality, words and things, nature and culture, can be understood in terms of the broader tendency to oppose subjects to objects. Course (2010) takes this argument a step further in suggesting that such an emphasis on subject/object oppositions is in part rooted in analogies derived from European languages. He suggests that, since this formulation of agency and subject/object relations can be seen in terms of specific cultural and historical contexts, we should be wary of importing these ideas into our analysis of Amerindian cosmology and social practice.

In the present chapter I follow Mahmood's suggestion that 'the meaning and sense of agency cannot be fixed in advance, but must emerge through an analysis of the particular concepts that enable specific modes of being, responsibility, and effectivity' (Mahmood 2005: 14–15). Mahmood's work, for example, illustrates the ways in which submission can be understood as a specific cultural expression of agency. I suggest that part of this openness to alternate, culturally-specific formulations of agency stands to benefit from viewing subjects and objects as points along a continuum of agency, rather than exclusive or opposed categories (Course 2010: 256). It is within this frame of reference that this chapter interprets Waorani understandings of human and non-human perspectives, as well as the cultural value placed on being prey rather than predators.

'Enemies' and 'Prey'

The Waorani live on a vast ethnic reserve of more than one million acres between the Napo and Curaray rivers in eastern Ecuador. Most of the total population of about 2,500 reside in more than thirty villages, many of which have airstrips and state-run schools. The past four decades have been marked by a dramatic transition from highly dispersed and nomadic longhouses to larger and more permanent settlements. Still, their long treks in the forest, residential movement between villages and temporary migration for employment with oil companies continue to constitute a mobile way of life.

Waorani people are best known in Ecuador and in anthropology for their relative isolation until the 1960s, and their famous spear-killing raids between household groups and against outsiders. The earliest ethnographic accounts describe a society on the verge of disappearance prior to mission settlement, primarily as a result of an intense cycle of internal revenge killings (Yost 1981). While the causes of this violence continue to be debated from diverse perspectives,[2] it is clear that Waorani people envisioned their conflicts with 'outsiders' (described by Waorani as *cohuori*) as a relationship of predation. Still today, elders describe how they once feared that all *cohuori* people were cannibals. This is part of a broader Waorani logic that locates personhood in the position of the 'prey' or victim of outside aggression (Rival 2002). Oral histories and commentaries about contemporary relations with *cohuori* tend to emphasise Waorani victimhood in the face of powerful outsiders, even after the dramatic decrease in violence following mission settlement in the 1960s. Despite the intensity of past violence, which may have accounted for as much as half of Waorani deaths in the decades preceding missionary settlement (Beckerman and Yost 2007), household and village life today is characterised by an often-expressed ideal of peaceful conviviality. As in previous times, the household (*nanicabo*) and a tightly knit endogamous group of closely related households (*waomoni*) remain the primary units of social organisation, even in large villages with as many as 200 residents. And yet, in recent decades missionaries, local schools, oil development and tourists have made relations between Waorani and *cohuori* people increasingly frequent and varied.

Until recently the Waorani were referred to as *aucas*, a derogatory term meaning 'wild', 'savage' or 'enemy' in Kichwa, the dominant language of indigenous Ecuador. This social categorisation as 'wild' Indians was amplified in 1956 when five North American evangelical missionaries were killed by Waorani during an attempt to make what was assumed to be 'first contact'.[3] In the years following the killings, Waorani became the target of an intensive and highly publicised evangelical mission campaign by the Summer Institute of Linguistics (SIL), which lasted until the SIL was expelled from Ecuador in 1981 (see Stoll 1982). The mission and subsequent settlement of Waorani people in larger villages has coincided with their increasing intermarriage with neighbouring Kichwa-speaking (Runa) people. Despite the relative peace that has emerged since the mission period, some Waorani continue to be involved in violent inter-family feuds and conflicts with loggers, oil workers and Kichwas who live and work on Waorani lands.

Shamans, Pets and Orphans

One of the odd things in writing about Waorani shamanism is that there are remarkably few Waorani shamans today. There is no doubt that the establishment of missionary settlements had a major role in discouraging shamanism. The missionary texts written about this period make clear the familiar missionary goal of replacing shamanic beliefs and practices with Christian teachings.[4] However, despite more than two decades of missionary presence, shamanism did not disappear during the missionary period, and a few practising shamans remain in some communities today. Despite the fact very few people claim to be shamans, what shamans do is something of much interest and concern to Waorani people. I suggest that understanding regional social transformations requires taking these contemporary Waorani concerns seriously, as they reveal not only specific notions of human and non-human agency but also fundamental ontological assumptions that underlie indigenous understandings of sociality.

To explain the apparent decline of shamanism requires understanding not only missionary history and the specific role of the shaman, but also the place of animals, spirits, and human enemies within a broader Waorani cosmos of alterity. Although little has been written about Waorani shamanism, it is clear that relationships between humans and animals have a central role. Shamans are described as people who develop a special kin relationship with jaguars through dreams in which a jaguar-spirit is 'adopted' by a shaman (Rival 2002). The jaguar-spirit subsequently visits the shaman and speaks through the voice of its human 'father' during trances experienced by the shaman while dreaming. As it temporarily inhabits the shaman's body, the jaguar-spirit tells its adopted father and his family where to find game animals. In the Waorani language, these shamans are called *meñera*, meaning 'jaguar father', and are sometimes referred to simply as *meñi* (jaguar).

In describing the process of becoming a shaman, my Waorani hosts emphasise that people do not themselves choose to become shamans. People who suffer near fatal illnesses or accidents are said to be particularly vulnerable to becoming shamans, especially if the calamity was caused by witchcraft. It is instead the jaguar-spirit who imposes its own perspective on an adoptive human father while dreaming, literally inhabiting and speaking through the shaman's body while he sleeps. As Laura Rival has explained: 'Waorani shamans do not take an active role in controlling their spirit helpers. On the contrary, they let the spirits possess them' (Rival 2005: 296). The relationship between shaman and jaguar-spirit is one of adoption because jaguar spirits are, like the most famous Waorani killers, seen as orphans. That is, an orphan, someone without kin with whom to engage in proper relations of sociality, is akin to the position of a predator. Following a similar logic that revenge should be taken after the death of a kinsman, many of the most notorious killers in local oral histories are described as orphans. This characterisation of predatory jaguars and human killers as orphans illustrates how the predatory point of view cannot simply be assimilated to the kind of personhood appropriate to Waorani humanity. Since the moral 'human' perspective is that of being prey surrounded by consubstantial kin, the challenge for shamans, according to their peers, is to remain in a subordinate position in their relations with animal spirits. In contrast to the predatory agency of jaguars, shamans thus ideally demonstrate their human agency through being controlled by non-human beings, rather than by controlling them.

While the title of 'shaman' is sometimes attributed to specific people, communication between animals and human beings is not restricted to shamanic practices. For example, a man described to me how his father, upon experiencing an unexpected encounter with a jaguar in the forest, angrily insisted to the jaguar that he was not afraid, since he too was an orphan.[5] Following descriptions of perspectivism, jaguars are attributed a human perspective because they share the same universal 'culture' as people. However, Waorani people themselves understand jaguars not only in terms of continuities with human perspective, but also as having a particular kind of agency that is antithetical to proper human sociality. As Londoño Sulkin notes among the Muinane of Colombian Amazonia, jaguars and other animals are seen as 'failures in moral sociality' to the extent that they 'create immoral subjective states' (Londoño Sulkin 2005: 12). Jaguars are dangerous because they have no kin and, like human 'enemies' (*cohuori*), they occupy a predatory subject position in relation to Waorani people. Since Waorani define themselves paradigmatically as 'prey' in relations of alterity, the subjectivity of jaguars and enemies is often expressed in contrast to the ideal of generosity and peaceful conviviality that Waorani people associate with their own sociality. When men become consumed with rage and kill people, they are seen as becoming temporarily detached from their human bodies (Rival 2005). This is because to be a real Waorani person is not to be a predator but instead to be prey.

Both the presence of missionaries and the conversion of indigenous peoples to Christianity have had an important impact on Amazonian logics of predation and personhood (Vilaça and Wright 2009). For example, local oral histories in which Waorani people situate themselves unambiguously as 'prey' to aggressive outsiders sometimes draw on imagery of Christian martyrdom promoted by missionaries in the 1960s (High 2008). Waorani people today emphasise that these missionaries were close relatives of the missionaries killed by Waorani in 1956. It appears that this narrative of self-sacrifice and the identification as kin of victims became a key discursive feature of the missionisation process. Although few Waorani today describe themselves as Christian, many adults reflect on the missionary period as a time of *civilización* ('civilisation') in which former 'enemy' groups came to live together in larger settlements. The missionary period also corresponded with the decline of Waorani shamanism – a process that continues up to the present day.

In discussing the close links between shamanism, warfare and jaguars in Amazonia, Fausto voices one of the central assertions of recent work on perspectivism in stating that, in Amazonia, 'the capacity for predation is a hallmark of powerful agency' (Fausto 2004: 170). Although this view resonates with Waorani understandings of shamanism, it is also important to recognise the different kinds of agency attributed to jaguars and human persons. In rejecting the predator subject position on moral grounds as a non-human perspective attributed to jaguars, enemies and killers, it appears that Waorani people do not understand jaguars as having the same 'culture' or agency as humans. So, if we are to suggest a common or analogous personhood shared by jaguars and human beings, we should be careful to recognise that indigenous peoples themselves often view these as radically different kinds of 'persons' or moral beings. For example, Londoño Sulkin's ethnography makes clear that jaguars and other animals 'cannot really be said to have a properly "human perspective"' because their affects toward their own co-specifics 'differ from those of Real People' (Londoño Sulkin 2005: 20). In contrast to the dangerously 'false' perspectives that animals attempt to impose on real people, the Muinane view their own 'true' perspective as having greater agency than others since, in contrast to non-humans, theirs is a moral perspective (ibid.: 16). While Waorani people share a similar vision of jaguars having a different and often morally problematic kind of agency when compared to their own, it is striking that they envision themselves as the victims of more powerful predatory agencies that in turn make real people into prey.

Regardless of the extent to which Waorani expressions of personhood intersect with missionary discourses, Waorani people today see themselves as properly human subjects insofar as they are objects of predation. This of course is not to say that they envision their own subject position as prey to be without a certain agency of its own. Whereas jaguars are predatory 'orphans', human agency is characterised by the capacity to create and maintain everyday sociality – a 'moral' agency that is often contrasted explicitly with other indigenous groups and mestizo Ecuadorians. What is central to Waorani understandings of alterity is not so much a rigid dichotomy between 'subjects' with agency and 'objects' without, rather it is a complex and overlapping matrix of humans and non-humans that interact in different ways. In this light, we might envision Amazonian cosmology and sociality not just as a struggle between different co-specifics to assert a generic 'human' perspective over other beings (Lima 1999; Course 2010), but also a set of multiple agencies that affect specific relationships in distinct ways. From this perspective, agency can be understood more as a capacity to create and affect particular kinds of relations than as a form of individual self-realisation often implied in conventional anthropological approaches to agency.

Witchcraft and the Direction of Agency

The key differences between the kinds of agency attributed to humans and non-humans can be seen in Waorani understandings of witchcraft. While hunting is an important part of Amazonian shamanism, until recently there has been relatively little attention to the 'darker' aspects of such practices that emerge when shamans use their powers to harm people (Whitehead 2002; Whitehead and Wright 2004). Waorani people, for example, complain that shamans are responsible for sickness, accidents and deaths through witchcraft. They describe how relations between shamans and their adopted jaguar-spirits may result in a shaman or an actual jaguar killing a person. This is particularly the case when shamans assert their ability to control spirit-animals. In this sense witchcraft appears to invert the expected direction of agency in relations between humans and non-humans. As Fausto has pointed out for Amazonia more generally, it is not always clear who adopts or controls whom in the adoptive father/son relationship between shamans and animal spirits (Fausto 2000: 938). He describes humans and animals as being 'immersed in a sociocosmic system in which the direction of predation and the production of kinship are in dispute' (Fausto 2007: 500).

This ambiguity in agency and perspective is in part what makes Waorani shamanism dangerous. Shamans perform witchcraft by communicating with an animal and sending it to kill enemies. In describing this process to me, my Waorani hosts compare the relationship between shamans and animals to a person having a domesticated 'pet'. Whereas in some cases the jaguar/predator perspective inhabits the body and voice of a human shaman, witchcraft appears to be a reversal of this relationship in which animal pets are controlled or domesticated by shamans for the purpose of attacking people. Shamans who practice witchcraft may engage not only the services of a jaguar but also a variety of different animals, such as poisonous snakes and insects. Like the jaguar-shaman (*meñera, meñi*), other shamans are identified with the name of the animal with whom they are involved in this kind of relation.

These misgivings about the relationship between shamans and jaguars provide an interesting contrast to the symbolic or actual 'domestication' of large predator animals among hunting peoples of Siberia. Whereas Waorani view jaguars as diametrically opposed to human sociality and equate the domestication of predatory animals by shamans with witchcraft, among Siberian hunters the domestication of 'house bears' historically constituted an attempt to create kinship and 'force the animal into a collective domain of sociality with other children and adults' (Kwon 1999: 378). The process of capturing bear cubs and fostering them in captivity in preparation for a 'bear feast' or 'bear play', in which bears were ritually killed and eaten, was associated with marriage and the 'growing' of children. Kwon suggests that 'bear play' constituted a double dialogue of hunting and marriage in which 'the role exchange between prey and hunter [was] a key to the inversion of meaning between the mythic and ritual violence' (ibid.: 387). This kind of inversion of perspectives between people and animals is familiar to studies of shamanism, myth and cosmology in Amazonia (see Viveiros de Castro 1998). Waorani people are particularly attuned to the potential for shamans to adopt the perspective of jaguars. However, the status of jaguars as quintessential predators makes them a dangerous site for sociality and 'domestication' by shamans that may lead to witchcraft. While Amazonian myths contain stories of confused and inverted perspectives akin to those told about bears in Siberia, it is telling that indigenous Amazonian people generally do not capture or domesticate jaguars or other large predator animals.

In some ways Waorani shamanism presents a striking contrast to the shamanic dreams described among Amazonian groups like the Brazilian Parakanã, where a shaman is said to become dangerous to his kin when he 'surrenders' his perspective to that of a jaguar, thus reversing the master/pet relationship (Fausto 2004). For my Waorani informants, it is the 'master' or 'predator' perspective itself that is antithetical to proper human sociality – a subject position associated with assault sorcery, enmity and vengeful rage. It is for this reason that shamans and their families should surrender to their jaguar-spirits rather than control them as pets. Waorani understandings of shamanism suggest that perspectivist ontologies in Amazonia do not necessarily constitute a universal struggle to impose a predatory human perspective on 'prey' objects, as moral human subjects are conceived as objects of aggressive non-human and enemy perspectives.

Shamanism in Decline?

In part as a result of their association with witchcraft, shamans are generally not seen in a positive light in Waorani villages, where people explain that many past revenge killings were inspired by the misdeeds of shamans. When children died of sickness, their kin sought revenge by attempting to kill the entire family of the suspected shaman. This was in part to prevent the possibility of counter-attacks, but it has also been explained to me that other members of a shaman's household may be directly responsible for witchcraft. This is because household members who are present when the shaman is inhabited by his 'jaguar-spirit' may speak to the latter, giving it names of people to kill. Waorani people speak literally about actual jaguars being sent by shamans to kill people. One also hears stories about people becoming seriously ill as a result of the witchcraft of these same shamans. Although they distinguish between being physically attacked by an animal and falling ill, these various misfortunes are attributed to the same general predatory agency – often expressed metaphorically as being eaten by a jaguar. Following a broader logic of perspectivist ontology, it appears that disease and warfare are understood as different perspectives on the same event (Fausto 2007: 501).

In recent years Waorani people have come to see shamans as one of the key obstacles to achieving peaceful sociality in the increasingly large villages established since the missionary period. These communities bring together groups who previously maintained a greater degree of household independence and geographical distance characteristic of many small-scale Amazonian societies. Since virtually every major accident, serious illness or death is attributed to some form of human responsibility, shamanism appears to have become a considerable threat within this new concentration of former 'enemy' groups. It appears that in this context Waorani people reject shamanism locally not because of a declining confidence or 'belief' in its power, but instead because they take the consequences of such practices so very seriously. Much like Fausto describes for the Parakanã, the predatory associations between shamans, warfare and jaguars make the shaman a 'stigmatised' and 'unfeasible figure' whose role is seldom publicly recognised (Fausto 2004: 160). Among the Waorani, this public recognition is very rarely claimed but instead attributed to specific people in cases of witchcraft.

Nevertheless, shamanism continues to figure prominently in Waorani social life, though in a different context. Today Kichwa-speaking (Runa) communities that line the boundary of Waorani lands have become the primary source of shamanic curing as well as a seemingly constant target of witchcraft accusations (High 2006). This has coincided with the increasing frequency of inter-ethnic marriage, especially between Waorani men and Kichwa women. Kichwa people have come to occupy a seemingly paradoxical position: they are described as enemy 'outsiders' (like all other non-Waorani people), as potential and actual affines, and as specialists in shamanic practices. Many Waorani travel to distant villages or even to the regional capital to pay Kichwa shamans for diagnosis or treatment, as they are said to be particularly adept at identifying who is responsible for illnesses and accidents. At the same time, witchcraft accusations against Kichwas are among the most common motivations for Waorani attacks against Kichwa people.[6]

Within this regional system of inter-ethnic relations, Kichwa shamans appear to have occupied a role similar to that attributed to predatory jaguar-spirits in Waorani shamanism. Whether as shamans, 'enemies' or actual affines, Kichwas are attributed a highly agentive predatory perspective associated with non-humans. In the communities where I work, it is in reference to this perceived moral deficiency of Kichwas that Waorani people often contrast their own position as victims or 'prey' to aggressive outsiders. It is not surprising that Kichwas and other outsiders are referred to as *cohuori*, a word that traditionally denoted a semi-human status of cannibalism. This is an example of how, in Amerindian cosmology, human culture or perspective is extended to things we associate with 'nature' (Descola 1994), such as animals and plants, whereas a non-human perspective is often attributed to people outside the local group (Viveiros de Castro 1998).

As we have seen, the Waorani externalisation of the predator perspective appears to invert the Amazonian model of ontological predation described by Viveiros de Castro and others (Rival 2002). However, it is also important to place Waorani discourses of victimhood and predation within a specific socio-historical context characterised by missionary settlement and the recent transition from widespread inter-group revenge killing to relative peace. Without reproducing the tendency to reify specific historical periods or societies as 'violent' or 'peaceful', it is striking that recent decades have marked a dramatic decrease in spear killings between Waorani groups. Although young Waorani men still occupy the position of 'wild' Amazonian warriors in certain inter-ethnic contexts (High 2009b), it may well be that previous generations identified more closely with the predator/jaguar perspective in past times of intense violence, when men were said to be actively trained as killers. I suggest that the current marginalisation of Waorani shamanism and the increasing importance of 'enemy' Kichwa shamans reflects the ways in which Waorani people have understood and engaged in changing relations of alterity through their own lens of predation. In order to live peacefully among human (Waorani) enemies today, it seems that openly engaging with jaguar-spirits poses too great a threat to the present ideal of 'community' (*comunidad*). And yet, there are clear continuities between the agency attributed to jaguars and the 'predatory' perspective projected onto Kichwa people, and particularly their shamans.

In this light, the marginal position and general lack of Waorani shamanism today can be understood not only as a result of missionary settlement but also as part of a larger indigenous project in which my informants envision the growth and expansion of their communities. Local historical narratives make clear that this ideal cannot be achieved without avoiding the revenge killings that have such a vivid presence in Waorani social memory. The broad range of misfortune attributed to witchcraft and the preoccupation with preventing conflicts between household groups leaves little moral space for local shamans today. On more than one occasion my Waorani friends have proudly assured me that, in contrast to other villages, theirs has no *brujos* (shamans, witches). The lack of Waorani shamans today is thus an important part of the broader emphasis on avoiding potential conflicts that would threaten what Waorani people envision as a current period of relatively peaceful relations between households. And yet, everyone knows that the village is still not safe from shamanic power. People still suffer the attacks of predatory 'jaguars'. The jaguars of today however, are not as frequently Waorani enemies and shamans, but rather Kichwa people.

Conclusion

As many anthropologists have warned, it is important to resist the temptation to simply project our own conceptual preoccupations and theoretical fashions onto the cultural contexts that we write about (Viveiros de Castro 2003; Henare, Holbraad and Wastell 2007). In particular, the focus on 'agency' in anthropology over the past few decades 'risks projecting onto native peoples our own most cherished cultural notions, those that positively define our contemporary subjective experience' (Fausto and Heckenberger 2007: 4). Much anthropological writing on agency appears to attribute a positive moral value to individual and collective action that demonstrates a kind of self-realisation and autonomy (Mahmood 2005). For example, in challenging historical approaches that emphasise the transformative role of European colonialism in the Americas, Peter Gow (2001) suggests that we should instead understand indigenous Amazonian people themselves as creative agents in their own histories. While approaches like these have made a valuable contribution to understanding other lived worlds on their own terms, I suggest that we should also be open to the ways in which agency itself is construed in ways that may diverge from our own.

In contrast to the positive moral connotations of individual agency in some of our own anthropological and philosophical traditions, Waorani people appear to be more concerned with the dangers of specific people who claim or acquire too much agency. This is as much the case in Waorani understandings of relations between humans and non-humans in shamanism as it is in contemporary indigenous politics (High 2007). Like jaguars, people associated with an excessive degree of intentionality, control and power may become predators who harm even their own kin. Despite the apparent contrast between the position of jaguars in Waorani shamanism and the 'bear play' of Siberia, in these two geographically distant areas one finds a common emphasis on the agency of animals, rather than that of individual leaders or ancestors.[7] Just as the famous Waorani killers of past times are described as orphans who were able to bring other people under their own influence and control, shamans become sorcerers when they assert their abilities to control or impose too much of their own will upon non-human 'pets'. In this light, I suggest that many Waorani people today are suspicious of shamans in much the same way that they challenge the moral legitimacy of their own political leadership: they know all too well from the stories of elders how the potential excesses of agency pose a threat to the idealised conditions of human sociality.

Notes

1. The fieldwork on which this chapter is based (2002–2004) was made possible by grants from the Wenner-Gren Foundation, the Fulbright Commission and the Central Research Fund of the University of London. I also wish to thank Magnus Course and Mette High for their insightful comments on earlier drafts of the present chapter. A post-doctoral position at the Centre National de la Recherche Scientifique (CNRS), University of Paris X-Nanterre, provided me valuable time to develop the chapter's theme. I also owe thanks

to my Waorani friends, hosts and informants for sharing their stories and homes with me during fieldwork.
2. These include ethno-psychology (Robarchek and Robarchek 1998), ethnohistory (Cabodevilla 1999; Cipolletti 2002), indigenous cosmology (Rival 2002, 2005), and sociobiology (Beckerman and Yost 2007).
3. This event subsequently became the subject of several popular Christian books published in North America and Europe.
4. See, e.g., Elliot (1957, 1961), Wallis (1960, 1973), Kingsland (1980), Liefeld (1990) and Saint (2005).
5. Implicit in this story was the man's refusal to be recognised as prey (and thus killed) in his encounter with the jaguar.
6. Ethnographic and historical research has pointed to the key position of Kichwa-speaking people in regional inter-ethnic relations (Taylor 1999, 2007; Whitten and Whitten 2007). As Amerindian groups who were assigned the category of 'tame' or 'civilised' Indians at missions during the colonial period, they became intermediaries between whites and forest-dwelling *auca* groups in a regional system of economic and shamanic exchange. It was groups like these who became renowned for powerful shamanism in part as a result of their experience in regional inter-ethnic relations. Gow (1993) suggests that much of this shamanic complex itself emerged during the colonial period in response to the European diseases that decimated Amerindian populations on early mission settlements.
7. Morton Pedersen has suggested that the striking parallels between the animist and perspectivist social ontologies of Amazonia and Siberia may be related to a common emphasis on horizontal (rather than vertical) relations. Whereas relatively egalitarian Amazonian peoples like the Waorani and North Asian hunters both understand perspectivism in terms of relations of 'analogous identification' between humans and non-humans, Pedersen notes that the shamanic traditions of relatively hierarchical societies in southern North Asia (such as Mongolia) appear to prioritise 'homologous differentiation' in engaging the perspectives of human ancestors (Pedersen 2001: 419).

References

Århem, K. 1996. 'The Cosmic Food Web: Human–Nature Relatedness in the Northwest Amazon', in P. Descola and G. Pálsson (eds), *Nature and Society: Anthropological Perspectives*. London: Routledge, pp. 185–209.
Beckerman, S., and J. Yost. 2007. 'Upper Amazonian Warfare', in R. Chacon and R. Mendoza (eds), *Latin American Indigenous Warfare and Ritual Violence*. Tucson: University of Arizona Press, pp. 142–79.
Bonilla, O. 2007. Des proies si desirables. Soumission et predation pour les Paumari d'Amazonie bresilienne. PhD. Dissertation, Ecole des huate etudes en sciences sociales. Paris, France.
Cabodevilla, M. 1999. *Los Huaorani en la historia del Oriente*. Quito: CICAME.
Cipolletti, M. 2002. 'El testimonio de Joaquina Grefa, una cautiva Quichua entre los Huaorani (Ecuador, 1945)', *Journal de la Societé des Américanistes* 88: 111–35.
Course, M.E. 2010. 'Of Words and Fog: Linguistic Relativity and Amerindian Ontology', *Anthropological Theory* 10(3): 247–63..
Descola, P. 1992. 'Societies of Nature and the Nature of Society', in A. Kuper (ed.), *Conceptualizing Society*. London: Routledge, pp. 107–26.

―――― 1994. *In the Society of Nature: A Native Ecology in Amazonia*. Cambridge: Cambridge University Press.
Elliot, E. 1957. *Through the Gates of Splendor*. New York: Harper and Brothers.
―――― 1961. *The Savage My Kinsman*. New York: Harper and Brothers.
Fausto, C. 2000. 'Of Enemies and Pets: Warfare and Shamanism in Amazonia', *American Ethnologist* 26(4): 933–56.
―――― 2001. *Inimigos fiéis: história, guerra e xamanismo na Amazônia*. São Paulo: Universidade de São Paulo.
―――― 2004. 'A Blend of Blood and Tobacco: Shamans and Jaguars among the Parakanã of Eastern Amazonia', in N. Whitehead and R. Wright (eds), *In Darkness and Secrecy: The Anthropology of Assault Sorcery and Witchcraft in Amazonia*. Durham, NC: Duke University Press, pp. 157–78.
―――― 2007. 'Feasting on People: Eating Animals and Humans in Amazonia', *Current Anthropology* 48(4): 497–530.
Fausto, C., and M. Heckenberger. 2007. 'Introduction: Indigenous History and the History of the "Indians"', in C. Fausto and M. Heckenberger (eds), *Time and Memory in Indigenous Amazonia: Anthropological Perspectives*. Tallahassee: University of Florida Press, pp. 1–42.
Gow, P. 1993. 'Gringos and Wild Indians: Images of History in Western Amazonian Cultures', *L'Homme* 126–128: 331–51.
―――― 2001. *An Amazonian Myth and its History*. Oxford: Oxford University Press.
Henare, A., M. Holbraad and S. Wastell. 2007. 'Introduction: Thinking Through Things', in A. Henare, M. Holbraad and S. Wastell (eds), *Thinking Through Things: Theorising Artefacts Ethnographically*. New York: Routledge, pp. 1–31.
High, C. 2006. 'From Enemies to Affines: Conflict and Community among the Huaorani of Amazonian Ecuador', Ph.D. thesis. London: London School of Economics.
―――― 2007. 'Indigenous Organisations, Oil Development, and the Politics of Egalitarianism', *Cambridge Anthropology* 26(2): 34–46.
―――― 2008. 'End of the Spear: Re-imagining Amazonian History and Ethnography through Film', in L. Chua, C. High and T. Lau (eds), *How Do We Know? Evidence, Ethnography and the Making of Anthropological Knowledge*. Newcastle: Cambridge Scholars Publishing, pp. 76–96.
―――― 2009a. 'Victims and Martyrs: Converging Histories of Violence in Amazonian Anthropology and U.S. Cinema', *Anthropology and Humanism* 34(1): 41–50.
―――― 2009b. 'Remembering the Auca: Violence and Generational Memory in Amazonian Ecuador', *Journal of the Royal Anthropological Institute* 15: 719–36.
Hugh-Jones, S. 1994. 'Shamans, Prophets, Priests, and Pastors', in N. Thomas and C. Humphrey (eds), *Shamanism, History, and the State*. Ann Arbor: University of Michigan Press, pp. 32–75.
Keane, W. 2007. *Christian Moderns: Freedom and Fetish in the Mission Encounter*. Berkeley: University of California Press.
Kingsland, R. 1980. *A Saint among Savages*. London: Collins.
Kirsch, S. 2006. *Reverse Anthropology: Indigenous Analysis of Social and Environmental Relations in New Guinea*. Stanford: Stanford University Press.
Kwon, H. 1999. 'Play the Bear: Myth and Ritual in East Siberia', *History of Religions* 38(4): 373–87.
Liefield, O. 1990. *Unfolding Destinies: The Untold Story of Peter Fleming and the Auca Mission*. Grand Rapids, MI: Harper Collins.

Lima, T.S. 1999. 'The Two and its Many: Reflections on Perspectivism in Tupi Cosmology', *Ethnos* 64(1): 107–31.

Londoño Sulkin, C. 2005. 'Inhuman Beings: Morality and Perspectivism among Muinane People (Colombian Amazon)', *Ethnos* 70(1): 7–30.

Mahmood, S. 2005. *Politics of Piety: The Islamic Revival and the Feminist Subject*. Princeton, NJ: Princeton University Press.

Pedersen, M. 2001. 'Totemism, Animism and North Asian Indigenous Ontologies', *Journal of the Royal Anthropological Institute* 7: 411–27.

Pedersen, M., R. Empson, and C. Humphrey. 2007. Inner Asian Perspectivisms. *Inner Asia* 9(2): 141–52.

Rival, L. 2002. *Trekking Through History: The Huaorani of Amazonian Ecuador*. New York: Columbia University Press.

——— 2005. 'The Attachment of the Soul to the Body among the Huaorani of Amazonian Ecuador', *Ethnos* 70(3): 285–310.

Robarchek, C., and C. Robarchek. 1998. *Waorani: The Contexts of Violence and War*. Fort Worth, TX: Harcourt Brace.

Saint, S. 2005. *End of the Spear*. Carol Stream: Tyndale House.

Stoll, D. 1982. *Fishers of Men or Founders of Empire? The Wycliffe Bible Translators in Latin America*. London: Zed Books.

Taylor, A.-C.1999. 'The Western Margins of Amazonia from the Early Sixteenth to the Early Nineteenth Century', in F. Salomon and S. Schwartz (eds), *The Cambridge History of the Native Peoples of the Americas*, Vol.3: *South America*. Cambridge: Cambridge University Press, pp. 188–256.

——— 2007. 'Sick of History: Contrasting Regimes of Historicity in the Upper Amazon', in C. Fausto and M. Heckenberger (eds), *Time and Memory in Indigenous Amazonia: Anthropological Perspectives*. Gainesville: University of Florida Press, pp. 133–68.

Vilaça, A., and R. Wright (eds). 2009. *Native Christians: Modes and Effects of Christianity among Indigenous Peoples of the Americas*. Aldershot: Ashgate.

Viveiros de Castro, E. 1992. *From the Enemy's Point of View: Humanity and Divinity in an Amazonian Society*. Chicago: University of Chicago Press.

——— 1998. 'Cosmological Deixis and Amerindian Perspectivism', *Journal of the Royal Anthropological Institute* 4(3): 469–88.

——— 2003. 'Anthropology and Science', *Manchester Papers in Social Anthropology 7*. Manchester: Manchester University Press.

Walker, H. 2009. 'Baby Hammocks and Stone Bowls: Urarina Technologies of Companionship and Subjection', in F. Santos Granero (ed.), *The Occult Life of Things: Native Amazonian Theories of Materiality and Personhood*. Tucson: University of Arizona Press, pp. 81–102.

Wallis, E. 1960. *The Dayuma Story: Life Under Auca Spears*. New York: Harper and Brothers.

——— 1973. *Aucas Downriver*. New York: Harper and Row.

Whitehead, N. 2002. *Dark Shamans: Kanaima and the Poetics of Violent Death*. Durham, NC: Duke University Press.

Whitehead, N., and R. Wright. 2004. 'Introduction: Dark Shamanism', in N. Whitehead and R. Wright (eds), *In Darkness and Secrecy: The Anthropology of Assault Sorcery and Witchcraft in Amazonia*. Durham, NC: Duke University Press, pp. 1–19.

Whitten, N., and D. Whitten. 2007. *Napo Runa: Imagery and Power in Modern Amazonia*. Urbana: University of Illinois Press.

Willerslev, R. 2004. 'Not Animal, Not *Not*-Animal: Hunting, Imitation and Empathetic Knowledge among the Siberian Yukaghirs', *Journal of the Royal Anthropological Institute* 10: 629–52.

——— 2007. *Soul Hunters: Hunting, Animism, and Personhood among the Siberian Yukaghirs.* Berkeley: University of California Press.

Yost, J. 1981. 'Twenty Years of Contact: The Mechanisms of Change in Wao (Auca) Culture', in N. Whitten (ed.), *Cultural Transformations and Ethnicity in Modern Ecuador.* Urbana: University of Illinois Press, pp. 677–704.

CHAPTER 8

Expressions and Experiences of Personhood: Spatiality and Objects in the Nenets Tundra Home

Vera Skvirskaja

This chapter examines some of the ways in which Nenets tundra dwellers on the Yamal peninsula experience patrilineal clan identity and establish a relational sense of themselves via the mobile tundra dwelling, or *choom* (Nenets, *mia*).[1] My take on the Nenets *choom* draws on Lévi-Strauss's concept of the house as a 'moral person', recognising it as a social entity that commands material and immaterial wealth and perpetuates a name (Lévi-Strauss 1987). But while for Lévi-Strauss the house objectifies a relation of alliance in what he calls 'house societies', I am more interested in looking at how the *choom* enables the objectification of certain aspects of personhood. Just as among some Amazonian groups (e.g., Hugh-Jones 1995), the traditional 'house' provides rural Nenets with a means of conceptualising their personhood in relation to social structure. This is possible because Nenets tundra dwellers, like many native Amazonian peoples (e.g., McCallum 2001, Erikson, n.d), experience certain things as extensions of the self and as symbols of individual and collective relationships with both kin and non-kin.

Methodologically, this chapter adopts an approach that emphasises an analytic focus on materiality and explicitly recognises that 'the things that people make, make people' (Miller 2005: 38). Recent moves away from anthropological perspectives that reduce materiality to the 'semiotic representation of some bedrock of social relations' (ibid.: 3) have been followed by attempts to deal with things 'as they present themselves' (Henare, Holbraad and Wastell 2007: 2). The proponents of this analytical position suggest that instead of assuming that things signify or stand for something else, we have to consider how the material form enunciates meaning, what it illuminates and how people 'think through things'. Whilst recognising the advantages of this methodology, I also wish to take into account the thinking political subject, that is to say a subject engaged with forms of power that (re)produce wider society.

Acknowledging political subjects in the broader sense has important implications for discussions of the status of indigenous ontologies. For instance, following Viveiros de Castro's (e.g., 1998) theorisations of Amerindian cosmology Henare, Holbraad and Wastell (2007) have been critical of anthropologists' tendency to postulate one, universal nature and to reduce alien or different ontologies to different epistemological positions or different cultural accounts of one world. As a way out of the 'impasse' posed by our ontology ('one ontology'), the authors suggest that we take others seriously and understand their articulations not as mere 'cultural perspectives' but 'as enunciations of different "worlds" or "natures"' (ibid.: 10). In present-day indigenous Siberia it is precisely by paying close attention to people's articulations that we can see the limitations of this ontological alterity paradigm. What the subjects of this chapter – the tundra Nenets of Yamal – share with those anthropologists criticised for their inability to overcome the 'one ontology' paradigm is the assumption 'that differences … are a matter of cultural perspective' (ibid.: 10).

This premise, based on scientific ontology – or 'naturalism' in Descola's (1996) terms – was introduced to the geographically remote and hardly accessible indigenous hunters and herders by means of Soviet education and cultural representations. For indigenous Siberian minorities – known in Russia as 'small peoples of the North' (R. *malye narody severa*) – this naturalist ontology had a crucial political dimension to it. A Soviet version of the 'one nature, many cultures' view of the world gained currency because it offered the 'small peoples' a vision of coevalness (Grant 1995: esp. 157–58). The price of coevalness was an awareness of the necessary rupture with an ontological alterity embodied in, and politically identified as, indigenous cosmologies and shamanism.

That is not to say that the cosmological ideas, complex sets of actions upon the world and collections of representations that comprise shamanism (Humphrey 1994) have entirely vanished from Yamal (cf. Znamenski 2007: 345). Judging by my interlocutors' utterances, they have acquired the status of museum relics ('what ancient Nenets used to be/to have') as well as that of alternative epistemologies that can be challenged, ignored, extolled or defended as traditional knowledge. For some of my Nenets hosts, traditional knowledge is something that merits respect, in practice or in the abstract, an attitude that has been encouraged by post-Soviet cultural revival movements. For others, cultural revival notwithstanding, traditional epistemologies have largely remained obsolete. Despite verbal disagreements and uncertainties about the truth status or validity of traditional ideas, in their practices many tundra Nenets accommodate, in Chakrabarty's (2000: 243) terms, 'the temporal heterogeneity of the "now"'. The point Charkrabarty seeks to highlight is that the modern individual is neither bound by nor free from the past, and that the 'diversity of life practices' does not have to fit one single overarching framework. It is this 'heterogeneity of the now' that makes any consistent or coherent representation of Nenets 'world-view(s)' an ethnographic fiction.

Using a dynamic approach to things, this chapter deals with two ethnographic themes – the spatiality of the *choom* and its sacred objects. I attempt to go beyond consciously articulated narratives of my informants and explore how the *choom* as an institution and actual dwelling elucidates those aspects of personhood that are usually kept muted and the validity of which is often contested or even verbally denied. In so doing I wish to avoid reconstructing indigenous models ('ontologies') on the basis of isolated concepts. Instead, my focus on 'things' brings to the fore manoeuvres and negotiations that (re)produce cultural forms, including expressions of personhood.

The Linguistic Reality of Nenets Clans

The significance of the *choom*'s spatiality in foregrounding relations based on conceptual sameness and otherness, consanguinity and affinity, cannot be properly appreciated without an overview of the construction and deconstruction of Nenets clans in local discourse and marriage practices. Indigenous clans and other units of traditional indigenous social organisation have been the subject of substantial ethnographic and political debate in post-Soviet Russia. Public interest in clans emerged in tandem with the breakdown in the early 1990s of the state and collective farms that had formerly been the principal employers of rural indigenous inhabitants. Indigenous clan or kin communes (R. *rodovaia obshchina*) were designed by Russian social scientists as potential alternatives to the vanishing state and collective farms.[2] At the time of my research among Yamal Nenets in 2000/2001, the idea of a supposedly clan-based collective enterprise caused undisguised confusion. There was no single way of talking about or understanding the 'clan' (R. *rod*). I start by discussing the linguistic reality of Nenets 'clans' before turning in the next section to the ways in which a clan-centred perspective on personhood is articulated in and via the *choom*.

The Asiatic Nenets (also known as Samoyed) are a Finno-Ugrian speaking reindeer-herding people who moved to the territory of what is today the Yamal-Nenets Autonomous Okrug in the late seventeenth century. At the turn of the millennium, there were some twenty-six thousand Nenets in the Okrug and the majority lived in the countryside, with approximately forty per cent leading a mobile way of life on the land all year round. Many tundra dwellers (R. *tundraviki*) visit multiethnic settlements and villages two or three times a year to buy provisions. Tundra Nenets are bilingual (only children of pre-school age and a handful of elders do not speak Russian) and the majority, both men and women, have experienced village or urban life through boarding school education, further studies, work in state institutions, obligatory military service or previous marriages to sedentary villagers. Although the tundra and the village represent different physical and, to a certain extent, social environments, people share many attitudes and ideas across the village–tundra divide. As I shall show, mixed popular attitudes in relation to traditional Nenets kinship, which emphasises agnatic relations and exogamous patrilineal clans, are characteristic of both sedentary and nomadic spaces.

Genealogical memory among the Nenets does not go deeper than two to four generations.[3] What we know about the Nenets' historical clan structure and rules of exogamy is based largely on reconstructions by generations of Soviet ethnographers who relied on Russian colonial tax records and mythical stories of clan and lineage origin. The latter, which are still in circulation, usually centre on the creation of new lineage names resulting from the separation of mythical brothers from their natal home. The Russian colonial records are, in turn, rather unclear from the terminological point of view. The Russian term 'clan' (R. *rod*) was used interchangeably with 'tribe' (R. *plemia*) and 'band' (R. *vataga*) (Khomich 1995: 158). There is no certainty about how these terms corresponded to the Nenets' notions of *erkar* and *tenz* that today both designate 'clan'/lineage' (R. *rod*) and 'surname' (R. *familia*).

Terminological muddles aside, everybody in rural Yamal seems to know, in the words of one young informant of mine, that 'the Nenets nation (R. *natsia*) is divided in two', and that in the old days marriage between the two halves was forbidden. This image of Nenets social structure has been popularised in Russian ethnographies and textbooks made available in (post-)Soviet state institutions (such as schools) and disseminated by local politicians, native activists and entrepreneurs. (In classic Soviet ethnographies the two exogamous 'halves' are called phratries and for the lack of a better term I will also use it). Furthermore, this popular conceptualisation has also been made possible by the Soviet system of registered surnames and state policies aimed at ordering and restricting the movements of the pastoral population.

Registered surnames that mark patrilineal descent were introduced in the 1920s and they have effectively cemented people's memory of ancestral names. There is no reason to suppose that prior to the system of registered surnames new lineage names did not over time replace the name of a common ancestor. Some elders still refer to their registered surnames as 'our Russian names' and identify more intimately with their unofficial lineage names. The overall effect of the state codification of naming practices is that the number of Nenets surnames ('clan' or 'lineage' names) is kept constant; bearers of the same surnames who live far away from each other, migrate in different tundra and never come in contact with each other can still be formally identified as belonging to the same exogamous clan and phratry.

The Soviet system that made the idea of the Nenets 'nation divided in two' possible also taught that clans and exogamy are survivals (R. *perezhitki*) of primitive society incompatible with the modern self. Non-exogamous marriage has become widespread both in the tundra and the village. Several of my tundra hostesses in their late forties told me proudly that they were the first in their locality to marry a man with the same surname and to break with the 'old rules' of exogamy. Many people stated that they did not care about exogamous clans because of the connotations of backwardness. In response to my question about potential marriage partners for his daughter, one middle-aged herder replied: 'We have already stepped over this threshold! She can marry anyone'. People are also uneasy about clan exogamy because it can bring together people who are seen as too closely related by blood (for example, a marriage between a woman's younger brother and her daughter or between a woman's sister and her son). People's reservations are conditioned by their adoption of a popular-scientific perspective that 'inbreeding' – that is, marriage between people too closely related by blood – can have negative consequences. All the same, where spouses are namesakes or belong to the same phratry, there may be a vague sense of unease associated with the Nenets notion of *khivy* (sin or taboo violation), as for instance when one young woman I knew in the village was worried that the poor health of her baby might be related to the sin she had committed by marrying a namesake.

The breakdown of clan exogamy and people's conscious departure from the idea of a 'clan-based society' signify that Nenets clans, and even more so phratries, have very limited social vitality. In practice, only localised lineages still tend to regulate exogamy in immediate tundra neighbourhoods and kinship networks. Where namesakes are deemed eligible partners, people argue that outside particular localities or kinship networks there is no kinship among people bearing these surnames; namesakes are not 'the same'. For many ordinary Nenets, surnames cum clan names indicate a similar level of abstraction to that of the surname Ivanov for the Russians. As one elder said of his namesakes in the village: 'Maybe a long time ago, our ancestors were real kin but we know nothing about it and we are no longer related'. It is against the background of these dismissive and uncertain articulations and concomitant marriages that more clear-cut modes of manifesting personhood entangled in clan structure are sustained by the *choom*'s materiality.

Two Orders of the *Choom*

The perception that artefacts are a resting point capable of resolving uncertain perspectives is, as Miller (1987: 106) argued, 'quite illusory'. An object can evoke different perspectives: one man's sacred possession, an old icon for example, is another man's tourist souvenir or merchandise. Among rural Nenets, there is, of course, more than one way of thinking about the symbolic order of the *choom*, but there are, nonetheless, shared norms that govern its everyday life. The maintenance of specific spatial arrangements unique to the tundra dwelling implies that its materiality, as we will see below, promotes particular perspectives. Whereas attitudes to clan identities do not change as people move between the tundra and the village, the *choom* allows for a visualisation of relations that has no equivalent in differently designed village houses.

The *choom*, a tepee-like structure built with wooden poles and covered with reindeer hides (or a tarpaulin in summer) is the only type of tundra dwelling used by herding families and is often the only 'house' they have at their disposal. Sedentary native villagers who live in modern houses with central heating, electric stoves and running water are not strangers to the *choom* – it is common for tundra dwellers to accommodate their village-based relatives and friends during the summer holidays and sporadic visits. And in the *choom* every person is physically positioned with reference to two spatial templates that I respectively call the invariable and the relational order.

The spatial organisation of the Nenets *choom* is well-documented in ethnographic accounts (e.g., Sokolova 1998; Golovnev and Osherenko 1999), and these focus exclusively on the fixed, invariable order of domestic space. This order is invariable because it is established, both vertically and horizontally, in relation to a fixed centre, the hearth (see Fig. 8.1), which defines the immutable spatial realms of the sacred and accentuates gender in relation to the sacred and 'pure' domains. The space behind the fireplace and opposite the entrance is a sacred zone marked by two sacred poles (N. *siamzy*). In the past it was used to accommodate carved wooden images of spirits (N. *siadai*). My tundra hosts kept only their food provisions in the sacred zone and on rare occasions they acknowledged invisible spirits residing there by an offering of a few drops of vodka.

The sacred, 'pure' domains are acknowledged by various prohibitions applied to women of child-bearing age who are considered 'dirty' (N. *siamei*). During their reproductive years women do not cross the sacred zone, neither inside nor outside the *choom*, do not dry the clothes that cover the lower part of their body above the fire and so on. Inside the *choom*, there are female sectors that are situated on both sides of the entrance and used to store women's belongings. Male sectors, located next to the sacred poles, are deemed 'pure' and serve as designated areas for respected visitors and guests. The bed of the household head and his wife is located in the intermediate space between the male and female sectors. Nenets women I talked to were critical of their being designated by 'the ugly word' *siamei* and mocked their men's supposed 'pureness'. Yet, these women might also interpret a repeated violation of the spatial taboos, especially a crossing of the sacred zone, not only as disrespect for customs but also as a sign of a mental illness expressed by the inability to navigate domestic space in an appropriate female manner. People's observance of the *choom*'s invariable order does not mean that some patriarchal ideas about gender have been frozen in time. It

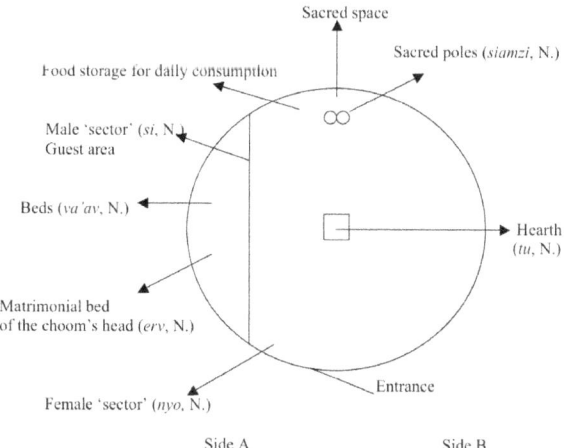

Figure 8.1: Layout of a *choom*

simply shows people's embodied relation to space and the capacity of 'things' to objectify some forms of gender relations at the expense of others.

This embodied, even visceral, relation to space, as well as the capacity of things to make certain relations visible, also underlies a different spatial ordering in the *choom*, one which is centred on the matrimonial bed and on a relational enactment of kinship. Studies of the Nenets *choom* and clans seem to have overlooked this mode of *choom* spatiality. It is this relational order of the *choom*, however, that actualises patrilineal clans in people's consciousness. It can recast each individual as the 'same' or 'other' on the basis of clan identity – a distinction that is not realised in references to people's surnames ('clan' names) outside one's network of established relations, as we have already seen. Let me now explain how this clan/kinship-focused ordering works inside the *choom*.

Beds, Clans and Conjugal Sentiments

In contrast to the village house, *choom* hospitality is taken for granted and offered to all. Much like the hospitality of Inner Mongolian pastoralists, the *choom*'s daily consumption is 'public in that it [is] generally open to visitors' (Sneath 2000: 187). Complete strangers and people from neighbouring encampments who come to exchange news or help with practical tasks are offered, at the very least, a cup of tea. Hospitality creates a social setting within which clan identity as an undeniable aspect of personhood is often revealed to all people present. The relational order of the *choom* can thus challenge established perspectives: if, for example, a poor neighbour next door in the village bearing the same surname is designated a 'stranger' or a 'namesake', inside the *choom* this distancing vision is undermined.

There are two areas where guests and visitors are accommodated: in the 'male', pure sector, as I mentioned already, and on the matrimonial bed, which during the daytime is not visually any different from other floor areas covered by hides. At meal times or when hosts entertain their guests with drink and a game of cards or chess, the matrimonial bed is transformed into a seating area, near which a low table is set up. The pattern of seating arrangements on the bed provides a ground plan for clan relations and relations of seniority. One's positioning on the matrimonial bed also brings to the fore kin distinctions that are not expressed by linguistic means, such as Nenets polite modes of address and classificatory kinship terminology (which itself is not uniformly remembered or used, often being partially replaced by Nenets translations of Russian descriptive kinship terms).

Visitors are accommodated as follows: all men senior to the wife's husband, both from his agnatic lineage and from his group of clans (or the phratry) are not welcome to sit on the couple's bed. Similar restrictions apply to women: they are free to sit on the beds of any men from their own phratry but would not accommodate themselves on the beds of any men from the other phratry who are senior to their husbands. The term a married woman uses for her father-in-law and all her senior male affines is the same word she would use for senior men (older than her father) in her own group (a respectful *iri-* 'grandfather', N.). In seating arrangements, by contrast, agnates and affines of all ages are clearly differentiated and each person is acknowledged as a member not only of her agnatic lineage (marked by surname), but also as a member of a phratry.

As seating arrangements presuppose a detailed knowledge of relations between individuals, so they also constitute a technology of remembering and discovering these relations. At times when the *choom* is crowded with visitors, the hosts may cover the bed with an old woman's coat to make this space clearly demarcated, and hence, to prevent potentially 'wrong' people from landing on the bed accidentally. Novel constellations of people can present a challenge to both hosts and visitors. It is not unusual for new members in the encampment and strangers to learn specific clan relations and relations of seniority by making embarrassing mistakes in the process of accommodation itself.

The situation is further complicated by the proliferation of non-exogamous marriage, which blurs the conceptual distinction between 'sameness' and 'otherness'. In cases of non-exogamous unions that I observed, seating arrangements on the matrimonial bed were more restrictive than usual: married women demonstratively 'denied' belonging to their own patrilineage (N. *erkar*) by being allocated or by allocating themselves places to sit only with reference to their husbands' lineage and seniority. The obvious paradox of this 'solution' is that even when the idea of exogamous clans is undermined by the very practice of non-exogamous marriages, the *choom*'s structure (the bed) supports the idea of marriage as a union of people who do not share 'sameness'.

The conjugal sentiments aimed at sustaining the 'house' in time, rather than an adherence to 'rules', are crucial here. The bed is not just any object in the *choom*. When an old coat is used to cover the bed, it signals a transformation of the bed from a public space into an intimate place of the couple. The bed is perceived as a spatial extension of the joint body of the husband and wife and it emphasises the principle of unity. As a public space that accommodates various visitors is should be open only to those who cannot violate the intimacy of matrimonial relations. It is in the interests of the couple that none of those who sit on the bed can be 'seen' as someone who might also 'sleep' in this bed. To sit on somebody's bed is to compel that person's attention; the sight of the 'wrong' person (a non-agnate) on one's bed transforms him or her into a potential sexual rival or partner.

Married women make sure from the start that the wives of their younger affines and of men from the same group of surnames as their husbands do not approach their beds. People are particular about who sits on their beds even when their spouses or family members are not around. In other words, this is not just a matter of public etiquette or the controlling gaze of elders enforcing 'old rules'. People might not care about exogamy and clans in the abstract and treat them verbally as the relics of the past, but they care about the integrity of their families.

My tundra hostesses who had themselves contracted non-exogamous marriages told me that there exists one 'irresolvable' problem with a non-exogamous marriage: jealousy. However hard a woman in a non-exogamous marriage might try to observe seating arrangements in her own *choom* by treating her actual and conceptual agnates as her affines, nobody expects that she would always restrict herself in this manner when enjoying the company of her brothers and uncles in her natal *choom*, and that is something her husband finds somewhat emotionally disturbing. From his vantage point, even in the intimacy of her natal house, his wife is surrounded by his male kinsmen who, being the 'same' as him, share his sexualised perspective on the woman.

In this way the *choom*'s spatiality and objects such as the (matrimonial) bed actualise the clan-centred identity of the person and mediate an experience of the self as either 'same' or 'other' in relation to other people present. In the *choom*, social, geographical and genealogical distances are temporarily suspended – people's affiliation to clans and phratries lingers on in material structures in spite of verbal deconstructions or declared indifference. In this cultural perspective mediated by the *choom* there are no 'namesakes' and each person is projected either as kin or affine. Uncertain or discrepant perspectives on clan-based personhood are resolved on and by the matrimonial bed.

The *Choom*'s Immaterial Wealth and Invisible Hierarchies

So far I have discussed how, within the *choom*, people experience their belonging to patrilineal clans as if they had remained immune to 'opportunistic' marriage practices and hostile ideological currents. In the remaining part of this chapter I consider the role of sacred objects of the tundra 'house' in the construction of Nenets personhood as enmeshed in virtually invisible hierarchies and in tune with a shamanic imagery. Sacred objects (N. *khekhe*) and the sacred sledge (N. *khekhe-khan*) comprise the *choom*'s spiritual wealth that is transmitted between generations and follows a different path from the other key item of inheritance: reindeer. The collection of sacred objects ensures a recognition of the self as a member of the *choom* entitled (ideally) to transcendental permanence.

Tundra Nenets practice patrilineal inheritance, whereby the youngest son who is expected to reside with his parents inherits the *choom*, his father's livestock and the sacred sledge. Elder sons meanwhile receive a share of their father's livestock upon separation from the natal household, usually after they marry and set up their own *choom*. Throughout the Soviet period, reindeer herders attempted to fit this pattern of residence and inheritance with their employment status and responsibilities. Nenets customary rules of inheritance appear to endorse an egalitarian spirit, in that they are not designed to create property inequality in livestock per se. An heir inherits his father's livestock when his elder male siblings have received their, more or less equal, shares.

All the same, the sacred sledge and the sacred objects that it transports and which have no value outside Nenets communities establish people as members of hierarchically ranked 'houses' (*chooms*). The sacred sledge is not divided between the siblings, but is handed down from generation to generation via the principal heir. The indivisibility of the sacred sledge establishes the imaginative hierarchy between *chooms* as being unequally endowed with sacred power. When in our discussions of inheritance people occasionally referred to some *choom*s as 'big' or 'head' ones, this designated the volume of its sacred sledge and the generations of ancestors that it represented.

Classic accounts of the Nenets sacred sledge emphasise different sacred objects as forms of representation – for example, representations of the spirit of the locality, parts of some 'main' spirits (taken from sacred places in the tundra), ancestral images (N. *ngitarma*), domestic spirits, *choom* guardians, and so on (e.g., Prokof'yeva 1953, cited in Diószegi 1978: 152). A classification of sacred objects into clearly demarcated symbolic categories ('things' that stand for something else) does not, however, help us understand the various ways in which a relationship between people and sacred objects is formed and how the concentration of meaning and power in sacred things is achieved. It is these processes, based, as it were, on indigenous epistemology and people's phenomenological engagement with the natural environment, that contribute to the constitution of a person as a member of the *choom* that claims permanence in time. I cannot here account for all the different types of Nenets sacred objects. To make my argument clear I shall look in detail at only one type of object that acquires the status of *khekhe*, objects (such as a stone or a tree trunk) that have 'chosen' a particular individual or group of people.

The Importance of Being Chosen

If I were to ask my tundra hosts directly whether an object such as a stone or a man-made ancestral image (N. *ngitarma*) has a spirit or soul of its own, the answer, more often than not, would be negative. In detached reflections on the subject, people described even their most treasured *ngitarma* as a dead doll. One of my interlocutors, a woman in her fifties, recalled that when her old mother tried to explain her something about spirits in sacred things (N. *khekhe*), she simply rejected her explanation as 'lies'. There was a consensus of sorts among my interlocutors that perhaps shamans and some, often unspecified, elders might have a different and deeper insight into the nature of (sacred) objects, but shamans were no more and ordinary elders were not keen on claiming to possess any deeper knowledge. With the exception of new Protestant converts in the area, sacred objects were, however, respected as things integral to Nenets ethnic identity: 'Russians have icons, we have *khekhe*' (see Skvirskaja in press). A more nuanced vision of sacred objects emerges from people's descriptions of their own encounters with things that became sacred and stories about the old sacred things' origin.

Khekhe fall into the category of 'inalienable possessions' (Weiner 1992): not only are they personally important to their owners but they also do not lend themselves to replication, exchange and purchase. Indeed, these objects' sacredness lies in the fact that unlike reindeer they cannot be accumulated at will by a human being; a person cannot look for a sacred object to add to his sacred sledge.[4] A relationship between people and sacred-objects-to-be is initially formed by engaging the sensory or emotional capacities of both parties involved. Family histories and stories of a sacred object's origin capture the process of sacred objects' discovery and transformation.

In one narrative, which describes events dating back to the early twentieth century, the narrator's grandfather became possessed and ran into the woods until he got stuck between two tree trunks. To free the grandfather, his rescuers had to cut down one tree and sometime later a shaman suggested that an idol (N. *siadai*) should be carved out of this tree's trunk because it saved the man. The *siadai* became a sacred thing of his *choom* and is kept in the sacred sledge of his grandson who inherited it from his father.

In a less dramatic scenario, one of my interlocutors in his early thirties found a small stone on the surface of freshly fallen snow. By his own admission, the only thing he knew about sacred things is that he would recognise one when he saw it (that is what his father had told him). The herder was so struck by the impossible positioning of the stone that he was in no doubt that the stone 'wanted' to be noticed and that it was there for him. In a similar manner, the Nenets ethnographer Galina Kharuchi (2001: 82) recalls how in her childhood she discovered a *khekhe*. Once, when out with her friends, she lost her way in the tundra fog. After some wandering, the children decided not to panic but to stop on a hill and have a rest. At this spot they noticed a stone in the shape of a sitting person. They thought that it could be a spirit of the hill; they took it and when the fog was over they easily found their way back to the *choom*. Kharuchi's father stored the stone on his sacred sledge.

A common theme in these stories is that an object becomes sacred due to unusual circumstances or by 'showing' itself to a particular individual. These two occurrences are conceptualised as the same thing: the specific materiality of the object and its non-ordinariness (its shape or location) command people's attention. A *khekhe*'s agency lies in its phenomenological abilities to attract attention, to stand in the way, to reveal itself to, or to 'choose' a particular person directly, without any symbolic mediation.[5] Once an object is seen, this means that it has revealed itself and must be taken.

Thus, people turn acquired objects into symbols upon incorporating them into the *choom*, like the tree trunk that was transformed into an idol upon the shaman's order. Some *khekhe* are given names – 'the watchman', 'the grandma', 'the doctor' and so on. Others remain nameless, but people attribute them different genders and dress them accordingly. Although these *khekhe* are not conceptualised as ancestral spirits, they resemble the *ongon* (an ancestral spirit vessel) found in Siberian and Inner Asian shamanic groups in that they are seen as protectors and helpers (see, e.g., Humphrey 1971; Petersen 2007: 150–56). From early ethnographic records of the first half of the twentieth century we learn that Nenets *khekhe* were explicitly understood as containers of spirits, i.e. a spirit could leave or enter a (sacred) object (see Yevladov 1992: 150), and the sacred sledge itself was fashioned after a reindeer and perceived as a 'body' animated by spirit (Prokof'yeva 1953, cited in Diószegi 1978).

Just like *ongon*, *khekhe* (and the sacred sledge) can be conceived of as an 'amalgamation of events, social relationships and material substances' (Petersen 2007:

155). As generations replace generations, the shape of a *khekhe* changes and it acquires a collection of different things: cloth, shawls, belts, coins and beards. It grows larger as it is given new things by its owners or by the wider circle of the owner's relations, as expressions of gratitude or care on special occasions. Later on, these pieces of clothing can be detached and given to the non-heirs, both elder sons and daughters who have left the natal *choom*, as tokens of goodwill and parental blessing; they circulate, marking links between various people, without compromising the integrity of the sacred sledge. *Khekhe* may not lend themselves to reproduction, but they can 'reproduce' and become a source of new sacred things.

New *chooms* that do not inherit a sacred sledge start the process of accumulation of their own sacred things by incorporating objects that have revealed themselves to the *choom*'s members and that are given by kin to kin. *Khekhe* then actualise two types of relations: relations based on separation between the living and relations between the living and their dead ancestors. Even though *khekhe* and the sacred sledge are seen today as the material remnants of half-forgotten, half-dismissed indigenous epistemology, they have not ceased to produce a sense of 'dynastic' continuity and permanence among *choom* members.

Securing an Heir and Perpetuating the Tundra 'House'

Provided that a person is integrated into kinship networks and occasionally 'chosen' by sacred objects-to-be, every Nenets can amass some inalienable possessions of their own. The initial accumulation of sacred things is not unlike laying the foundation of the tundra 'house'. The relationship between the *choom*/'house' and the sledge is one of ordinary metonymy – the sledge is a part that stands for the *choom*, the whole. Inheritance of the sacred sledge aims at preserving the *choom* with its sacred patrimony at full strength, and this shows that the *choom* is deemed an entity of great importance, independently of its members. In the late socialist period (from the late 1960s onwards), when there was very little property (e.g., reindeer) left at the disposal of a pastoral household, and many people chose different lives for themselves (moving, temporarily or permanently, away from the tundra), the sacred sledge with its ancestral *khekhe* was an inalienable possession that was 'good to think with' about the pastoral 'house'.

There is also a ritual means of conveying the metonymic relationship between the sacred sledge and the *choom*. The sledge is acknowledged by the annual sacrifice of a reindeer in January to mark the beginning of the new year ('new sun'). Where there are several sacred sledges in the encampment, people sacrifice to each sacred sledge individually. In the flexible and often changing residential patterns that characterise tundra life, the sacrifice marks each *choom*/tundra 'house' with its sacred sledge as a separate entity.

Popular understandings of the sacred sledge and sacred objects may have changed historically, their cosmological premises being substantially eroded, but their durable materiality continues to produce effects in its own right: persons, living and dead, are emphasised as members of transcendental 'houses' so long as the living continue to take care of their *khekhe-khan*. Tundra dwellers envision and desire different futures for their children, but prospective heirs are cultivated from early on as persons responsible for the perpetuation of the *choom*. Heirs have to ensure that the *choom* does not vanish in history.

An heir's failure to comply with parental and ancestral mandates is seen as inviting misfortune for the individual and his family. One of my tundra hosts, in his early forties, told me that he had had to give up his life in the village to become a herder because he was the youngest son. I asked him why his brothers, all of whom had never left the tundra, did not join the encampment of their elderly parents; he explained that it was, of course, also a possible scenario and, indeed, personal circumstances had always calibrated the pathways of inheritance. However, it was also important to have 'some kind of special inclination' to have the *khekhe-khan*, and that was analogous to an inexplicable 'shamanic calling'. One had to feel (and not just know) that it was one's task to take care of one's elderly parents and their sacred possessions. It is this inclination that is cultivated in, and expected from, people who will see the tundra 'house' into the future.

Conclusion

In conclusion, let us return to the Nenets tundra 'house' as a composite thing. The spatial and material structures of the *choom* enable people to experience and express implicit hierarchies and those instances of 'sameness' and 'otherness' that often remain invisible or are challenged by an epistemology which operates by supposedly more progressive attitudes and perspectives. The coexistence of different epistemological traditions in a society where 'naturalism' dominates warns us against using reconstructions of Nenets cosmology as an explanatory framework for understanding present-day Nenets personhood. I have attempted to show that whereas tundra Nenets can rely on different epistemologies in their lives, certain things have the power to override these differences and evoke clan- and *choom*-centred visions of the person.

The Nenets' mode of indexing relations in the *choom*, via the matrimonial bed and *khekhe*, facilitates the reaffirmation of diverse relations, often bypassing verbal negotiations of meaning across the available epistemological spectrum. One might argue that the Nenets' mode of indexing relations in things is not so much about expressing or experiencing certain aspects of personhood as it is a strategy aimed at maintaining social relations and relatedness. In her study of objects that can be found in every Mongolian household – photographic displays, things kept inside the family chest, like pieces of offerings from *oboos* (ritual sites), people's hair – Rebecca Empson (2007: 134) suggests precisely that. She points out that indexing relations in things is necessary because in pastoral communities people are unable to enact relations in shared places. When people are dispersed across the landscape, things act as sites for containing aspects of people's relations in the absence of people and maintain relations in time as open possibilities.

In the case of Yamal Nenets, this line of reasoning could be applied as well, but it would fall short of explaining why in the instance of *choom* hospitality people who are otherwise deemed namesakes only (for example, in the village context or in people's narratives) should be recognised as clansmen, and why there should be a need to reckon the relations that constitute phratries. Here, an argument that reifies 'the social' (the need to maintain relations, to connect) obscures the import of materiality itself.

If we move away from the idea that for rural Nenets visualising relations through things is a function of sociality alone, the Lévi-Straussian point that the 'house' is a moral person can be extended to draw an analogy between the Nenets *choom* and the urban post-Soviet shaman in Ulan-Ude, Buriatiia, as analysed by Humphrey (1999). The urban shaman reconnects city people with their ancestors. In the shaman's perspective, which she confers on her urban clients, individuals are actualised as belonging to familial or descent groups whose origins lie far away. The shaman sets a process of kinship rediscovery in motion, for without this data a seance would fail. In a somewhat similar vein, the *choom* sustains an ongoing process of reaffirmation and the learning of multiple real and abstract connections. Like the shaman, it not only provides a way of conceptualising certain relations – such as gender – but it also transmits its perspective to its members and visitors; people are moved (literally and metaphorically) to recognise and present themselves to themselves and others as making up entities of a different order – from the 'house' in history and patrilineage to an abstract phratry. The *choom*'s spatiality and sacred objects elicit people's emotional engagements and are maintained by them, and these are the same operations that were at play in the erstwhile practices of Nenets shamanism.

Notes

1. Hereafter, Nenets words and phrases are indicated by N. and Russian words and phrases by R.
2. The concept of indigenous commune (R. *obshchina*) – that is, a particular form of social and economic organisation attributed to all Russian indigenous Northern minorities – was first developed by a group of Russian ethnographers under the heading of 'Northern neo-traditionalism' (see Pika and Prokhorov 1994). Since its conception, the indigenous *obshchina* has become both a new theoretical doctrine and an explicit programme for political action, and has come to designate a special category of land tenure recognised by Russian federal law.
3. The absence of genealogies, together with a customary tundra requirement that a deceased person's personal belongings are left with her corpse rather than inherited, bring to mind the 'genealogical amnesia' widespread among native Amazonians (see, e.g., Erikson n.d.).
4. Those things that have, in fact, been taken from sacred places in the tundra tend to be considered 'borrowed' and should, ideally, one day be returned.
5. The idea of objects choosing the persons with whom they want to form relationships is a common one across indigenous Siberia (see, e.g., Vitebsky 2002).

References

Chakrabarty, D. 2000. *Provincializing Europe: Postcolonial Thought and Historical Difference*. Princeton, NJ: Princeton University Press.
Descola, P. 1996. 'Constructing Natures: Symbolic Ecologies and Social Practice', in P. Descola and G. Pálsson (eds), *Nature and Society: Anthropological Perspectives*. London: Routledge, pp. 82–102.
Diószegi, V. 1978. 'Pre-Islamic Shamanism of the Baraba Turks and Some Ethnogenetic Conclusions', in V. Diószegi and M. Hoppál (eds), *Shamanism in Siberia*. Budapest: Akadémiai Kaidó, pp. 83–168.
Empson, R. 2007. 'Separating and Containing People and Things in Mongolia', in A. Henare, M. Holbraad and S. Wastel (eds), *Thinking Through Things: Theorising Artefacts Ethnographically*. New York: Routledge, pp. 113–40.
Erikson, P. n.d. 'Obedient Things: Reflections on the Matis Theory of Materiality', unpublished paper.
Golovnev, A., and G. Osherenko. 1999. *Siberian Survival: The Nenets and Their Story*. Ithaca, NY: Cornell University Press.
Grant, B. 1995. *In the Soviet House of Culture: A Century of Perestroikas*. Princeton, NJ: Princeton University Press.
Henare, A., M. Holbraad and S.Wastell. 2007. 'Introduction: Thinking through Things', in A. Henare, M. Holbraad and S. Wastel (eds), *Thinking Through Things: Theorising Artefacts Ethnographically*. New York: Routledge, pp. 1–31.
Hugh-Jones, S. 1995. 'Inside-out and Back-to-front: The Androgynous House in Northwest Amazonia', in J. Carsten and S. Hugh-Jones (eds), *About the House: Lévi-Strauss and Beyond*. Cambridge: Cambridge University Press, pp. 226–52.
Humphrey, C. 1971. 'Some Ideas of Saussure Applied to Buryat Magical Drawings', in E. Ardner (ed.), *Social Anthropology and Language*. London: Tavistock, pp. 271–90.
——— 1994. 'Shamanic Practices and the State in Northern Asia: Views from the Centre and Periphery', in N. Thomas and C. Humphrey (eds), *Shamanism, History, and the State*. Ann Arbor: University of Michigan Press, pp. 191–210.
——— 1999. 'Shamans in the City', *Anthropology Today* 15(3): 3–10.
Kharuchi, G.P. 2001. *Traditsii i innovatsii v kul'ture nenetskogo etnosa*. Tomsk: Izdatel'stvo Tomskogo Universiteta.
Khomich, L.V. 1995. *Nentsy. Ocherki traditsionnoi kul'tury*. St Petersburg: Russkii Dvor.
Lévi-Strauss, C. 1987. *Anthropology and Myth: Lectures 1951–1982*. Oxford: Blackwell.
McCallum, C. 2001. *Gender and Sociality in Amazonia: How Real People are Made*. Oxford: Berg.
Miller, D. 1987. *Material Culture and Mass Consumption*. Oxford: Blackwell.
——— 2005. 'Introduction', in D. Miller (ed.), *Materiality: Politics, History, and Culture*. Durham, NC: Duke University Press, pp. 1–50.
Petersen, M. 2007. 'Talismans of Thought: Shamanist Ontologies and Extended Cognition in Northern Mongolia', in A. Henare, M. Holbraad and S. Wastel (eds), *Thinking Through Things: Theorising Artefacts Ethnographically*. New York: Routledge, pp. 141–66.
Pika, A., and B. Prokhorov. 1994. *Neotraditsionalizm na rossiiskom severe*. Moskva: INP.
Skvirskaja, V. 'Contested Souls: Christianisation, Millenarianism and Sentiments of Belonging on Indigenous Rural Yamal, Russia', *Études mongoles et sibériennes, centrasiatiques et tibétaines*, in press.

Sneath, D. 2000. *Changing Inner Mongolia: Pastoral Mongolian Society and the Chinese State.* Oxford: Oxford University Press.

Sokolova, Z. 1998. *Zhilishche Narodov Sibiri: Opyt tipologii.* Moskva: IPA 'Tri Li'.

Vitebsky, P. 2002. 'Withdrawing from the Land: Social and Spiritual Crisis in the Indigenous Russian Arctic', in C.M. Hann (ed.), *Postsocialism: Ideals, Ideologies and Practices in Eurasia.* London: Routledge, pp. 180–95.

Viveiros de Castro, V. 1998. 'Cosmological Deixis and Amerindian Perspectivism', *Journal of the Royal Anthropological Institute* 4(3): 469–88.

Weiner, A.B. 1992. *Inalienable Possessions: The Paradox of Keeping-while-giving.* Berkeley: University of California Press.

Yevladov, V.P. 1992. *Po tundram Yamala k Belomu Ostrovu.* Tiumen: Institut problem osvoeniia severa SORAN.

Znamenski, A. 2007. *The Beauty of the Primitive: Shamanism and the Western Imagination.* Oxford: Oxford University Press.

Chapter 9
Humanity, Personhood and Transformability in Northern Amazonia

Vanessa Elisa Grotti and Marc Brightman

In the native cosmologies of Amazonia and Siberia, the ability to transform one's body and one's perspective in order to act beyond the human sphere has conventionally been associated with specialist practitioners: shamans. Amazonian societies are also known to thrive and, indeed, depend on the appropriation of alterity for their continuity (Overing 1983/1984), but the fact that affinity or alterity remain volatile at the heart of the social sphere has only recently been established (Vilaça 2005) and requires further development. Discussions of native Amazonian sociality tend to rely on a notion of humanity which is more or less exclusive to a group of subjects, or persons with shared subjectivity (Viveiros de Castro 1998), and a notion of personhood understood as a quality shared by non-human beings (animals, plants and spirits) (Descola 1986). Previous authors have understood native Amazonian conceptions of humanity in terms of commensality (Gow 1991; Vilaça 2002) and body ornamentation (Erikson 1996), but these refer to qualities of humanity that are shared by non-humans in a perspectivist universe.

In this chapter we offer an explanation of the difference between humanity and personhood based on observations of the importance given by native Amazonians to a certain capacity of subjects to transform themselves. This implies that humanity is a power to be feared as well as to be cultivated, and represents a challenge to the traditional view of human beings as constituting a convivial community synonymous with kinship. Meanwhile, it supports previous theoretical interpretations of the Amazonian social subject as lacking a centre, not only as hybrid (Santos Granero 2009) but also composed of recursive or nested oppositions corresponding to the relationship between consanguinity and affinity (Viveiros de Castro 2001).

The Trio, Wayana and Akuriyo are Carib-speaking Amerindians who live clustered near centres of healthcare and education in mission posts around the triple border area separating Suriname, French Guiana and Brazil. In this chapter we will discuss their relationship with each other, and how they relate to other types of persons, in terms of their corporeality (Seeger, Da Matta and Viveiros de Castro 1979) or their bodily ontology. From a relational and indigenous physiological point of view, these interactions may be expressed in terms of humanity and non-humanity. Various forms of social relations can be distinguished from the point of view of the body, and the processes that constitute these relations allow the cultivation and nurture of the quality of humanity throughout the lifetime of a given subject. By emphasising the fact that humanity is a quality that must be cultivated, we underline the ambiguous status of the human body as an object of continuous making rather than a given. However, while the need constantly to make and maintain humanity has already been established by various Amazonianist authors, who have situated it in a socialised, village context (Gow 1991; Overing and Passes 2000), we would like to add another dimension to the definition of Amazonian humanity: we will focus on the connection between humanity and transformability – that is, the propensity of a person to change from one bodily state to another. The ability to transform is a quality associated with humanity in a way which sometimes transcends other social categories. By considering the nature of this transcendence, we will be able to shed light on the distinction between humanity and non-humanity among agentive persons.

The distinction between bodies is frequently approached in Amazonian anthropology in terms of the relationship between humanity and non-humanity (Viveiros de Castro 1992), which may differentiate living beings from one another. The means by which these different persons interact or are engaged with have previously been discussed in terms of predatory or reciprocal relationships (e.g., Descola 1986 and Århem 1996 respectively; see also Rivière 2001). Authors who emphasise commensality and nurture have focused upon the dissolution of social difference through the sharing and merging of substance (Overing and Passes 2000), and the making of kin out of 'others' such as enemies (Taylor 2000; Fausto 2002; Vilaça 2002), wild people and pets (Howard 2001). Recently, researchers focusing on material culture have analysed the relationship between persons and the various forms of bodies they make, including their offspring but also the objects which come to inhabit their everyday lives: in the case of women, the cotton hammocks in which they sleep, the strings of beads they adorn themselves with, or the manioc bread they mould and 'scarify' with the same patterns which are used on human skin (Van Velthem 2001, 2003). This raises the question of whether these socialising processes necessarily generate human subjects, or whether in fact a distinction needs to be made between sociability and humanity. According to Viveiros de Castro's theory of Amerindian perspectivism (Viveiros de Castro 1998), humanity is a subjective condition dependent upon social perspective: creatures which appear to be non-human in fact appear to themselves as human, and from their own perspectives satisfy the criteria for humanity, particularly through kinship and eating practices. The theory of perspectivism may conceivably provide the key to defining the difference between humanity and sociability. However, for this to be possible the theory must be successfully applied to the ethnography of contemporary everyday life and the management of social relationships on a daily basis.

Human Persons and Other Persons in Amazonia

Daily nurturing and educational processes among the Trio and Wayana reflect the emphasis placed on humanity as a condition that must be actively cultivated throughout one's lifetime. At the very early stages of life in particular, various techniques are used in order to ensure that children grow into human beings. Indeed, the Trio's word for a mother's upbringing of her child is *arimika*, which literally means 'to undo the spider-monkey'. This does not mean that the Trio think of their babies as animals who should be nurtured into human beings, but that at birth the elements of the baby's personhood are not yet secure, and it therefore needs to be gradually moulded into kin to prevent it from being made into the kin of 'other' living beings such as spider-monkeys. Nurture and upbringing are constructions which fix the perspective of a child into one social sphere. As the child grows into a fully developed adult, it will acquire the capacity to handle interaction with 'others' without losing its human point of view in the process.

Let us first take two examples: the ways in which the Trio relate to their hunting dogs and to 'wild people' respectively. Hunting dogs are 'moulded', educated and physically and morally transformed from a young age, usually by old women, who feed them proper human foods such as cassava bread, wash them in the river, delouse them and twist their tails to give them their characteristic curl, and address them as 'my son' (*jimuku*). The Akuriyo, who used to be 'wild people' (*wajarikure*) – that is, people who live in the forest as hunter-gatherers and are considered dangerous predators – were 'captured' by some Trio at the instigation of Protestant evangelical missionaries in the late 1960s and settled under their close supervision in the Trio village of Tëpu in southern Suriname; since then, they have become de facto servants of the families of the men involved in their capture. They are social marginals, and at the same time they are regarded as having great power in the forest where they are said to be able to move faster and develop superhuman predatory abilities. Although Akuriyo families are parcelled out through their attachment to Trio families, they are not considered members of the household and, unlike hunting dogs, are not referred to in kinship terms. The Akuriyo seem to exemplify a tendency among Amazonian peoples to regard humanity and transformability as matters of degree, which are not the preserve of real human beings, and indeed which may be possessed in extraordinary quantities by those on the margins of, or outside, human society.

It would appear that dogs are socialised creatures which are not considered to be human, whereas the Akuriyo have a high degree of humanity without being considered socialised. Accordingly, if we were to consider the status of material objects (in the sense of things, or artefacts), it might be expected that they will turn out to be like dogs: at first glance, they do not have human bodies but, in the case of artefacts, they can be moulded into socially practical forms. They can also be traded, like dogs, but unlike the Akuriyo: hunting dogs were the principal item of trade with Maroon trading partners from downriver for two centuries, and are still often traded with outsiders; the Akuriyo, on the other hand, although they are considered as property, are treated as such only in the sense that they are 'owned' by their Trio masters, and they are not traded in exchange for objects or money (Brightman 2010). Objects are often said to have human features such as mouths, heads and limbs, and when items of material culture are made by highly skilled individuals they are sometimes believed to have souls: as reproductions of primordial archetypes, if they are recreated too perfectly they may develop their own intentionality. There are numerous myths describing how certain items of material culture once had intentionality and motive force of their own. Arrows, for example, flew of their own accord at the bidding of the ancients, until they were treated with disrespect, and from then on they vowed stubbornly to remain immobile and rely on the strength and aim of people (Koelewijn and Rivière 1987). However, today objects exist in relation to people who make them, whereas people are the product of their own making – first by their kin who bring them up, and then by themselves and by their interactions with a network of relatives.

This distinction between humans, who are linked by kinship networks, and who control their own perspectives, and objects, which are made by people, also explains why objects can be exchanged whereas human persons cannot. A human person is irreplaceable because of the love and affection of close kin. Because all entities, objects and people, are the product of the moulding and design that create new bodies, the difference between the replaceable and the irreplaceable is a matter of emphasis, and this emphasis is determined by perspective: entities of the same kind share the same perspective, and are bound by affection. Nurture, care and commensality are therefore not the sole conditions of human personhood, as some elements of humanity and consanguinity spring from (pro) creation and are therefore given and inalienable. Bodily substances can be more taming than foods, although foods and nurture are more socially ingrained. This raises the question of how the human body is moulded in practice.

The Making of the Human Body

In a paper from the early 1960s, one of the earliest biomedical studies of the development of medical care in the Wayana villages of the upper reaches of the Maroni river, in southern French Guiana, Dr Etienne Bois noted that, when collecting blood samples from villagers for analysis, he was requested by the Wayana to give in return a little of his own blood to the head of each family (Bois n.d.). From a Wayana perspective, giving blood was part of a ritual exchange with a highly specific meaning. Piercing or cutting the skin in order to obtain blood (Wayana, *mïwu*), a powerful source of strength and life, and letting a stranger, a potential enemy, take it, is inconceivable. The cutting of skin and drinking of blood is strictly performed between hitherto enemy warriors who have agreed upon an alliance and peaceful interaction through the mixing of their vital substance. By mixing the very origin of their vitality, warriors thus open themselves up to each other's influence. This exchange of blood is a merging of substance which was frequently referred to by my Trio, Wayana and Katxuyana interlocutors when remembering the end of the wars of the past.

There is, however, a rather ambivalent relationship to the substance, illustrated by the fact that one of the historical groups of the Trio, the Pijanakoto, are known to have been particularly fierce because they used to drink the blood of their enemies: such cannibalistic, predatory ingestion is considered a vitality-enhancing strategy. This in turn explains the attitude of the Wayana to the French doctor's collecting of blood samples: in order to prevent the doctor from becoming a fierce enemy charged with the Wayana's own strength, he had to give them his own blood in return for theirs. The mutual drinking of blood seals the end of warfare and the beginning of peaceful interaction: by giving away some of one's own strength, one exposes oneself to the increased strength of the former enemy. This suggests an important nuance to be made in the distinction between commensality and cannibalism established by Fausto (2007). Fausto observed that 'eating together' and 'eating each other' afford the promotion of consubstantiality and the predatory accumulation of power, corresponding to the consumption of cooked and raw meat respectively. The evidence given above of the consumption of the raw blood of enemies to seal peace treaties between rival groups shows that the mutual prestation of vital substance can also be used to promote peace, while maintaining a certain ontological difference between the parties concerned. The price of peaceful life in today's large villages around health and education posts, in close physical proximity to non-relatives (and thus potential enemies), is the increased exposure to these ambiguous 'others' which must be regularly mediated through domesticating procedures such as communal feasts and the ingestion and regurgitation of the highly socialising substance of manioc beer.

To the Trio and the Wayana alike, pacification and the willingness to engage in convivial relationships are expressed in terms of the way one's body is exposed to the gaze of village co-residents. Each treatment of the body is taken to indicate the innermost intentions of a person and, for this reason, sociable daily activities such as washing, cooking and eating are performed in parts of the village which are communal, such as the river landing, or in sections of the household which are open to the gaze of neighbours and passers-by. The cookhouse, the hearth and, in broadest terms, the communal space located between the various buildings comprising a household are never sealed off with planks or low roofs, but rather offer a possibility for any villager to determine, at a fair distance, the activities taking place there: manioc processing, weaving, the preparation of game for a family meal, all activities which are conducted preferably in broad daylight or rarely, in the case of the preparation of game, by a big fire at night time. By careful exposure to social interaction, one demonstrates the innocuous nature of one's activities: poisons and curses are said to be prepared in the deepest corners of the house.

Individual character and the quality of social interaction are also determined by certain treatments of the human body itself: some are said to induce peaceful behaviour and others nurture a certain form of warlike fierceness. The choice of foods is a marker of peaceful or bellicose intentions: strong foods such as chilli pepper and salt are said to have socialising qualities; warriors who wish to cultivate fierceness must not eat them. The wish to eat strong foods is taken to express a social desire for convivial affinal interaction. In this sense, bodily practice corresponds to these two ideal states, providing techniques and markers of each. They are represented in myth as alternating possibilities in the collective experience and identity of the Wayana and the Trio alike, and are often used to describe differences between two ways of life, one marked by warfare and the other by peaceful conviviality between affines.

These two ideal states can be adapted to transformative states in which specific qualities are required for interaction with different types of stranger. For example, travelling to the city to visit a governmental office requires specific bodily preparations, just as entering the forest on a hunting expedition does. To go to a gold mine, a Trio or Wayana will need to wear the clothes worn by gold miners, such as trainers, baggy shorts, a sleeveless mesh tee-shirt and a tight nylon hat, and may dye his hair blond, wear gold and have his public nickname tattooed on a visible part of his body. On the other hand, to visit an administrative office, a Trio or Wayana may wear long trousers and a short-sleeved shirt, comb his hair and carry a folder with papers inside. The capacity to transform thus lies in the outer as well as the inner layers of the body. In a recent article Santos Granero showed in a similar vein how the Yanesha use of 'traditional' and 'modern' clothing and body ornaments testifies to the 'hybrid' nature of Amazonian bodies (Santos Granero 2009), but the sophistication and versatility of Trio and Wayana strategies of self-transformation and their manipulation of visible and invisible attributes suggest that there is something more profound going on. This balance between inner and outer body is manifested by the attention paid to the appearance and the feeding of the body.

The Human Body and Creativity

We shall now dwell a bit longer on bodily decorations, creativity and transformability as essential components of humanity in Amazonia and suggest that transformability is a fundamental feature of human personhood in that a properly human person can willingly and creatively transform their corporeality to fit specific social purposes. Here it is important to understand that by 'transformability' we refer to the possibility of transforming temporarily, which can be contrasted with the irreversible process of metamorphosis (Monod Becquelin 1982). To the Trio and Wayana, human persons are persons who can adorn themselves, beautify their bodies at times of celebration, but also neutralise themselves, make themselves as bland as possible before entering the other world of the forest to go hunting, thus removing all social attributes. In the Trio village of

Tëpu today, a man will remove his red loincloth and bodily adornments before going into the forest and put on some old white people's clothes in order to cover his social skin; the white people's clothes also act as a disguise, because the role associated with them is not that of a hunter. In this way, a change of perspective, or passage from a given state to another, was always described to us as a change of clothes. For example, a shaman on the hunt for spirit-matter will take off his Trio clothes and put on his jaguar clothes and thus see through the eyes of this predatory being. Transformability as such is not solely a human capacity which is given but a quality which is cultivated through rigorous training and appropriation of the knowledge of the outside.

The Trio and Wayana express awe at the capacity of some entities to transform, particularly the caterpillar, which is the subject of many mythical narratives. However, the caterpillar's transformability is above all interesting in that it shows that this quality must be used appropriately and creatively to be effective. For instance, there is a myth that recounts that, after having caught the eye of a young Wayana woman in the forest who admired its beauty aloud, a caterpillar transforms itself into a handsome young man, leaves the forest and enters the young lady's village with the hope of seducing her. Upon arrival, he is admired by all the young women for his elaborate feather ornaments, body paint and the beauty of his body. He turns out to behave like a perfect husband to the young Wayana lady who becomes his wife. But his beautiful attire and social composure eventually raise suspicions among the villagers who start to question this constant perfection.

Unlike a normal person, whose beautifully adorned body would progressively turn back to a 'normal' state as everyday activities wear off the paint, the caterpillar husband remains unchanged. This flawless perfection turns out to be what exposes him as a non-human person. He is eventually rejected as a stranger by the community of villagers and disappears, never to be seen again.

The incompleteness of the caterpillar's transformation into a Wayana man is betrayed by his perfection, and this may seem paradoxical until one remembers that the very nature of humanity is imperfect (though in a sense very different from that associated with Christian teaching). The distinction between a human being, *wïtoto*, and something that has the appearance of one but is not intrinsically human, *wïtoto-me*, is very salient in Trio discourse. The suffix *-me* exists in the Trio language precisely to express this distinction between the apparent and true nature of things, and is employed in a variety of situations. And this very distinction relates to the inherent ambiguity of bodily transformations: perspectival changes are rarely portrayed as a straightforward passage from a given state of being to another. With the change of 'clothes', although the perspective may appear to have changed and spirits or animals appear to a human person to have become fellow humans, the 'sight' is frequently confused, and it is often through commensality and sharing foods with 'others' that the change becomes more stable and settled. It is because of the profound transformational characteristic of commensality and the sharing of substance that a shaman distinguishes himself from other village residents: he has familiars in the spirit world and thus shares substance with them. His body is connected to the spirit world in an intimate, substantial manner. So even though his transformational capacities are extremely developed, his marginal status in the social life of the village attests to his ambiguity, and his every move will be studied to determine whether he is dangerous or not.

And yet, as the story of the caterpillar attests, a person who is human in appearance remains singled out when there is something in his daily practice which does not correspond to the social norm; in this case, what betrays the caterpillar-spirit is his frozen bodily flawlessness: the transformation was not complete because not creative enough. This and the case of the shaman's social role, lead us to underline a fundamental clue to the understanding of the relationship between humanity and transformability: appearances are deceptive and one must always look out for the 'other' under the clothes of the familiar (cf. Viveiros de Castro 2007). Because of this, humanity is never a straightforward matter, and always an ambiguous condition. Lúcia Van Velthem has recently suggested that humans are the only ones in whose nature it is to modify bodily painting and thus appearance, 'the rest are condemned to wearing the same decorations forever' (Van Velthem 2001: 213). However, the story mentioned above shows that this is the case only in an ideal world: it is desirable for humans to transform themselves but not for 'others' to do so, but there are 'others' who have the same capacity to transform, the same intentionality which enables them to adopt several guises. This is further underlined by the fact that non-humans in certain cases (especially of social animals) must also follow ritual rules and prohibitions: for example, a Wayana culture hero is said to have learned about the *maraké* initiation ceremony, male initiation songs and healing songs by secretly watching and listening to the yellow-rumped cacique bird (*Payakwa* in Wayana; *Cacicus cela*) (Chapuis and Rivière 2003: 388–89; Brightman 2011). In another example, a Trio myth describes how a shaman visits the village of the white lipped peccary, dressed as though for a dance, and finds them all together, drinking, eating and laughing, and he engages in a ceremonial dialogue with the master of peccaries (Rivière 2001). As Rivière suggests (ibid.), it may be that the presence of a high level of sociability among animals correlates with human–animal relations of reciprocity (as opposed to predation). In any case, as demonstrated above, the modification of the outer body shell, by adopting variations based on models but also invention, are qualities that human persons nurture and develop. We will now turn to what is physiologically necessary for a body to be human.

Human Bodies are Tubes

Up to now, we have discussed concepts of humanity in terms of intentionality and transformability. However, we have not been inclined to refer to any idea of 'soul' or 'soul matter' in our discussion of the interaction between various types of beings, because the very idea of 'souls' appears to render less appropriately Trio and Wayana ideas about the body and its socialisation. The possession of one or several souls (depending on the entity concerned) may not be the only determining factor enabling the mastery of transformation. Some entities, such as woven artefacts, have remnants of souls which are considered fixed – that is, not unstable. They do not have intentionality of their own but as extensions of the highly socialised and skilled persons who shape them, and they carry the intentionality of their maker.[5] For this reason, a Trio or Wayana avoids having any form of contact, either visual or physical, with an object hanging in the house of a shaman.[6]

Although Trio and Wayana human beings are said to possess various souls, such as an eye-soul and a skin-soul, as well as a generic soul which rests in the liver, these souls are not the seat of humanity. This is a feature well illustrated in the anthropological literature of Lowland South America, which describes how, among a significant number of Amerindian populations, the spirits of the dead are perceived as disembodied, incomplete, miserable beings which cannot see properly and crave to inhabit another body (Descola 1993). The material things and 'clothes' of a dead person are destroyed, the name erased from the memory of the living. Among the Trio and Wayana, the skin of game animals, in which one of the souls rests, is cooked and eaten to ensure that the leftover spirit does not come back to attack the hunter and his kin. But what is left of the dead is deprived of transformability; spirits of the dead can only inhabit existing receptacles; humanity is thus a fully embodied condition, as only the bodily envelope, the 'clothes', can provide the perspective. The body's aptitude as receptacle interests us here and we suggest that its transformability derives from its tubular qualities.

Trio accounts of their past recount how a new form of 'other' was made human by the Trio and Wayana by making it into a tube. The Maroons, descendants of African slaves who escaped Dutch colonial sugarcane plantations in the seventeenth and eighteenth centuries, fleeing to the interior of present-day Suriname and French Guiana, became important trading partners for the Trio and Wayana. Our Trio host said that through the many years of interaction he established and developed with his Maroon trading partner, he 'educated' him in various ways by telling him and showing him how the Trio live well. He also stressed that the Trio have always educated the Maroons, and he told us how, in the past (that is, in mythical times), a Trio 'saved' the first Maroon who was still then a miserable, wretched spirit, by giving him an anus: this archetypal Trio first pierced the spirit's bottom, then one of his bones, thus allowing the Maroon spirit to enter a cycle of humanising bodily transformations.

Humanity is fundamentally a condition generated by the circulation of some vital substances and influences through a properly shaped body. Intentionality or transformability are thus intrinsically connected to bodily 'physiological' movement, and to bodily orifices which allow circulation; and in this sense, human bodies are tubes which function as 'energy transformers' (Rivière 1969b), transformational entities activated by breath and the circulation of vital fluids (Hugh-Jones 2001; Goldman 2004; Costa, this volume). This emphasis on tubes and the control of vital substance finds clear expression across Amazonia in the ritual use and symbolism of flutes (Chaumeil and Hill 2011).

Among the Trio and the Wayana, the control of one's bodily orifices and the socialising apprenticeship of their highly controlled use is a fundamental feature of the educative process of children and their maturation into fully developed adults: through positive encouragement, young children are taught to urinate and defecate in appropriate places. Children also learn to regurgitate manioc beer, and young men develop specific techniques of regurgitation in competitions at times of communal celebrations. If we recognise in turn the central importance of foodstuffs and the movement of substances through the body, in and out of either different orifices or the same one, it becomes easier to explain the stress on an early apprenticeship of language, proper communication and the control of breath being a direct manifestation of the humanising process. This humanising attribute of the tube is taken to its most exuberant level with the use of flutes during collective feasts: in such contexts, flutes become agents which, as both containers and contained, act as mediators between consanguinity and affinity, allowing the transformation of alterity and the ritual expression and promotion of humanity (Brightman 2011).

In the light of these observations on the tubular quality of the human body, it should be clear why we have emphasised that transformability or the changing of bodies should not be conceived in a way which simply and radically divides an invisible soul, or essence, from a visible bodily envelope. Soul(s) are constitutive of the body, and the two are intimately implied in each other. The seat of the soul is also partially located in bodily fluids and air, and as such it is the use of breath and the beating of the heart that stimulates the movement of these fluids and provides the soul with a perspective. As the Wayana say that life is the movement of vital components such as air, blood and water through the body, and that death is characterised by the stopping of this continuous flow (cf. Chapuis 1998), transformability or perspectival change, and therefore humanity itself, is a nurtured quality based upon and stimulated by movement.

Conclusion

In Lowland South American ethnography, the body is often shown to be a place of incessant modification, yet previous authors have said little about differences among Amerindian bodies themselves and the relationships among a wider spectrum of bodies which inhabit the same social environment. Whereas all bodies are constantly subjected to nurturing techniques, some are attributed special levels of socialisation, because they appear to have a greater propensity to transform. Humanity is not only a matter of sociability, but it is also about transformability. And this transformability in turn is a creative quality cultivated throughout a person's lifetime, in order to allow changes of perspective which do not result in incomplete or confused shape shifting. Bodily strength, or instability, may, paradoxically, be connected to an excess of humanity rather than a lack of it, an ability to transform that is only achieved by highly trained individuals such as shamans, and by 'wild people' such as the Akuriyo, these nomadic forest dwellers who were captured by the Trio in a missionary-led expedition and brought back to a Trio village to live an existence of social marginality because of their widely known and feared bodily strength and transformability. The case of the Akuriyo, and also those of hunting dogs and objects made by the Trio and Wayana, suggest that in northern Amazonia and arguably throughout Lowland South America as a whole, humanity is a fully embodied condition, strategically developed by bodily enhancing techniques rooted in the physiology of the human body itself. Because human bodies are tubes, they can master the movement of vital substances through themselves, using socialising practices such as commensality. Humanity, among the Trio, Wayana and Akuriyo of northern Amazonia, is thus both social and physiological, or, to be more precise, it arises from a carefully nurtured interplay between social convention and bodily transformation.

Notes

1. All italicised non-English words are Trio unless otherwise stated.
2. Cf. Viveiros de Castro: '"Personitude" and "perspectivity" – the capacity to occupy a point of view – is a question of degree, of context and of position, rather than of a distinctive property of one species or another. Certain non-humans realise this potentiality in a more complete way than others; certain among them, indeed, manifest it with an intensity superior to that of our own species and, in this sense, they are "more human" than humans (Hallowell 1960: 69)' (Viveiros de Castro 2009: 23).
3. We use the term 'intentionality' in order to refer to both the various 'souls' (Wayana, *omole*) and the blood (Wayana, *mïwu*) of a person which all contribute to their life force and existence as a person. As in some other parts of Amazonia (e.g., Taylor 1998; Vilaça 2005), the Trio and Wayana do not demonstrate an interest in determining with precision the origin of bodily substances and the mechanical role they play in the constitution of the human person. See also Chapuis (1998).
4. On chilli peppers, see Chapuis and Rivière (2003: 457).
5. On the notion of the 'extended person', see Grotti (in press).
6. As Van Velthem also rightly observes, people avoid 'seeing' the woven artefacts of a shaman (Van Velthem 2001). In turn, this helps explain the fact that shamans tend to accumulate things more than other people (see Hugh-Jones 1992).

References

Århem, K. 1996. 'The Cosmic Food Web: Human-nature Relatedness in the Northwest Amazon', in P. Descola and G. Pálsson (eds), *Nature and Society: Anthropological Perspectives*. London: Routledge, pp. 185–204.
Bois, E. n.d. 'The Last of the Oayanas', *World Reality*.
Brightman, M. 2010. 'Creativity and Control: Property in Guianese Amazonia', *Journal de la Société des Américanistes* 96(1): 135–167.
——— 2011. 'Archetypal Agents of Affinity: "Sacred" Musical Instruments in the Guianas?' in J.-P. Chaumeil and J. Hill (eds), *Burst of Breath: New Research on Indigenous Ritual Flutes in Lowland South America*. Lincoln: University of Nebraska, pp. 158–72.
Chapuis, J. 1998. 'La personne wayana entre sang et ciel', Ph.D. thesis. Aix-Provence: Université d'Aix-Marseilles.

Chapuis, J., and H. Rivière (eds). 2003. *Wayana eitoponpë: (Une) histoire (orale) des Indiens Wayana*. Guyane: Ibis Rouge.
Chaumeil, J.-P., and J. Hill (eds). 2011. *Burst of Breath: New Research on Indigenous Ritual Flutes in Lowland South America*. Lincoln: University of Nebraska.
Descola, P. 1986. *La nature domestique: symbolisme et praxis dans l'écologie des Achuar*. Paris: Editions de la Maison des Sciences de l'Homme.
───── 1993. *Les lances du crépuscule: relations jivaros, Haute Amazonie*. Paris: Plon.
Erikson, P. 1996. *La griffe des aïeux: marquage du corps et démarquages ethniques chez les Matis d'Amazonie*. Louvain: Peeters/SELAF.
Fausto, C. 2002. 'Banquete de gente: comensalidade e canibalismo na Amazonia', *Mana* 8(2): 7–44.
───── 2007. 'Feasting on People: Eating Animals and Humans in Amazonia', *Current Anthropology* 48(4): 497–530.
Goldman, I. 2004. *Cubeo Hehénawa Religious Thought*, ed. P. Wilson. New York: Columbia University Press.
Gow, P. 1991. *Of Mixed Blood: Kinship and History in Peruvian Amazonia*. Oxford: Clarendon Press.
Grotti, V. in press. 'The Wealth of the Body: Trade Relations, Objects and Personhood in Northeastern Amazonia', *Journal of Latin American and Caribbean Anthropology*.
Howard, C. 2001. 'Wrought Identities: The Waiwai Expeditions in Search of the "Unseen Tribes" of Northern Amazonia', Ph.D. thesis. Chicago: University of Chicago.
Hugh-Jones, S. 1992. 'Yesterday's Luxuries, Tomorrow's Necessities: Business and Barter in Northwest Amazonia', in C. Humphrey and S.Hugh-Jones (eds), *Barter, Exchange and Value: An Anthropological Approach*. Cambridge: Cambridge University Press, pp. 42–74.
───── 2001. 'The Gender of Some Amazonian Gifts: An Experiment with an Experiment', in T. Gregor and D. Tuzin (eds), *Gender in Amazonia and Melanesia: An Exploration of the Comparative Method*. Berkeley: University of California Press.
Koelewijn, C., and P. Rivière. 1987. *Oral Literature of the Trio Indians of Suriname*. Dordrecht: Foris.
Monod Becquelin, A. 1982 'La métamorphose: contribution à l'étude de la propriété de transformabilité dans la pensée trumai (haut Xingu, Brésil)', *Journal de la Société des Américanistes* 68(1): 133–47.
Overing, J. 1983–1984. Elementary Structures of Reciprocity: A Comparative Note on Guianese, Central Brazilian, and North–west Amazon Socio–political Thought. *Antropológica* 56–62: 331–48.
Overing, J., and A. Passes (eds). 2000. *The Anthropology of Love and Anger: The Aesthetics of Conviviality in Amazonia*. London: Routledge.
Rivière, P. 1969a. *Marriage among the Trio: A Principle of Social Organisation*. Oxford: Oxford University Press.
───── 1969b. 'Myth and Material Culture: Some Symbolic Interrelations', in R. Spencer (ed.), *Forms of Symbolic Action*. Seattle: University of Washington Press, pp. 151–66.
───── 1984. *Individual and Society in Guiana: A Comparative Study of Amerindian Social Organisation*. Cambridge: Cambridge University Press.
───── 2001. 'A predação, a reciprocidade, e o caso das Guianas', *Mana* 7(1): 251–73.
Santos Granero, F. 2009. 'Hybrid Bodyscapes: A Visual History of Yanesha Patterns of Cultural Change', *Current Anthropology* 50(4): 477–512.
Seeger, A., R. Da Matta, E. Viveiros de Castro. 1979. 'A construção da pessoa nas sociedades indígenas brasileiras', *Boletim do Museu Nacional* 32: 2–19.

Taylor, A.-C. 1998. 'Corps immortels, devoir d'oubli: formes humaines et trajectoires de vie chez les Achuar', in M. Godelier and M. Panoff (eds), *La production du corps: approches anthropologiques et historiques*. Amsterdam: Editions des Archives Contemporaines, pp. 317–38.

—— 2000. 'Le sexe de la proie: représentations jivaro du lien de parenté', *L'Homme* 154/155: 309–34.

Van Velthem, L. 2001. 'The Woven Universe: Carib Basketry', in C. McEwan, C. Barreto and E. Neves (eds), *Unknown Amazon: Culture in Nature in Ancient Brazil*. London: British Museum Press, pp. 198–213.

—— 2003. *O belo é a fera: a estética da produção e da predação entre os Wayana*. Lisbon: Museu Nacional de Etnologia.

Vilaça, A. 2002. 'Making Kin out of Others in Amazonia', *Journal of the Royal Anthropological Institute* 8: 347–65.

—— 2005. 'Chronically Unstable Bodies: Reflections on Amazonian Corporealities', *Journal of the Royal Anthropological Institute* 11: 445–64.

Viveiros de Castro, E. 1992. *From the Enemy's Point of View: Humanity and Divinity in an Amazonian Society*. Chicago: University of Chicago Press.

—— 1998. 'Cosmological Deixis and Amerindian Perspectivism', *Journal of the Royal Anthropological Institute* 4: 469–85.

—— 2001. 'GUT Feelings about Amazonia: Potential Affinity and the Construction of Sociality', in L. Rival and N. Whitehead (eds), *Beyond the Visible and the Material: The Amerindianization of Society in the Work of Peter Rivière*. Oxford: Oxford University Press.

—— 2007. 'La forêt des miroirs: quelques notes sur l'ontologie des esprits amazoniens', in F. Laugrand and J. Oosten (eds), *La nature des esprits dans les cosmologies autochtones*. Montreal: Presses de l'Université Laval, pp. 45–74.

—— 2009. *Métaphysiques Cannibales*. Paris: Presses Universitaires de France.

Chapter 10

Masked Predation, Hierarchy and the Scaling of Extractive Relations in Inner Asia and Beyond

Katherine Swancutt

Predation – as an everyday phenomenon and as an important lynchpin in many shamanic cosmologies – has been a leitmotif in anthropological studies of personhood in Amazonia and the Siberian tundra.[1] A classic theme, such as predation, is often a wellspring of ideas. Not surprisingly, then, the study of predation has helped reveal what it means to be a person, spirit, animal, plant, stone or even a 'thing' in these two regions. The spirit of ontological unwrapping has since caught the widespread attention of anthropologists, who have honed the Amazonia–Siberian comparison,[2] or exported it as a 'thought experiment' to see how far people in different regions, such as Inner Asia, might ascribe similar qualities of personhood to other beings – including those beings regarded as prey (Pedersen 2001: 421–22; Pedersen, Empson and Humphrey 2007). Thus, while Amazonian and Siberian anthropology have extended beyond their geographical remits, they have given rise to telling permutations of their own themes, set amidst different ethnographic horizons (Holbraad and Willerslev 2007: 330–33).

In dialogue with the Amazonia–Siberian comparison, this chapter introduces a sliding-scale model for predation and hierarchy, which is intended to be applicable across Inner Asia, and possibly beyond. The thrust of my idea is simple, namely that predation and hierarchy can be placed along a continuum, wherein groups who overtly pursue 'predatory' or 'extractive' relations simultaneously veil their social hierarchies. Conversely, I suggest that groups who explicitly uphold social hierarchies also mask their predatory relations. Any given 'rise' in predation thus tends to precipitate a corresponding 'fall' in the explicit quality of hierarchical relations, and vice-versa. But while, for purposes of analysis, predation and hierarchy can be seen as notionally distinct, in practice these phenomena constantly move along a sliding scale, so that they often 'overlap' or 'shade into' one another, just as Willerslev and Ulturgasheva (this volume) have shown the finer elements of animistic and totemic ontologies do.

My proposed scaling between predation and hierarchy is thus intended to reflect their interdependence in practice, rather than being just 'an abstract model, detached from the real experiences of people in a life-world' (Willerslev 2004: 630). Of course, it is possible to find notional ideals which clash with this scaling of predation or hierarchy, such as the 'ultimate' predatory ideal of extracting resources from a person, whilst openly calling attention to their lower social status. Some Nuosu people (known in Chinese as Liangshan Yizu) I knew in Southwest China, whose forebears had been slaveholders, occasionally appeared to have been fond of pairing explicit predation with explicit hierarchy – which, incidentally, also appears to have been favourable to some of the groups in Santos-Granero's historical study of Amerindian slavery (Santos Granero 2009: 2). Still, it is important to bear in mind that notional ideals are abstractions of the mind, which only ever approximate their 'spatio-temporal realization in a state of affairs' (Deleuze 1990: 53). Even religious virtuosi, such as Nuosu text-reading shamans (*bimo*), never gain complete mastery over predation and hierarchy. However, as we shall see, they may gain an unusual degree of control over them.

The Amazonian, Siberian and Inner Asian ethnography has shown that virtuoso shamans, hunters, game players and other elite practitioners come closest to mastering notional ideals, such as the shaman's ideal of taking on different species' perspectives at will.[3] Through regular practice, virtuosi nearly obtain what Holbraad and Willerslev (2007: 340–41), drawing on Merleau-Ponty (1964) and Holenstein (1999) call the 'view from everywhere', which is an omnipresent view on their craft that reveals all the necessary steps for putting an ideal into practice (see also Vilaça 2005: 456–58). However, master practitioners always fall some degree short of obtaining this bird's-eye perception, which as a notional ideal is usually attributed to the spirits and gods alone. Master practitioners, then, only obtain close approximations of the 'view from everywhere' – and I suggest that they do this by progressively making their actual practices shade into their notional ideals (Swancutt 2007: 253–5). As this chapter shows, master practitioners (and some ordinary people) can encourage this shading between practices and ideals in any kind of setting, such as the 'animistic', 'totemic', 'naturalistic' or 'analogic' ontologies described by Descola (2005: 176). Alternatively, a kind of 'double shading' can arise when practitioners – in an effort to put their ideals into practice – trigger a movement between different ontological fields, as Willerslev and Ulturgasheva (this volume) have shown for Siberians who traffic between animistic and totemic settings. In either case, what master practitioners gain from controlling these different kinds of shading is ontological leverage regarding the situation at hand, which is a form of raw power that can be used to expertly mask their predatory motives, among other things.

Consider, for instance, how easily ordinary people, animals and even spirits of the dead (not all of whom are master practitioners) mask their predatory motives by manipulating the relation between hierarchy and predation so that they shade into one another. As I have shown elsewhere, Aga Buryat Mongols hold that when unvirtuous people die, they become vampiric imps (*chötgör*) because they refuse to meet the spirit bureaucracy (an explicit hierarchy) which regulates the cycle of laypersons' rebirths and the afterlife for shamans (Swancutt 2008: 847). These vampiric imps remain on earth, preying upon their consanguineal relatives' livestock, food stores and eventually their bodies. At the same time, the imps encourage their kin to commit suicide or suffer accidental deaths, so that they too can contravene the authority of the spirit bureaucracy and become imps (ibid.: 846). Intriguingly, the scaling between hierarchy and predation can be manipulated in even subtler ways, through a more expertly masked predation. Willerslev has shown that the Siberian Yukaghir 'hunter's "double perspective" implies a kind of optical oscillation', whereby the hunter rapidly shifts between retaining his own perspective as the predator preparing to kill an animal (an explicit hierarchy between hunter and prey), and adopting the perspective of the animal who watches the hunter insidiously mimic its own beautiful likeness (masked predation), until the hunter has lured the animal close enough to kill it (Willerslev 2004: 641). In yet another vein, Deed Mongol ethnography suggests that, where herders make a joint effort with their dogs to corral an animal, the herder's intent to capture is sometimes magnified by their dogs, who act as extensions of the herder's 'distributed personhood' with the aim of confusing the corralled animal through the tactic of split pursuit (Swancutt 2007: 251). Even as it is being pursued, the corralled animal runs the risk of being caught unawares by the increasingly coordinated efforts of herdsman and dog, which simultaneously magnify and mask the personhood of the herder. Fausto (this volume), gives a parallel example from the Amerindian world, where he invites us to imagine 'a world of owners and the owner as a model of the magnified person'.

To show ethnographically how my proposed scaling of predation and hierarchy actually changes over time, this chapter moves the reader southwards, across a large expanse of Asia, to the Nuosu of Yunnan Province, China, who live mainly in high alpine forests, practising pastoralism, swidden cultivation, hunting and their own text-based shamanic religion. Classed under the Chinese umbrella ethnonym of Yi, the Nuosu are a Tibeto-Burman group. My fieldwork among the Nuosu was carried out during the last four months of 2007, in a rural village of Ninglang County, where, as I was told, the parents or grandparents of present-day villagers had migrated one hundred and fifty years earlier from the Greater Cool Mountains (*Da Liangshan*) of neighbouring Sichuan Province. Famous for their 'serf' and 'slaveholding' practices, which were only forcibly disbanded by the Chinese during the Democratic Reforms of 1956-1957, the Nuosu afford a remarkable springboard for the study of 'masked predation'. Central to this masked predation is the Nuosu notion that the human soul is in fact a predatory 'soul-spider' (*yyr*) residing on the outer surface of the human body. As we will see, the Nuosu soul-spider underpins a host of analogies between people, spiders and web-like attachments to their ranked lineages and the human home, so that spider imagery is pivotal to their masked predation – as it appears to be further afield (see Swancutt in press).[4]

Drawing upon Nuosu materials, then, I propose in this chapter that predation and hierarchy are interdependent elements of social life. At the level of cross-cultural comparison, I also suggest that those groups with explicit hierarchies, such as the Nuosu, mask their predatory metaphors and economy of relations.[5] By contrast, the comparatively 'egalitarian' groups of Amazonia and Siberia often use predatory metaphors to describe their personhood and economy of relations, whilst masking their hierarchies. Certainly the Amazonian literature is replete with studies on fairly egalitarian groups, who go so far as to notionally pair predators with consanguines and prey with affines, regarding this opposition as a cornerstone of their ontology of personhood.[6] Santos-Granero suggests that different scales of predation and hierarchy have underpinned the social production of Amazonian groups for some time (Santos-Granero 2009: 5–14). Recent work by Brightman (2007: 14–23, see also 3, 46–49, 189) also reveals that more explicit forms of hierarchy are present in the Guianas, a region classically associated with Amazonian egalitarianism. These findings suggest it is necessary to rethink the general tendency among some Amazonian scholars of linking egalitarianism to simple political formations.[7] Equating egalitarianism with simple political forms is itself a dangerous masking technique, which downplays the predatory and hierarchical elements that underpin core Amazonian concerns about the 'instability' (Ewart 2003: 268, 270; Vilaça 2005: 445, 452, 457, 460) or the making and undoing (Lepri 2005: 708–11) of kinship and other social roles.

Unequal Shades of Predation, Hierarchy and Morality

Before turning to my Nuosu ethnography, I want to briefly explain how the shading of predation and hierarchy can give rise to 'loopholes' in local morality, as well as to what Bateson, in his classic study, has called 'schismogenesis' (Bateson 2000: 61–72). According to Bateson, schismogenesis arises whenever inter-personal competition destabilises either of two modes of social organisation: 'symmetrical differentiation', where competitive relations exist between categorical equals (egalitarian relations); and 'complementary differentiation', where competitive relations hold between categorical unequals (hierarchical relations) (ibid.: 68–72). Bateson describes the precise patterns of exchange which characterise symmetrical and complementary forms of competition, and suggests that each person tries to outdo their exchange partner, such that their collective rivalry finally pushes social organisation to its breaking point (ibid.: 68). Taking Bateson's argument in a somewhat different direction, I propose that each schismogenesis-like shift also happens whenever predation and hierarchy shade dramatically into one another, producing widespread moral ambiguities about whether one is living amidst explicit predation – that is, symmetrical differentiation – or masked predation – that is, complementary differentiation. But while this dramatic near-merging of predation and hierarchy can lead to schismogenesis, I suggest that it is actually more common to find a subtle shading between predation and hierarchy, which produces loopholes in local morality without overturning the current mode of social organisation.

It is this subtle shading which ensures that, across Inner Asia, everyday forms of masked predation are not trumped by moral ambiguities about the 'self-cultivation' that is so widespread among hierarchical groups subscribing to Buddhism – including groups who mix shamanic and Buddhist cosmologies, such as the Buryats of northeast Mongolia, among whom I carried out my first fieldwork in 1999 and 2000. In line with their self-cultivating morality, these Buryats hold that shamanic spirits and Buddhist gods often express their pleasure when observing a person acting virtuously (*buyantai*) by sending that person blessings (*buyan*) and boons of fortune (*khiimor'*). These 'gifts from the gods' are especially associated with philanthropic acts, in which there is a triangular relation between the virtuous donor, the recipient of the gift and those spirits who bestow blessings when witnessing the philanthropic act. Occasionally, this triangular relation encourages so-called virtuous acts which are not necessarily purely selfless or philanthropic, but are instead loopholes in the conventional morality. One month's fieldwork in summer 2005, among Deed Mongols in the district of Züün Sum (Chinese: Zongjia), in Qinghai Province, China, provided me with several instances where a young man told me openly, at his home and in front of relatives and friends, that not only could a person carry out ordinary virtuous deeds but that the same person could even make ritual sacrifices, with the explicit purpose of attracting disproportionately more blessings from the spirits than any peers carrying out similar deeds or rites alongside them. This man gave the following rationale behind his thoughts: those people who make their virtuous behaviour the most evident to the Buddhist gods are best able to attract their attention and receive their blessings; whereas, more modest people fail to attract the necessary attention of the gods, and by extension their blessings. Although this man received embarrassed rebukes from kin and friends involved in the conversation, who told me in lowered tones that he should not have said 'such things', these same people confessed the man had spoken truthfully after all, allowing that the hypothetical situation he had described could be 'possible' – even if it highlighted unvirtuous behaviour, competition and ambiguity in their morality of self-cultivation.

I was given similar moral anecdotes by Buryats during my first fieldwork, some of which revolved around interactions between the poor person and the philanthropic rich person, which I discuss in detail below. Curiously, the Mongol strategy of attracting a disproportionate number of blessings resonates with the medieval Catholic practice of selling indulgences, or documents from the Church declaring the extraordinarily good behaviour of the purchasers, which absolved them of their sins. Notoriously attractive, these documents were avidly sought by wealthy people, who hoped to buy up all the indulgences on offer from travelling churchmen. So the logic of carrying out seemingly selfless acts to curry favour with the gods, whilst masking one's own extractive motives, has not been exclusive to Inner Asia. But there appears to have been a tendency in Inner Asia for the shading between predation and hierarchy to elicit these moral loopholes, especially when resources are shifted asymmetrically through, first, 'circulated exchanges' made between the philanthropic donor, the person receiving the gift and the spirits as witnesses of exchange; or, secondly, 'extractions' of resources which are one-sided but carried out in ways that mask the intention of rendering the 'other' or the 'outsider' as prey.

While Inner Asian notions of fortune – and the Mongol principle of attracting the favour of spirits or gods with virtuous behaviour – do not have exact Amazonian equivalents, similar loopholes in morality appear to arise within the Amazonian 'symbolic economy of alterity' (Viveiros de Castro 1996: 190; Santos-Granero 2009: 202, 209). The crux of this symbolic economy of alterity is the basic distinction between 'other/outsider' and 'non-other/insider', which corresponds to the Amazonian notion that outsiders must be captured and incorporated into the group in order to successfully reproduce society.[8] Capturing outsiders is even vital to Amazonian societies in cases where, as Lepri has shown for the Ese Ejja, 'otherness must constantly be made and undone within the group of kin who are *uapapojiama*, non-other' – that is, close relatives who fall under the incest taboo (Lepri 2005: 711). Thus Amazonian people – as well as animals, spirits, plants and sometimes other 'agents' such as diseases – strategically draw outsiders into the consanguineal sphere by eliciting 'intimate' relations with them through: marriage, seduction and hunting (Taylor 2001: 47–54); kidnapping, illness or disease (Vilaça 2002: 357–58), which may be linked to warfare (Fausto 2007: 501–2, 508–9); or food consumption and the adoption of pets (Taylor 2001: 47–50; Fausto 2007: 502).

Given this vast scaling of 'predatory' relations in Amazonia, Taylor suggests that we keep abreast of its various registers:

> In the work of Viveiros de Castro and of most anthropologists of structuralist bent, 'predation' is a purely analytic construct: it is the label for a highly abstract scheme predicated on the subsumption of one term of a relation ('other') by the other term ('self'). It does not refer as such to empirical forms of killing and consuming 'others'. However, it is often understood as a category of actual practice. I think, therefore, that we need to distinguish between three distinct levels lumped within the same category: predation in the abstract sense (perhaps best renamed 'incorporation', though this is admittedly an unsatisfactory term), predation as the symbolic form taken by 'incorporation' in a given cultural context, and finally the specific modes of killing and consuming 'living' others: hunting, exo- and endocannibalism, and so forth. (Taylor 2001: 55)

Taylor's three levels of predation all exist in Inner Asia, but in this chapter I use mainly her first and second – that is, the abstract and symbolic – registers, to present my ideas about masked predation. These abstract and symbolic registers are especially pronounced in cases where the shading between predation and hierarchy gives rise to loopholes in local morality.

With this in mind, I next offer an in-depth look at Nuosu notions about the soul-spider, which I propose is the backbone of their shamanic cosmology and extractive economy of relations. Following this, I make a brief comparison with the Buryat morality of self-cultivation, where predatory notions are often filtered through a veneer of virtuous acts. Different analytic purchases onto masked predation are afforded by these two Inner Asian examples, where predation and hierarchy are scaled in similar ways, affording evidence that this scaling model might be fruitfully transported back to Amazonia, Siberia and beyond.

The Cosmology of Soul-spiders

At the heart of Nuosu shamanic cosmology is the spider's life-world and the web of predatory motifs surrounding it. I learned about the salience of spiders from different Nuosu villagers, but it was the shaman in my field home, whom I call Fijy, who told me the finer points of knowledge about the Nuosu person's soul-spider whilst elucidating how Nuosu sociality is underpinned by notions about the spider-like capture of resources. According to Fijy, the soul-spider is actually a dual concept at the notional and linguistic levels, since the same Nuosu word (*yyr*) can alternatively mean 'human soul', 'spider' or even 'soul-spider', while text-reading shamans (*bimo*) say that their ancient and modern script forms for this word physically resemble a spider (see Fig. 10.1). Fijy also confirmed that the word for soul-spider is a component part of the Nuosu idiom of 'fate-fortune' (*rrep bbo yyr lup*; *zza zze ke po*), which refers to the propagation of the household's livestock, grain and other resources – including attachments to other lineage members – so that it is routinely incorporated into the final chanting of the text-reading shaman's ceremony. He then expanded upon notions about the soul-spider, which are known to shamans and laypersons alike, as other Nuosu in Fijy's village confirmed for me.

Every Nuosu person's soul-spider, Fijy said, resides on the outside surface of the body and crawls along its contours. Resembling the smallest and whitest of spiders, or a newly hatched spider, the soul-spider can be seen with the naked eye and is visible to both laypersons and shamans. Typically, the Nuosu see their own soul-spiders crossing their household thresholds during a soul-calling ceremony. Sometimes, though, the Nuosu see soul-spiders walking along the surface of their own bodies, or on the surface of other people's bodies, possibly leaving web tracings in their wake. On rare occasions, the soul-spider may even be seen to spin a thread which takes it some distance away from its owner – for instance when using its filament to lower itself from a person's fingertip, before climbing back up that thread and crawling again along the person's body. The soul-spider does not actually lose contact with its owner during these threaded excursions – it simply extends the range of its territory – because the 'home' of the soul-spider is its human host, plus any web filaments spun on top of them. Thus, the Nuosu would never remove the soul-spider or its web tracings from the surface of any person's body, as this would cause soul loss. Moreover, the Nuosu prohibit killing actual spiders, which although never confused with soul-spiders bear too close of a resemblance to them. These notions about the soul-spider suggest, at

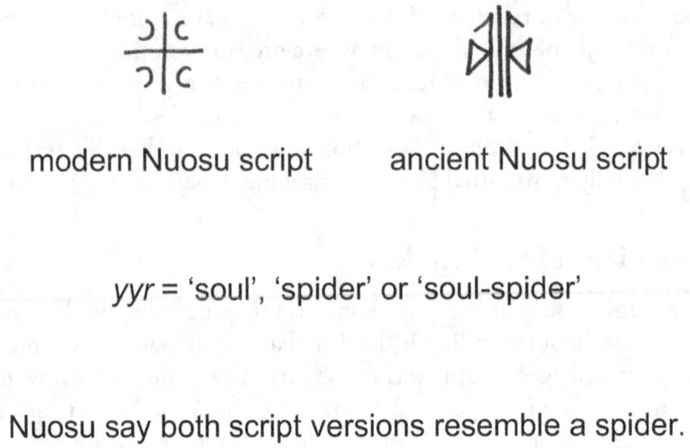

ᗡ|ᴄ
ᗡ|ᴄ

modern Nuosu script   ancient Nuosu script

yyr = 'soul', 'spider' or 'soul-spider'

Nuosu say both script versions resemble a spider.

Figure 10.1: The Nuosu 'soul-spider', written in the author's hand.

the micro-level of the Nuosu person, that the human soul and the propagation of household fortunes actually exist within a 'centripetal' sociality, where resources are drawn into the household and amassed in abundance there.

Revealingly, the soul-spider notion underscores both traditional Nuosu lineage rankings and their now historical practice of keeping lower-ranked lineage members as slaves and serfs (see Pan 1997: 109; Harrell 2001: 50; Hill and Diehl 2001: 54; Heberer 2007: 28–29). Nuosu lineage rankings are still firmly upheld today and comprise different categories of person: 'the *nuo*, or elites; the *qunuo*, or commoners, making up the majority of Nuosu people in Ninglang; the *mgajie*, a residual category of semi-independent farmers; and the *gaxy*, or recent captives and their immediate descendants' (Hill and Diehl 2001: 54). These lineage rankings are actually part of a larger two-tiered system, in which the 'Black Nuosu' nobility (the *nuo*) are regarded as superior to 'White Nuosu' commoners, who are comprised of *qunuo, mgajie* and *gaxy* (Pan 1997: 108; Heberer 2007: 26–27). Pan has shown that Nuosu lineage rankings historically have been underpinned by their 'theory of blood superiority', which propounds essential differences in the purity of blood and hardness of bone between Nuosu of different lineage rankings, as well as between Nuosu and non-Nuosu (Pan 1997: 109, see also 108, 115–16, 119, 121). Moreover, Hill and Diehl's findings suggest that, in Ninglang, the lowest-ranked Nuosu people have been perceived as only quasi-Nuosu, since 'in thinking about the system, the Nuosu regard the *mgajie* and *gaxy* as not of the same order as *nuo* or *qunuo*, as somehow outside the system, perhaps because they were so closely identified with ethnic origins outside Nuosu society and attached as individuals to particular Nuosu households' (Hill and Diehl 2001: 54). Frequently, the lowest-ranked sectors of Nuosu society had been populated by Han Chinese (the majority ethnic group within China) who had been captured in Nuosu slave raids, but who over time could attach themselves to a higher-ranking Nuosu lineage (Lin 1961: 94–95; Hill 2001: 1033–41; Hill and Diehl 2001: 54). Hill even shows that incorporation into the lineage (*cyt vi*) was the only way for a non-Nuosu person to transcend their 'slave status', so that former slaves often claimed attachments to a prestigious lineage (an explicit reference to hierarchy) whilst masking information about their slave origins (viewed by established lineage members as predatory social-climbing) (Hill 2001: 1033–44). A neat parallel, then, arises between these three chief Nuosu concerns: firstly, highlighting attachments to the lineage, 'Nuosu-ness' and prestige; second, keeping the soul-spider attached to the person's body; and third, attaching business opportunities, health and, historically, even captives to the household.

My fieldwork in Fijy's village was carried out among people of the high-ranking White Nuosu commoner lineage (*qunuo* or *quho*), among whom there were many text-reading shamans (*bimo*) who, as Harrell notes, 'almost always are *quho*, usually from a few prominent clans, in which the knowledge is passed down from father to son' (Harrell 2001: 97). During fieldwork, I learned that these Nuosu strengthen their lineage attachments and household prestige by balancing masked predation against explicit hierarchy. Many villagers still prefer their lineage-based, rank-specific marital endogamy (which, however, entails choosing a marriage partner from a different clan), because this helps to propagate their lineage across the generations. But these same Nuosu also espouse meritocratic ideals, which offer a convenient rhetoric for masked predation since they eulogize the spider-like extraction of resources and prestige that occurs within the Nuosu web of human relations.

A Meritocratic Extraction of Resources

Take, for instance, the Nuosu saying which Fijy paraphrased to me: spiders are the animals which eat the most meat, since they regularly catch insects in their webs, while text-reading shamans are the people who eat the most meat because in seasons where people do not regularly slaughter livestock shamans who travel from house to house to hold rituals eat sacrificial meat on a daily basis. According to Fijy, this saying underscores the meritocratic ideal that the hard-working shaman has regular access to meat in times of scarcity. Tellingly, Fijy also felt the saying confirmed that humanity is ideally spider-like. It follows that text-reading shamans, who are the most spider-like of people, are held to be the repositories of Nuosu 'higher morality', who selflessly help people in their time of need (Heberer 2007: 31–32). Thus, on several different occasions I observed very aged men offer young shamans, such as Fijy, their honorary seating positions within the home, showing their recognition of the shaman's merited status.

Significantly, though, every Nuosu person has some amount of spider-like humanity, which implicates them within this merit- and lineage-driven economy of relations. Fijy expressed the general capacity for spider-like humanity to me with a Nuosu proverb, which he cited in two different versions, using Mandarin

Chinese: 'Men and text-reading shamans are of the heavens, women and the home are of the earth' (*Nan bi tian; nü jia di*). This version of the proverb stresses the hierarchy of male–female relations, where men who undertake text-reading shamanic practices are associated with the heavens – since the Nuosu written script version of the /*bi*/ in *bimo* (text-reading shaman) resembles the flying shaman or an aeroplane – and women are associated with agricultural work – both of which contribute to the fullness of life within the home. In its alternative version, the proverb states: 'Ordinary men and text-reading shamans travel to the outside; women stay inside the home' (*Nan bi wai; nü jia nei*). Fijy said that this second version stresses the idea that men lure business prospects into the household, like the spider which leaves its den to hunt and returns home with its prey. Women, on the other hand, build up strong homesteads in which to capture prey, like the spider that continually rebuilds and expands its web. Nuosu men and women thus work together as the husband-and-wife team of the neolocal household, drawing people and resources into the home.

Intriguingly, the centripetal – or inward moving – sociality of the Nuosu resonates with the above-mentioned Amazonian symbolic economy of alterity, where outsiders are drawn into the consanguineal sphere for the reproduction of society. Grotti has shown that the Trio of southern Suriname occasionally pursue a 'centripetal sociality', circulating goods with the aim of accumulating them (Grotti 2007: 150–57), whilst their women especially attract 'external influences to the core' of the household (ibid.: 183–84, 187). Holding drinking festivals which attract residential affines into a single communal house, these Trio partake in drinking manioc beer, and games and circle dances around a central pole, with the aim of renewing society through their temporary, 'liminal' emphasis on centripetal relationality (ibid.: 63–65, see also 71–77, 104–6; 2009: 80–89). Most remarkably, though, the centripetal quality which Grotti ascribes to hierarchical and predatory elements within inter-ethnic relations between the Trio, Wayana and their so-called 'captives', the Akuriyo, parallels the centripetal sociality of the Nuosu, who draw resources into the home and amass them in abundance there (Grotti 2007: 114, 110–18). As already mentioned, the Nuosu strategy of masked predation is used to claim lineage membership, or to meritocratically attract resources and prestige. Beyond this, the Nuosu use masked predation to draw outsiders into the home as 'captive guests' (see Swancutt in press) during hunting and post-mortuary rites (more on this below), and even during ceremonies to call back their lost soul-spiders.

On several occasions I observed the Nuosu soul-calling ceremony in Fijy's village, which is in fact a ceremonial ambush of the lost soul-spider. Cajoled into the home with promises of warmth and good things to eat, the soul-spider is encouraged to climb a white thread laid across the household threshold, which is meant to resemble a real spider's thread. Usually the owner of the lost soul-spider, or a close relative, handles this thread and a small basket (often used for winnowing) – or a lacquer compote box – which contains a piece of meat (or fat) and a swatch of cloth, to which the thread is tied. Everyone attending the ceremony watches for the moment when the soul-spider starts climbing the thread, whispering to each other when they have seen it, and monitor its travel. When the soul-spider has reached the basket, the person handling the thread winds it up, possibly wrapping the soul-spider within the thread, and then places it in the basket, shutting the lid on top of it. The basket is opened on the next good astrological day that arises, to release the captured soul-spider within the home, whereupon it willingly crawls onto the surface of its owner's body. Recovering the soul-spider strengthens the person's health, business opportunities, lineage attachments and the fullness of life.

A similar strategy of 'ambush by basket' features in the Nuosu hunt for live pheasants, which are domesticated for their eggs. Fijy explained that when the Nuosu hunter travels to the forest to capture these pheasants he wears a round cape woven from hemp and a large woven conical hat with a pointed tip (the kind worn by Han Chinese for protection against the sun during agricultural labour). The Nuosu hunter also brings along a broad oval basket, which is about five feet tall, carrying within it an already domesticated pheasant. Significantly, Fijy said that these baskets resemble the scrub and bushes which comprise the 'homes' of wild pheasants. Once the hunter has found a suitable spot for capturing pheasants, he squats down behind his basket, hidden beneath his hemp cloak and hat. Soon the domesticated pheasant begins to cry out, acting as the hunter's bait, since it attracts wild pheasants seeking a mate. When a wild pheasant approaches the basket, the hunter carefully lifts one edge of the basket so that it can enter, then lowers the basket to the ground to capture the wild bird. More than one wild pheasant can be captured like this during a single trip to the forest (depending on the number of baskets brought on the hunt), and captured pheasants are conveniently carried home in the hunter's basket(s). When Nuosu hunters return home, they place their captured pheasants in separate wooden hutches, located outdoors and along the edges of the household courtyard. Captured pheasants are occasionally paired for mating, but they otherwise live alone to prevent them from fighting, and are fed the same dried maize kernels and other grains that the Nuosu give to their chickens.

Basket capture also features in elaborate Nuosu post-mortuary rites (*nimu cobi*) which, Fijy explained, invite the deceased ancestor home one or more years after the funeral. During my stay in 2007, I observed the post-mortuary rites that Fijy held for his father. Carving a 'spirit vessel' (*madu*), which takes the form of a cylindrical container made of hawthorn wood, Fijy explained that he would enclose a small effigy of his father in this vessel and then, at the appropriate moment in the rites, the vessel would be placed on a bamboo mat, 'representing a bed for the soul' (Ma 2000: 55). Ideally, the bamboo mat is suspended from the ceiling of the deceased's home (or the home of their descendants) to produce a basket-like shape (ibid.: 55–56). Fijy told me that the rite ensures the deceased returns to the original Nuosu lineage location or 'the land of the ancestors… [called] Zyzypuvy, near present-day Zhaotong, in northeastern Yunnan' (ibid.: 55). Then Fijy confirmed that when the deceased reached this ancestral land, they were also stably transformed into a guardian spirit (*jjyp lup*) residing within the home, where they helped their descendants to obtain the fullness of life.

Tipping the Scale of Masked Predation

Intriguingly, the dissolution of Nuosu slavery and more recent Chinese economic influences appear to have tipped the balance of Nuosu sociality subtly in favour of explicit predation. I occasionally observed Nuosu in Fijy's village trying to extract labour and resources from other Nuosu in their 'clan village' (Lin 1961: 29). This recent competition amongst Nuosu contrasts with what Heberer, in his study of rural Nuosu business, has suggested are more traditional codes of conduct (Heberer 2007: 7, 150–51). Significantly, the catalyst for this change has been both dramatic and 'external' to Nuosu sociality, namely, China's increasingly liberal marketing ethos, which propounds seemingly 'ahierarchical', merit-based opportunities for everyone to accumulate wealth. However, the meritocratic element of liberal marketing also may have meshed with indigenous Nuosu views about meritocracy and the spider-like extraction of resources. Feuchtwang has shown that the liberal marketing ethos has encouraged Han Chinese to pursue a rather extractive economy of relations, which ironically shades into that same philanthropic register of 'Buddhist' morality which (as mentioned above) Mongols recognise as 'selfless' gifting:

> One very common Chinese image of the realm of freedom in which money reigns as a measure of success is the ocean ... The ocean is the economy decollectivized and removed from direct state control. It is therefore an economy that has lost its moral dimension ... Now they mark out a set of obligations beyond whose seclusion an ocean of fortune, instrumentality and exploitation – regulated or not – is continuously expanding ... [B]eyond human responsiveness is the realm of gain, which comes either through luck (*fuqi*) or fairness, or through the unfair development of personal connections or the amoral skills of instrumental networking. It is an ocean full of money fish to be ruthlessly and opportunistically pursued. Regulation and the investigation of corruption can make the pursuit fairer, but negotiation and mutual back-scratching are the norm. Yet from this amoral economy reserves flow into the moral sphere. From oceanic wealth come contributions to the economy of gifts, reciprocity and donations to public works, such as the building of ancestral halls and temples, which build reputations for beneficence. (Feuchtwang 2002: 202–3)

Market rhetoric and tactics thus often only ostensibly level hierarchies – whilst exacerbating divides between rich and poor – which nonetheless can be used to accumulate prestige in an economy built upon resources and philanthropy. Among the Nuosu, increasingly explicit hierarchical divides have become an inescapable vehicle of prosperity, and have made an undeniable impact on how the Nuosu, at least in Fijy's village, have shifted the balance in favour of a more explicit predation. Only time will tell how far this shift will go. But the present emphasis on explicit predation appears to explain some of the rising interest in shamanic practices among the younger generation. Young Nuosu shamans accumulate resources and merit by holding ceremonies that purge unwanted ghosts from the home, thus reversing failed business prospects, illnesses and those spider-like relations in which they – or their clients – had become entangled.

A Veneer of Virtuous Acts

Let us now turn to the Buryats of Bayandun, Dornod Province, Mongolia, who refer to themselves as Aga Buryat since either they, or a previous generation of their family, migrated to north-east Mongolia from the Aga Buryat Autonomous District in southern Russia, which they regard as their ancestral 'homeland' (*nutag*). Although located 8,000km north-east of the Nuosu, the Aga Buryats have evidenced a similar shift towards explicit predation. Primarily shamanic, but also Buddhist, social ranking among these Buryats works differently to Nuosu lineage rankings. Humphrey contrasts the more flexible Russian Buryat hierarchy, where 'Buryat rank was established within each clan separately, i.e. "vertically"', to Nuosu hierarchies in which lineages were ranked against each other (Humphrey 1999: 64–65, see also 60–63). Thus, Humphrey explains that among the Buryats:

> unlike among the Yi [i.e., Nuosu], the inter-clan system of relations was not hierarchical. Clans or local lineages were conceived as essentially different from one another, as conveying qualities such as bravery or cunning, or as fitting their members for certain tasks (e.g. some were 'good hunters', others 'smiths', others 'herders', and so on), but these qualities and abilities were clearly not ranked. It was inside clans that rank was perceived, the hereditary titled aristocrats of the senior line more or less coinciding with the wealthy and the unmarked or junior lines containing the livestock-less labourers at the bottom. Because the aristocrats sat at the head of separate, 'different' exogamous clans/lineages, and did not constitute an in-marrying circle of their own, the notion of honour/status was more dispersed than among the Yi. (ibid.: 64)

In line with Humphrey's findings, I observed that the Buryats in Bayandun, who esteem age over youth and men over women, nonetheless have far more room to manoeuvre within their patrilineal hierarchies than do the Nuosu. These Buryats subscribe to the Buddhist morality of self-cultivation, which emphasises that people who undertake virtuous acts or worship frequently (*ongon shütdekh, burkhan shütdekh*) tend to receive boons of fortune from the spirits and gods. In addition, these Buryats hold that only some spirits and gods regularly watch after people (these are usually the shamanic spirits of close relatives, no more than five to six generations distant from their living descendants). Inevitably, then, some people's virtuous deeds go unnoticed and unrewarded. Still, these Buryats consider that the person who regularly performs virtuous deeds is likely to receive blessings and boosts of fortune fairly often.

Recall that a significant loophole in the Buryat (and wider Mongol) morality of merit making allows people to accumulate a disproportionately large amount of blessings and fortune through continuous acts of virtue and worship. Shamans in Bayandun gave me local anecdotes and actual stories about people who tried to draw these blessings towards themselves alone, which suggest that the Buryat scaling of hierarchy and predation also has been tipping increasingly towards the pole of explicit predation. Yaruu, the shaman whose home I lived in during my fieldwork, gave me this anecdote on several different occasions in 2000:

> The shamanic spirits and Buddhist gods like seeing people help others, without expecting anything in return, and treating each other as equals. There is a well-known anecdote about the rich person who looked askance at a poor person, and who was seen to have done this by the spirits and gods. This was not a good way of behaving, and the spirits and gods punished the rich man for looking down on the poor person. People should not look down on someone, just because of poverty ... But then again, there are many people who look askance at others because they are poor, and the spirits and gods do not always see them doing this. So it is possible for people to behave in this way and not be punished ... It is also possible for people to behave virtuously, in the effort to attract good things and fortune to them, but the spirits and gods only send people boons of fortune when they notice them acting especially virtuously.

Echoing this potential for attracting a disproportionate amount of fortune and blessings to oneself, the husband-and-wife shaman team whom I call by the names Galanjav and Chimegee told me in late 1999 about an old man in Bayandun who had a reputation locally of being very knowledgeable about Buddhism but also of being somewhat 'crazy' (*tenegtei*) with enthusiasm for worshipping the spirits. According to Galanjav and Chimegee, this old man recently had built many stone cairns (*ovoo*) in the style of those which traditionally demarcated the territorial boundaries of Mongol living spaces. Many Buryats in Bayandun considered that the man's new cairns were a form of explicit predation, because the old man would have known that other locals in the area could have guessed that he had built the new cairns to attract a disproportionate amount of blessings and fortune to himself. Galanjav explained that:

> Yes, that old man is very knowledgeable about Buddhism. And he worships a lot. But I tell you, what he does is wrong. You know that huge stone cairn in the western wing of the district centre? It is shaped like a turtle and has several ceremonial scarves, erected like flags, flying on top of it. That old man is the one who made it. He collected all the large stones for it himself and put it together in the shape of a turtle, maybe because the turtle is a water animal that lives in the underground kingdom of the Nature God (*lus*) – that old man is always thinking about Buddhist things. But no one worships at that cairn except for the old man. It just sits there unused. And I'll tell you something else. He's built so many cairns. Actually, he's built cairns all around the edges of Bayandun and has even built many of them leading out to the neighbouring district in the east, Dashbalbar. This is really wrong. The reason why it's wrong is that we have this idea: a newly-made cairn attracts blessings and fortune to the patriline of the person who made it. So every time an offering is left at such a cairn, blessings and fortune go towards the person who built the cairn, no matter who leaves the offering. But people are obliged

to leave offerings at cairns whenever they pass them, provided that these are legitimate, ancient cairns erected for worshipping the local nature spirits (*savdag*), who then impart blessings and fortune upon everyone living in the local area. New cairns, like the ones built by that old man, are sinful (*nügeltei*) because they do not properly attract offerings to nature spirits or shamanic spirits (*ongon*), who would then pass their blessings and fortune onto the local people. Instead, the old man's new cairns attract numerous blessings to his patriline alone, especially when you consider how many cairns he has made. They clearly outnumber the old cairns by dozens. Everyone from this area knows that the old man's cairns are newly made and ignores them. Occasionally, though, some newcomers to the area find themselves constantly making offerings, when passing along the roads between Dashbalbar and Bayandun, where the old man built his many cairns. Newcomers also go to see that turtle-shaped cairn, which looks impressive. Notice, though, that no one from this district pays any attention to it, because it was built to direct fortune and good things towards the old man's family alone.

Yaruu's and Galanjav's anecdotes show that Buryats are aware of the shading between predation and hierarchy, which gives rise to the loopholes in their morality of self-cultivation. Either looking askance at a poor person or building numerous cairns is an explicit form of predation which insidiously masks Buryat (and wider Mongol) hierarchies. Looking askance at a poor person only hints at disdain, which is neither spoken aloud nor publicly declared, so that it may be concealed from the shamanic spirits, Buddhist gods or other people. Similarly, building many stone cairns suggests the desire to attract disproportionate blessings and fortune to one's own family line, but it could be said that the cairns were built out of the general (and virtuous) enthusiasm for worshipping nature spirits – so that, actually, criticism of this enthusiastic worshipping is what is sinful! Significantly, though, these Buryat examples suggest that there is a cyclical relation between, on the one hand, the shading of predation into hierarchy and, on the other, the moral loopholes which this shading generates. Thus when left unchecked these moral loopholes can increase the shading between hierarchy and predation, eventually tipping the scale towards a more explicit predation.

Varying Degrees of Difference within and between Ontological Fields

Having compared Nuosu and Buryat scales of predation and hierarchy, I now come full circle to discuss their relevance for debates about ontology in the Inner Asian region and beyond. Recently, the Amazonia–Siberian comparison has been fuelled by the question of how 'whole' or 'intact' any given ontology happens to be. In different ways, Descola's classification of ontologies around the world (Descola 1996: 85–98; 2005: 176) and Viveiros de Castro's enthusiasm for the 'molar' models of Amazonian cosmology (Viveiros de Castro 2007: 155, 158, 164, 167) have emphasised that animistic ontologies are pervasive within the Amazonian region, allowing that occasional 'hints' of other ontologies, whether classed as 'naturalistic', 'totemic', or 'analogic', arise as just fleeting 'gaps' in the constitution of an otherwise animistic world. Pedersen has given a similar argument for Siberia, or the region of 'Northern North Asia' which he classes as 'predominantly animistic in nature', and for Inner Asia, or the region of 'Southern North Asia' which he considers to be 'predominantly totemistic' (Pedersen 2001: 411). According to Pedersen, animism all across North Asia is in fact occasionally 'ruptured by countless asocial entities, thus giving rise to a cosmology strangely reminiscent of a Swiss cheese', so that like the descriptions of animism given by Descola and Viveiros de Castro, it becomes temporarily unsettled by gaps in its constitution (ibid.: 415). But he points out that, within the predominantly totemistic ontology of Southern North Asia, only shamans have 'the ability to move between its numerous, discrete domains' (ibid.: 418).[9] Even more tellingly, Pedersen acknowledges the instability of the North Asian animistic ontology, and the potential for moving between different ontological registers in this region, with the caveat that his Swiss cheese metaphor:

> only really works for a snapshot of a given animist ontology ... because one given object might come to acquire spirit-power just as the spirit-power of another given object might come to an end. The holes in the animist cheese, as it were, constantly change position, as what before was empty becomes filled up and what before was filled up becomes empty. (ibid.: 425)

Pedersen's caveat is in fact the keystone of his argument, because it suggests that our analytic focus is best placed upon the ruptures, shadings, overlaps or loopholes caused by the instability of ontological fields found across North Asia. We are still, though, left with the following questions: Can the movement between different ontological fields (at the molar level) – as well as between the different elements within a given ontology (at the molecular level) – be scaled? And if they can be scaled, how interdependent might the different (molar or molecular) qualities of ontology be?

The sliding scale presented in this chapter shows how two important elements within Inner Asian sociality – namely, hierarchy and predation – evolve interdependently, such that they frequently produce loopholes in local morality. This finding can be taken to a more general level of analytic purchase. Recent studies on perspectivism have suggested that studies of ontology should start from the understanding that the 'viewpoint' of each 'subject' (person, animal, spirit, and so on) is actually scalable in terms of varying degrees of intensity (Viveiros de Castro 2007: 164; see also Swancutt 2007: 239–44, 256). Scaling becomes a critical element in the study of ontology at three different levels: first, the scaling of ontologies at the molar level; second, the scaling of ontologies at the molecular level; and third, the scaling of different subjects' viewpoints in terms of their varying degrees of intensity – which may be a response to the instability within and between ontological fields.

Note how the hierarchical, and fragmented, 'analogical' ontology which Descola has proposed for the Inner Asian region shades into a more 'animistic' ontology

(Descola 2005: 505–14), when – as I have shown in this chapter – Nuosu or Buryats tip the scale from masked predation towards explicit predation. This shading of predation and hierarchy is equally revealing for so-called 'animistic' Siberia, where – as Willerslev and Ulturgasheva (this volume) show – the first hunt of Eveny reindeer herders entails a triangular relationship between the adult hunter, the animal spirit, and the child hunter used as 'bait' for eliciting the 'move within the spectrum of relations from hierarchical predation to horizontal exchange and between symmetry of human and non-human components and their asymmetry'. I cannot resist drawing a parallel between this baited first hunt of the Eveny child and the similar manipulation of the Mongolian triangular relation between those people who, in seemingly selfless acts of philanthropy towards yet another person, acquire disproportionately numerous blessings and fortune from the shamanic spirits or Buddhist gods. As mentioned above, the crafty handling of this triangular relation between donor, receiver and the Christian God underpinned the medieval commodification of Catholic indulgences, suggesting that further examples of masked predation, including those which hail from a frequently 'naturalistic' ethnographic field, could readily be put forth (Descola 1996: 88–89, 96–97). What, then, the study of masked predation holds in store for the Amazonia–Siberian comparison – and for the comparative anthropological enterprise more broadly – is leverage for demonstrating that people regularly move not just between different ontological fields, but also between the differently scaled elements within any given ontology.

Notes

1. For Amazonia, see Descola (1992: 115–21; 1996: 90, 94), Viveiros de Castro (1998: 470–72, 480; 2004: 466, 470, 476, 480) and Fausto (2007: 497–98, 500–3, 505–13). For Siberia, see Shirokogoroff (1935: 138–45), Ingold (1987: 103–6; 1993: 108–11, 116–17; 2000: 69–76), Hamayon (1994: 113–18; 1996: 79–81), Kwon (1998: 116, 119, 122–24; 1999: 378, 381–83, 386), Willerslev (2004: 629–30, 633, 635, 642, 646; 2007: 85, 99–100, 117–18) and Vitebsky (2005: 24–25, 263–65).
2. See Willerslev (2004: 629–30, 635, 637) and Brightman, Grotti and Ulturgasheva (2006).
3. See Viveiros de Castro (1998: 471–72, 482–83; 2004: 468–69, 478–79; 2007: 164), Willerslev (2004: 639–42) and Swancutt (2007: 239–42, 247–55).
4. See also Lavrillier (this volume), who shows that Evenki consider spiders to be ancestor protectors of the home.
5. See Fausto (2007: 498 n.2), who describes a similar scaling of masked predation and explicit hierarchy in Amazonia.
6. See, e.g., Descola (1996: 90), Viveiros de Castro (1998: 480, also 471–72; 2004: 480) and Fausto (2007: 507, 510, 517, 518–19, 523).
7. See, e.g., Rivière (1984: 72–86), Clastres (1987: 10–26), Overing (2000: 67, 76) and Overing and Passes (2000: 10, 13, 17).
8. See, e.g., Rivière (1984: 70–71, 80, 85, 103, 105), Vilaça (2002: 349–50; 2005: 453–54) and Fausto (2007: 502).
9. Here Pedersen makes reference to Humphrey (1995) and Pedersen (1998).

References

Bateson, G. 2000[1972]. *Steps to an Ecology of Mind*. Chicago: University of Chicago Press.
Brightman, M. 2007. 'Amerindian Leadership in Guianese Amazonia', Ph.D. thesis. Cambridge: University of Cambridge.
Brightman, M., V. Grotti, and O. Ulturgasheva. 2006. 'Introduction: Rethinking the "Frontier" in Amazonia and Siberia: Extractive Economies, Indigenous Politics and Social Transformations', *Cambridge Anthropology* 26(2): 1–12.
Clastres, P. 1987. *Society against the State: Essays in Political Anthropology*, trans. R. Hurley and A. Stein. New York: Zone Books.
Deleuze, G. 1990. 'Ninth Series of the Problematic', in *The Logic of Sense*, trans. M. Lester and C. Stivale. London: Athlone Press, pp. 52–57.
Descola, P. 1992. 'Societies of Nature and the Nature of Society', in A. Kuper (ed.), *Conceptualizing Society*. London: Routledge, pp. 107–26.
——— 1996. 'Constructing Natures: Symbolic Ecology and Social Practice', in P. Descola and G. Pálsson (eds), *Nature and Society: Anthropological Perspectives*. London: Routledge, pp. 82–102
——— 2005. *Par-delà nature et culture*. Paris: Gallimard.
Ewart, E. 2003. 'Lines and Circles: Images of Time in a Panará Village', *Journal of the Royal Anthropological Institute* 9(2): 261–79.
Fausto, C. 2007. 'Feasting on People: Eating Animals and Humans in Amazonia', *Current Anthropology* 48(4): 497–530.
Feuchtwang, S. 2002. 'Remnants of Revolution in China', in C.M. Hann (ed.), *Postsocialism: Ideals, Ideologies and Practices in Eurasia*. London: Routledge, pp. 196–214.
Grotti, V. 2007. 'Nurturing the Other: Wellbeing, Social Body and Transformability in Northeastern Amazonia', Ph.D. thesis. Cambridge: University of Cambridge.
——— 2009. 'Un corps en mouvement: parenté, "diffusion de l'influence" et transformations corporelles dans les fêtes de bière trio, Amazonie du nord-est', *Journal de la société des américanistes* 95(1): 73–96.
Guldin, G. 1994. *The Saga of Anthropology in China*. New York: M.E. Sharpe.
Hamayon, R. 1994. 'Shamanism: A Religion of Nature ?' in T. Irimoto and Y. Takako (eds), *Circumpolar Religion and Ecology: An Anthropology of the North*. Tokyo: University of Tokyo Press, pp. 109–23.
——— 1996. 'Shamanism in Siberia: From Partnership in Supernature to Counter-power in Society', in N. Thomas and C. Humphrey (eds), *Shamanism, History, and the State*. Ann Arbor: University of Michigan Press, pp. 76–89.
Harrell, S. 1995. 'The History of the History of the Yi', in S. Harrell (ed.), *Cultural Encounters on China's Ethnic Frontiers*. Seattle: University of Washington Press, pp. 63–91.
——— 2001. *Ways of Being Ethnic in Southwest China*. Seattle: University of Washington Press.
Heberer, T. 2007. *Doing Business in Rural China: Liangshan's New Ethnic Entrepreneurs*. Seattle: University of Washington Press.
Hill, A.M. 2001. 'Captives, Kin, and Slaves in Xiao Liangshan', *Journal of Asian Studies* 60(4): 1033–49.
Hill, A.M., and E. Diehl. 2001. 'A Comparative Approach to Lineages among the Xiao Liangshan Nuosu and Han', in S. Harrell (ed.), *Perspectives on the Yi of Southwest China*. Berkeley: University of California Press, pp. 51–67.
Holbraad, M., and R. Willerslev. 2007. 'Afterword: Transcendental Perspectivism: Anonymous Viewpoints from Inner Asia', *Inner Asia*, special issue 9(2): 329–45.

Holenstein, E. 1999. 'The Zero-Point Orientation: The Placement of the I in Perceived Space', in D. Welton (ed.), *The Body*. Oxford: Blackwell Publishers. Blackwell Readings in Continental Philosophy, pp. 57–94.
Humphrey, C. 1995. 'Chiefly and Shamanist Landscapes in Mongolia', in E. Hirsch and M. O'Hanlon (eds), *The Anthropology of Landscape: Perspectives on Place and Space*. Oxford: Oxford University Press, pp. 135–62
——— 1999. 'The Fate of Earlier Social Ranking in the Communist Regimes of Russia and China', in R. Guha and J. Parry (eds), *Institutions and Inequalities: Essays in Honour of André Béteille*. Oxford: Oxford University Press, pp. 56–87.
Ingold, T. 1987. *The Appropriation of Nature: Essays on Human Ecology and Social Relations*. Iowa City: University of Iowa Press.
——— 1993. 'The Reindeerman's Lasso', in P. Lemmonier (ed.), *Technological Choices: Transformation in Material Cultures since the Neolithic*. London: Routledge, pp. 108–25
——— 2000. *The Perception of the Environment: Essays on Livelihood, Dwelling and Skill*. London: Routledge.
Kwon, H. 1998. 'The Saddle and the Sledge: Hunting as Comparative Narrative in Siberia and Beyond', *Journal of the Royal Anthropological Institute* 4(1): 115–27.
——— 1999. 'Play the Bear: Myth and Ritual in East Siberia', *History of Religions* 38(4): 373–87.
Lepri, I. 2005. 'The Meanings of Kinship among the Ese Ejja of Northern Bolivia', *Journal of the Royal Anthropological Institute* 11(4): 703–24.
Lin Yueh-hua. 1961. *The Lolo of Liang Shan*, trans. Ju-Shan Pan and Wu-Chi Liu. New Haven, CT: Human Relations Area Files Press.
Ma Erzi. 2000. 'The Bimo, their Books and their Ritual Implements', trans. S. Harrell, in S. Harrell and Bamo Qubumo and Ma Erzi (eds), *Mountain Patterns: The Survival of Nuosu Culture in China*. Seattle and London: University of Washington Press. pp. 51–57.
Merleau-Ponty, M. 1964. *The Primacy of Perception and Other Essays on Phenomenological Psychology, the Philosophy of Art, History and Politics*. Evanston, IL: Northwestern University Press.
Overing, J. 2000. 'The Efficacy of Laughter: The Ludic Side of Magic within Amazonian Sociality', in J. Overing and A. Passes (eds), *The Anthropology of Love and Anger: The Aesthetics of Conviviality in Native Amazonia*. London: Routledge, pp. 64–81.
Overing, J., and A. Passes . 2000. 'Introduction: Conviviality and the Opening up of Amazonian Anthropology', in J. Overing and A. Passes (eds), *The Anthropology of Love and Anger: The Aesthetics of Conviviality in Native Amazonia*. London: Routledge, pp. 1–30.
Pan Jiao. 1997. 'The Maintenance of the LoLo Caste Idea in Socialist China', *Inner Asia* 2(1): 108–27.
Pedersen, M. 1998. 'Networking the Landscape: Spatial Economy and Ritual Movement among the Tsataang of Northern Mongolia', unpublished paper delivered at the Second Baltic-Scandinavian Research Workshop, 'Uses of Nature: Towards an Anthropology of the Environment'. Tartu, Estonia, 10–14 May.
——— 2001. 'Totemism, Animism, and North Asian Indigenous Ontologies', *Journal of the Royal Anthropological Institute* 7(3): 411–27.
Pedersen, M., R. Empson and C. Humphrey (eds). 2007. 'Perspectivism', *Inner Asia*, special issue 9(2): 141–348.
Rivière, P. 1984. *Individual and Society in Guiana: A Comparative Study of Amerindian Social Organization*. Cambridge: Cambridge University Press.

Santos-Granero, F. 2009. *Vital Enemies: Slavery, Predation and the Amerindian Political Economy of Life*. Austin: University of Texas Press.

Shirokogoroff, S. 1935. *Psychomental Complex of the Tungus*. London: Kegan Paul, Trench, Trubner.

Swancutt, K. 2007. 'The Ontological Spiral: Virtuosity and Transparency in Mongolian Games', *Inner Asia*, special issue 9(2): 237–59.

——— 2008. 'The Undead Genealogy: Omnipresence, Spirit Perspectives, and a Case of Mongolian Vampirism', *Journal of the Royal Anthropological Institute* 14(4): 843–64.

——— In Press. 'The Captive Guest: Spider Webs of Hospitality among the Nuosu of Southwest China', *Journal of the Royal Anthropological Institute*, Special Issue 2012, 18(S1).

Taylor, A.-C. 2001. 'Wives, Pets, and Affines: Marriage among the Jivaro', in L. Rival and N. Whitehead (eds), *Beyond the Visible and the Material: The Amerindianization of Society in the Work of Peter Rivière*. Oxford: Oxford University Press, pp. 45–56.

Viveiros, A. 2002. 'Making Kin Out of Others in Amazonia', *Journal of the Royal Anthropological Institute* 8(2): 347–65.

——— 2005. 'Chronically Unstable Bodies: Reflections on Amazonian Corporalities', *Journal of the Royal Anthropological Institute* 11(3): 445–64.

Vitebsky, P. 2005. *Reindeer People: Living with Animals and Spirits in Siberia*. London: HarperCollins.

Viveiros de Castro, E. 1996. 'Images of Nature and Society in Amazonian Ethnology', *Annual Review of Anthropology* 25: 179–200.

——— 1998. 'Cosmological Deixis and Amerindian Perspectivism', *Journal of the Royal Anthropological Institute* 4(3): 469–88.

——— 2004. 'Exchanging Perspectives: The Transformation of Objects into Subjects in Amerindian Ontologies', *Common Knowledge* 10(3): 463–84.

——— 2007. 'The Crystal Forest: Notes on the Ontology of Amazonian Spirits', *Inner Asia*, special issue 9(2): 153–72.

Willerslev, R. 2004. 'Not Animal, Not *Not*-animal: Hunting, Imitation and Empathetic Knowledge among the Siberian Yukaghirs', *Journal of the Royal Anthropological Institute* 10(3): 629–52.

——— 2007. *Soul Hunters: Hunting, Animism, and Personhood among the Siberian Yukaghirs*. Berkeley: University of California Press.

Afterword

Piers Vitebsky

This collection is no ordinary regional comparison. It is an encounter between two discourses, on both the ethnographic and the theoretical level, which have been prevented from meeting for nearly a century. The prehistoric peopling of the Americas, the colonial histories as resource frontiers creating communities of marginality and tribalism, the striking parallels in ontologies of human, animal and spirit: all of these cry out for systematic comparison. But our means of knowing and interpreting these societies and cultures have developed in quite different ways. There is no chapter here which in itself compares both regions, and (unlike some other regional comparisons) the person does not yet exist who is able to write such a chapter from the experience of their own fieldwork.

Ethnographic research on Amazonia has flourished through decades of international research, funding and publication in Spanish, Portuguese, German, French and English, allowing the region to provide material for major contributions to cosmopolitan anthropological theory, from moieties to cannibalism to structuralism. Awareness of Amazonian anthropology has become all the more accessible with the postwar rise of American anthropology and the English language.

Knowledge of Siberian peoples in the wider world comes by much more restricted and idiosyncratic routes, all of them offering obstacles to dialogue with the ethnography of other regions. Between 1917 and the late 1980s the Russian North was almost totally sealed off. No ethnographer from outside the Soviet Union and its East European satellites could do long-term fieldwork there (the achievements of the few Western pre-perestroika pioneers were all the more extraordinary given the shortness of their visits). Thus, whatever outsiders read, they could never relate it to their own experience of fieldwork in a neighbouring or related community – that is, they could never have the embodied experience that goes with regional specialisation. The greater part of the Arctic and sub-Arctic was removed from international anthropological debate, and it is surely this which helps to explain how the circumpolar North slipped from the important comparative and theoretical role which it played in the Boas era 100 years ago.

Soviet ethnographers were also barred from comparative work outside their own country. They were confined to fieldwork in territories inside the Soviet Union (Siberia, Central Asia, the Caucasus) and could not form understandings of other regions from first-hand experience. In Leningrad (now St Petersburg) in the 1980s I knew one anthropologist, Berezkin, who wrote about shamans and spirits in Amazonia ('The Voice of the Devil among Snows and Jungles', 1987, and 'Myths of the Indians of South America', 1994) – but he had never been there. He was in the same position as a Leningrad-based Indonesianist who told me, 'I'm not really an ethnographer, I'm an astronomer - I study Indonesia through a telescope!' At the same time, Russian anthropologists were extremely learned and worked hard at learning exotic languages. To take only Moscow specialists on the ethnography of the Chukchi, one was also fluent in Japanese and another in Malay.

Meanwhile, most anthropologists in the West did not return the compliment. Almost all research on Siberia remained locked up in Russian, and the Russian language and alphabet functioned as a banal but effective way of repelling involvement by foreign scholars. Reading sources in Russian was a specialist professional commitment, with none of the easy movement between languages and national traditions which characterised Amazonian scholarship. Even in the late 1980s, important comparative studies by Western authors relied for data from Russia on material written in English before the Revolution of 1917.

But the biggest barrier to communication was the gulf in theoretical frameworks, fieldwork techniques and ways of communicating what one found out. Soviet scholars asked quite different questions and came up with correspondingly different answers, working from the design and evolution of sledges and shamans' costumes to conclusions about surviving traces of primitive communism and stages of matriarchy. They were passionately dedicated to research and produced a huge literature which Amazonianists (if they had overcome the linguistic barrier) would have found fascinating, but ultimately frustrating. The Amazonianists would have been encouraged by the serious attention given to working with local languages. But instead of ontology and epistemology they would have found speculations or assertions about evolution; instead of long-term individual fieldwork they would have found mostly joint summer expeditions with archaeologists and biologists; instead of the fluidity of social processes they would have been told what 'the Chukchi' or 'the Nenets' say, do or believe, with little sense of the internal tensions that make these concepts and ethnonyms so problematic and fascinating for Western anthropologists.

The catastrophic Soviet persecution of anthropologists from the 1930s into the mid 1980s combined with the framework of evolutionary stages and survivals to render this essentialism strangely timeless. History was hard at work in these models – but only until the Revolution. After this there was only the finalisation of Soviet development, as if the division between before and after was the last moment in historical time. Again and again in the 1980s I would locate a book with a title to gladden the heart of any Amazonianist, only to be brought up short by the time-limit in the sub-title (e.g., Anon. 1976, Anon. 1981, Prokof'eva 1971, respectively 'Nature and Man in the Religious Representations of the Peoples of Siberia and the North (Second Half of the 19th - Beginning of the 20th Century)', 'Problems of the History of Social Consciousness of the Aborigines of Siberia (Based on Materials of the Second Half of the 19th - Beginning of the 20th Century)', and 'Shamanic Costumes of the Peoples of Siberia: Religious Representations and Rituals in the 19th and Early 20th Century').

These old Soviet-era ethnographers knew about many profoundly important things which are central to this book: shamanic flight, the souls of animals, the speech of plants, curses and hauntings, clan rivalries and the detailed texture of social life... But much of what they witnessed in the present was not published but relayed in kitchen-table conversations. My early ethnographic knowledge of Siberia was greatly enriched from the oral history of talking to ethnographers, and this is still an untapped treasury of material which goes deeper back in time than our new access to the field. If they published interesting books about more recent times these were given misleading, apotropaic titles. The astronomer's study of southeast Asian shamanism, though sub-titled 'Aspects of Spiritual Culture', used a positively valued word which could also mean 'intellectual' or 'non-material' culture and disguised the real topic under the misleading main title 'Peoples of Malaysia and Western Indonesia' (Revunenkova 1980). I did not fully understand the reasons until I myself was arrested on the Leningrad metro for reading a book openly called 'Chosen by the Spirits' (Basilov 1984).

Most research on Siberia is still published in Russian, but increasingly also in English. International symposia and publications about the region now usually involve a full partnership with Russian contributors. Ironically, just as scholars of a younger generation in Russia are free to write and publish more as they wish, the funding structure of the Russian Academy of Sciences is evaporating and they are being thrown onto an international grant market which they are not trained to manipulate, despite indeed coming from 'a strong school with noble traditions and achievements' (Tishkov 1998: 3). This situation is reflected in the contributors to this book, of whom only one is actually based inside Russia. The other contributors from the Siberian side all more or less illustrate a tendency for cosmopolitan anthropology to be carried out either by Westerners or by people who began their education in Russia before moving out to receive advanced training and make their careers in the West.

Yet the young scholars in the West do not always think as freely they might. In those first heady years of access to the field in the 1990s and 2000s, some of them were so mesmerised by the State that they hardly engaged with cosmology in the way even a political anthropologist might do in Amazonia. I had to defend Rane Willerslev when he was my student from criticisms by some Westerners of his own generation that he had not set up the State as the fundamental framework, one could even say as the primal ontology, of his analysis. In this situation, a dose of the Amazon can only be beneficial for the anthropology of Siberia.

Anyone who reads this book will start to see their own fieldwork experience and ideas from new perspectives. For me, the book's greatest contribution lies not only in the theoretical discussions but also in the rich new data which these debates have called forth and in the way these feed each other. The contributors use their ethnography both to lead us through all the dichotomies (horizontal versus vertical, animism versus totemism) and to deconstruct them: the book is an object lesson in how to use theory in the service of understanding real people and societies. By simultaneously building and dissolving paradigms, the authors acknowledge that theory always risks slipping dangerously away from indigenous categories, and they reveal the model-bending potential of lived experience. The richness of the ethnography and the sophistication of argument in this book give rise to many moments of sheer beauty. Yet because of their very refinement and accuracy they also give a sense of groping after something much bigger and yet unknown, and it may be that this comparison will ultimately lead to new formulations of a Lévi-Straussian vision of human unity.

Yet Lévi-Strauss's Amazonian roots also remind us of what is not here. Even in this comparative book, the theoretical agenda is set by powerful Amazonia-derived models. However persuasively these can be applied to Siberian material, the fact remains that they did not grow out of the minds either of Siberian peoples or of their anthropologists. In the spirit of exchange, Siberia has not yet been able to send a big theory back to Amazonia. Slightly earlier big theories associated with data from Siberia concerned topics such as the development of pastoralism and the State, issues which were related to Marxist theorising but hardly concerned Amazonian cosmologies at all.

During the years of Siberian isolation the old pre-Soviet literature continued to exert international influence, especially as purveyed by the few scholars working in the West who knew Russian. Eliade (1964) moved freely in his reading between Amazonia, Siberia and anywhere else in his quest for an essentialised, generic 'shamanism' set in an unfocused ethnographic present. Though obviously failing to cope with context, Eliade usefully pointed to sometimes astonishing similarities which continue to challenge interpretation whatever one's theory. A master or mistress of wild animals may perhaps be explained as only to be expected among subsistence hunters, and it can be argued that this is supported by the spiritual transformations which accompany the shift (in Siberia at least) to pastoralism. But what are we to make of the shaman's journey, as has been reported in both regions discussed here, in which he balances on a thread across a chasm at the bottom of which lie the bleached bones of his predecessors who failed to complete the tightrope walk?

For decades I have been captivated by the ontological *jouissance* of Amazonian ethnography, from Lévi-Strauss's Nambikwara photos to Goldman's description of a Cubeo butterfly dance. In 1972 Peter Rivière suggested I should do a thesis on the somewhat less enchanting topic of tobacco vomiting in north-eastern Amazonia. Somehow this did not happen, and instead I spent the 1970s studying shamans among the Sora of tribal India. Negotiating permits there was good practice for turning myself in the 1980s from an astronomer of the Siberian

Arctic into a long-term fieldworker. It was not until the 1990s that I visited Amazonia, and on the way there I met an international group of Amazonianist anthropologists who gave me the telephone numbers of their shamans and other local friends. Even now, access to fieldwork in Siberia remains politically sensitive and logistically difficult, and Siberianists would not be so instantly generous to a stranger. But I took this as a sign that the day may come when Siberianists lavishly dispense phone numbers to Amazonianist colleagues. Siberian hunters and reindeer herders love reading anthropology and would surely welcome this comparative project with open arms. I hope that this book will become a milestone in the development of a dialogue between specialists in these two regions which will also eventually extend to the communities they study.

References

Anon. (ed). 1976. *Priroda i chelovek v religioznykh predstavleniyakh narodov Sibiri i Severa (vtoraya polovina XIX - nachala XX v)*. Leningrad: PChRPNSS.
Anon. (ed). 1981. *Problemy istorii obschestvennogo soznaniya aborigenov Sibiri (po materialam vtoroy poloviny XIX - nachala XX v)*. Leningrad: PIOSAS.
Basilov, V.N. 1984. *Izbranniki dukhov*. Moscow: Politizdat.
Berezkin, Y.Y. 1987. *Golos d'yavola sredi snegov i djungley*. Leningrad: Lenizdat.
——— 1994. *Mify Indeytsev Yuzhnoy Ameriki*. St Petersburg: Yevropeyskiy Dom.
Eliade, M. 1964. *Shamanism: Archaic Techniques of Ecstasy*. New York: Pantheon
Prokof'eva, Y.D. 1971. *Shamanskie kostyumy narodov Sibiri: religioznyye predstavleniya i obraydy v XIX - nachale XX veka*. Leningrad: Nauka.
Revunenkova E.V. 1980 *Narody Malaysii i Zapadnoy Indonezii: nekotorye aspekty dukhovnoy kul'tury*. Moscow: Nauka.
Tishkov, V. 1998. 'U.S. and Russian Anthropology: Unequal Dialogue in a Time of Transition', *Current Anthropology* 39(1): 1–18.

Notes on Contributors

Marc Brightman is Marie Curie Intra-European Fellow at the Graduate Institute of International and Development Studies, Geneva. His research, based on fieldwork among the Trio, Wayana and Akuriyo of southern Suriname and French Guiana, covers subjects including indigenous leadership, native Amazonian forms of ownership and the politics of conservation. His publications include a previous collection of essays on Amazonia and Siberia co-edited with Vanessa Elisa Grotti and Olga Ulturgasheva, which appeared as a special issue of *Cambridge Anthropology* (2007).

Luiz Costa is Associate Professor in the Department of Cultural Anthropology, Universidade Federal do Rio de Janeiro. Since 2002 he has carried out fieldwork among the Kanamari of western Amazonia and his research has focused on the relationships between kinship, history and myth. He has published articles in the *Journal de la Société des Américanistes* and *Tipiti: The Journal of the Society for the Anthropology of Lowland South America*.

Carlos Fausto is Associate Professor in the Programa de Pós-Graduação em Antropologia Social, Museu Nacional, Universidade Federal do Rio de Janeiro, Brazil. He has carried out fieldwork in Amazonia since 1988, focusing on history, kinship, warfare, shamanism, ritual and art. He is the author of *Os Índios antes do Brasil* (2000), *Inimigos Fiéis: História, Guerra e Xamanismo na Amazônia* (2001), and co-editor of *Time and Memory: Anthropological Perspectives* (2007).

Vanessa Elisa Grotti received her Ph.D. in Social Anthropology from the University of Cambridge in 2007. Her research focused on change and social transformation among the Trio, Wayana and Akuriyo of southern Suriname and French Guiana. She is currently British Academy Postdoctoral Research Fellow at the Institute of Social and Cultural Anthropology, University of Oxford, studying relations between Trio and Wayana Amerindians and the health-care systems in Suriname and French Guiana. She has previously been Research Fellow at the Laboratoire d'Anthropologie Sociale, Ecole des Hautes Etudes en Sciences Sociales (EHESS), Collège de France, Paris, and at the London School of Hygiene and Tropical Medicine. She is the author of several articles analysing conversion to Christianity, corporeality, relations between humans and non-humans, and beer production and consumption among Carib-speaking populations of northern Amazonia.

Casey High is Lecturer in the Department of Anthropology at Goldsmiths College, London. His research with the Waorani communities of Amazonian Ecuador focuses on memory, violence, language and indigenous politics. He is co-editor of the volume *How Do We Know? Evidence, Ethnography, and the Making of Anthropological Knowledge* (2008) and he has recently published articles in the *Journal of the Royal Anthropological Institute* and *Anthropology and Humanism*.

Stephen Hugh-Jones is Emeritus Research Associate at the Department of Social Anthropology, Cambridge University, and a Life Fellow of King's College. His research and publications have focused on the indigenous peoples of northwest Amazonia but with an emphasis on intra- and inter-regional comparison. The thematic focus has ranged from symbolism, mythology and ritual, kinship and architecture, the cocaine business and the articulation of different economic systems, alternative systems of education, through to work on ethnobotany and ethnozoology.

Alexandra Lavrillier is Associate professor at the European Centre for the Arctic at the University of Versailles Saint-Quentin-en-Yvelines. Her research interests cover comparative studies of nomadism, hunting, reindeer herding, landscape management, representations of the natural environment, lifestyles and adaptations brought on by postsocialism, the market economy and climate change, as well as shamanism among Evenki, Eveny and Yakuty. She has published extensively on ritual, the use of space and landscape, orienteering and ethnolinguistics.

Laura Rival is University Lecturer in the Anthropology of Nature, Society and Development in the Department of International Development and the School of Anthropology, Oxford University. Since 1989 she has conducted research among the Huaorani of Amazonian Ecuador, on whom she has published numerous articles and books. She has also worked with the Makushi of southern Guyana and the Chachis (Cayapas) of the Ecuadorian Chocó. Her research interests include issues in Amerindian conceptualizations of nature and society; historical ecology; the impact of development and conservation policies on indigenous peoples; the governance of natural resources; and nationalism, citizenship and state education in Latin America.

Tatiana Safonova is a researcher at the Centre for Independent Social Research, St Petersburg. Her research interests focus on contemporary hunter-gatherers, environmentalism and Siberian anthropology. Her publications address concepts of reversibility and circularity in native Siberia, companionship and the working ethos of rangers in Russian nature reserves.

István Sántha is a postdoctoral fellow at the Anthropology Department of the Institute of Ethnography, Hungarian Academy of Sciences. He works with Evenki hunter-gatherers and Buryat pastoral nomads in the Baikal region of south-eastern Siberia. His has published on companionship, sociality, hunting strategies and human–animal relations.

Vera Skvirskaja is Research Associate in the Department of Social Anthropology, University of Cambridge. She has worked on kinship, new economic forms and religious change in rural communities of Nenets and Komi in Arctic Siberia. Her current research focuses on urban cosmopolitanism, coexistence and migration in the context of the post-Soviet city. She has recently published articles in *Studies of Ethnicity and Nationalism* and *Focaal*.

Katherine Swancutt is an AHRC-ESRC Research Fellow in Social Anthropology at the Institute of Social and Cultural Anthropology and Wolfson College, University of Oxford. She has carried out fieldwork among Buryat Mongol shamans in north-east Mongolia since 1999 and among Nuosu shamans in south-west China since 2007. Her research interests include the anthropology of religion, and her new research explores dreams, the soul and vestigial slavery among the Nuosu. She is the author of two recent articles in the *Journal of the Royal Anthropological Institute* and the author of a forthcoming monograph, *Fortune and the Cursed: The Sliding Scale of Time in Mongolian Divination*.

Olga Ulturgasheva is Research Fellow in Social Anthropology at Clare Hall and Research Associate at the Scott Polar Research Institute, University of Cambridge. Her research interests include the anthropology of childhood and youth in the Arctic, and the comparative study of Siberia and Amazonia. Her ethnographic monograph is currently titled "Ideas of the Future among Young Eveny in Northeastern Siberia" (Berghahn Books, in preparation).

Piers Vitebsky has been Head of Anthropology and Russian Northern Studies at the Scott Polar Research Institute, University of Cambridge, since 1986. He has carried out long-term fieldwork among shamans and shifting cultivators in tribal India since 1975, and among nomadic reindeer herders in the Siberian Arctic since 1988. In the Russian Arctic, he was the first Westerner since the Revolution to live as a long-term guest with an indigenous community. In the early 1980s, he also studied marginal subsistence agriculturalists in Sri Lanka.

Rane Willerslev is Director of the Museum of Cultural History, University of Oslo. He is the author of *Soul Hunters: Hunting, Animism and Personhood among the Siberian Yukaghirs* (2007) an *On the Run in Siberia* (in press).

Index

Achaiyayam, 61
affine, 33, 139, 152–4, 178, 184
affinity, xii, 29, 40, 42, 59, 148, 162, 167, 171
    meta-affinity, 42
Aga Buryat, 176, 187
agency, xii, 3, 6, 8, 13, 14, 16, 32, 34, 36, 53, 54, 70, 72, 73, 78, 123, 125, 127, 130–41, 156
    agential realism, 73
agentivity, 113, 131, 163
aggression, 85, 87
Akuriyo, 164, 162–72
alliance, 8, 42, 146, 166
alterity, 33, 130, 134–5, 137, 140, 147, 162, 171, 180
Amazonia and Siberia, comparisons of, xi, xiii, 4, 7, 9, 19, 142n7
Amerindians, 4–7, 9–13, 40
ancestrality, 38
    ancestors, 58
animal, 96–109, 113–28, 130–41
animism, xii, 3, 6, 16–19, 48–66, 69–79, 83–4, 90–91, 94, 127, 189, 191, 198
    animist ontology, 70–71, 96–7, 108, 127–8, 190
anthropocentrism, 73
Arara, 32
Araweté, 30
assault sorcery, 130, 138
astronomy, 196, 197
asymmetry, 29, 32, 40–42, 52, 54–6, 58–9, 66, 191
Australian Aborigines, 49
Ávila Runa, 39

Basilov, Vladimir, 197
basket, 184–5
Bateson, Gregory, 85, 88, 90, 92, 178
bear, 7–8, 58, 75, 117–21, 127, 138
bed, matrimonial, 151–4, 158
Berezkin, Yuri, 196
bird, 14, 98, 99, 119, 123, 124, 169, 185
Bird-David, Nurit, 71, 74, 83, 90
blood, 6, 62–4, 86, 92, 97, 99–102, 105–7, 110n8, 119n3, 123, 165–6, 171, 172n3, 182
Boas, Franz, xii, 10, 195
body, xii, 4, 5, 13–14, 31, 32, 49, 57, 70, 77, 83, 97, 99–108, 109n6, 110n8, 132, 156, 162–3, 181
    closed, 53
    and creativity, 167–9
    as Klein bottle, 32
    making, 165–7
    as maloca, 32
    as 'ontological operator', 78
    open, 51–3
    parts of, 97, 106
    and self-ownership, 34
    as tube, 169–71
body-soul dualism 70–71
Bogoras, Waldemar, 61
Boyer, Pascal, 72
Brazil, 162
Brightman, Marc, 178
Buddhism, 179, 188
Buryat, 176, 179, 181, 187–9, 191

captive, 8, 19, 31, 41, 44n13, 44n20, 182, 184
capture, 177, 180–82, 184–5
cannibalism, xiii, 96, 108–9, 166, 180

cannibal incorporation, 33
caterpillar, 168–9
centripetal sociality, 182, 184
chief, 31
child, 51, 58, 87
    childhood, 51
Chimane, 32
Chiriguano, 40
Christianity, 19, 58, 136
Chukchi, 48, 57, 58–66, 196
circumpolar peoples, 49
clan, 146–50, 152–4, 158
    commune (*obshchina*), 148
    identity, 146, 152
    name, 150, 152
    relations, 152–3
classification, 155
    ethnoclassification, 69, 70
clothing, 167–8, 196
coevalness, 147
commensality, 166
communication, 82–94
companionship, 94
comparison, xii, 3–9, 13–16, 19, 33, 189, 191, 195
consubstantiality, 166
corporeality, 4, 12, 163
corpse, 89, 100
    becoming-corpse, 102–4
Corsín Jiménez, Alberto, 65
cosmology, 7, 131–3, 137–8, 140
creativity, 167–9
Cree, 75

dance, 115, 117, 127
death, 15–16, 51–2, 57–9, 64, 75, 89–90, 100, 115, 120, 122, 128n8, 135, 137, 139, 171, 177
debt, 16, 60
debt peonage, 39
Deed Mongol, 177, 179
Deleuze, Gilles, 176
    and Félix Guattari, 13
descent, xii
Descola, Philippe, xii, 1, 4, 15, 17, 48, 70–71, 147, 176, 189–91
Diehl, Eric, 182, 183
dividual person, 83

dog, xii, 44n16, 82–94, 114, 117–9, 121–2, 127, 164
domestication, 18, 138
Doniger, Wendy, 64

Ecuador, 133–4
education, Soviet, 147–8
Eliade, Mircea, 198
enemy, 130–41
energy, 6, 16, 49, 59, 61, 64, 101, 110n8, 170
equality, 29
    egalitarianism, 65, 83, 84
Evans-Pritchard, Edward, 55, 62
Evenki, 82–94, 113–28
Eveny, 48, 57
exchange, 8, 12, 16, 54, 56, 59, 60, 118, 126, 142n6, 156, 165–6, 178, 180
exogamy, 149, 150, 153
extraction, 180, 183, 186

fabrication, 57
fate/fortune, 182
Fausto, Carlos, 177, 180
Feuchtwang, Stephan, 186
fieldwork, 196
filiation
    adoptive, 31
    meta-, 40
fire, 43n9, 89, 97, 99, 121, 127, 151, 166,
    board, 60
    spirit, 127
flesh, 96, 97, 99, 102–4
flute, 170–71
folklore, 10
food, 6, 43n9, 59, 70, 90, 96–109, 115, 119, 124, 151, 164, 165, 167, 171, 177
fortune, 179, 180, 182, 186–9, 191
freedom, 132
French Guiana, 162
frontier zones, xi
funding, 197

Gell, Alfred, 14, 53, 71–2, 75–6, 77
gender, 5, 42, 43n3, 59, 110n11, 151–2, 156, 159
gift, 16, 55, 115, 123, 126, 179–80, 186

Godelier, Maurice, 60
gods, 2, 15, 60, 176, 179, 180, 187–9, 191
gold, 86, 167
Grotti, Vanessa, 184
growth, organic, 78
Guarani-Kaiowá, 35
Guemple, Lee, 61

Hallowell, Irving, xii, 7, 8
Harrell, Stevan, 183
Heberer, Thomas, 186
herding, 114–6
hierarchy, 18, 29, 65, 175, 176, 178, 180, 181, 184, 188, 189
　explicit, 176, 177, 183, 191n5
Hill, Ann Maxwell, 182–3
history, 131
　idea of, 196
homology, 118, 127
horizontal, 50, 65
house, 31, 91, 133, 170
　as moral person, 146, 159
Hubert, Henri, 63
human, 4
　human vs. non-human, xii, 2–9, 13, 14, 15, 38, 61, 91, 113, 124, 130–41, 191
　humanity, 162–72
Hume, David, 3
Humphrey, Caroline, 147, 156, 159–60, 187
hunting, 48, 82–94, 96, 97, 98–9, 106–7, 110n13, 114–5, 127

identity, 34
image, ancestral (*ngitarma*), 155
imagery, shamanic, 154
imprint, 115–6, 125, 127
India, 198
individual, 114
Indonesia, 196, 197
indulgences, 197, 191
Ingold, Tim, xii, 1, 4, 49, 57
inheritance, 154–5, 157–8
insect, 6, 119, 121, 123, 124
intentionality, 70–73, 77–8, 113, 124, 125, 127, 170, 172n3
Inuit, 61

Inupiat, 57
Itzaj' Maya, 76

jaguar, 7–8, 33, 40, 130–31
　clothes, 168
　as father-in-law, 41
　jaguarisation, 38
　spirits, 131, 135
Jesup
　monographs, 9
　North Pacific Expedition, 9

Kadiwéu, 40
Kamchatka, 58
kamo, 125
Kanamari, 31, 96–109
Kichwa, 131, 134, 139–40
kinship, xii, 96, 97, 100, 103, 104, 108, 119, 125, 127
Kohn, Eduardo, 78
Koryak, 49
Kuikuro, 30

labour, 34, 39
Leach, Edmund, 1
Leenhardt, Maurice, 71
Lepri, Isabella, 180
Lévi-Strauss, Claude, xii, 9, 11–12, 49, 146, 159–60, 198
　Mythologiques, 11, 12
life, 76–9
　anthropology of, 76
lineage, 177, 182–5, 187
　rank, 182
Locke, John, 33–6
loopholes (in morality or ontology), 178–80, 187, 189–90

magnified person, *see* person
Maku, 40
Malay, Malaysia, 196, 197
mana, 125
manioc, 69–70, 79
Maroon, 165, 170
marriage, 148–50, 153–4
　jealousy, 153
Marubo, 31
Marx, Karl, 1

Marxism, 10–11, 19n1, 198
master, 8
　of animals, 16
　mastery, 18–19
mastery relation, 29–42
　herd mother, 124
　master of animals, 31, 198
　master of peccaries, 32
　master-pet relation, 39
maternity, 41–2
matriarchy, 196
Mauss, Marcel, 2, 60
meat, 96, 97, 99, 102, 103–8, 183
Meletinsky, Eleazar, 10–12
merit making, 187
Merleau-Ponty, Maurice, 176
metamessage, 85
Miller, Daniel, 146, 150, 160
mining, 167
Miraña, 36
missionaries, 39, 134, 136, 164, 172
money, 165, 186
Mongol, 176, 177, 179, 186, 188
Mongolia, 49, 179, 187, 191
morality, 135–8, 141, 178–81, 187, 189, 190
　amoral economy, 186
movement, 171
multiculturalism, 132
multinaturalism, 132
myth, 4, 7, 8, 11–13, 20n11, 35, 41, 42, 138, 149, 165, 167, 168
　mythic time, 34, 36

name, 2, 31, 51–7, 58–9, 85, 99, 106, 114, 130, 137, 139, 146, 149, 170
　namesake, 150, 152, 154, 159
　name-soul, 5
　nickname, 167
　surname, 40, 149–50, 152–3
nature, xii, 1, 35, 49, 76, 82, 84, 114, 126, 127, 188
　anthropology of, 1, 16, 19, 147
　vs. culture, xii, 1–2, 16–17, 19n2, 73, 74, 78, 132–3
　god, 188
　spirit, 189
natural law, 33
naturalism, 147, 158

naualaku, 125
Nenets, 146–60, 196
nomad, 114, 115
non-human, xii, 29, 31, 35, 49, 51, 53, 57, 70, 72, 77, 124, 162, 163, 168, 170, 172n2; *see also* human vs. non-human
North America, 8
Nuer, 62
Nuosu (Yi), 175–91
nurture, 163–5

object, 13, 163, 164–5
　and ethnic identity, 155
　idol, 156
　ongon, 156
　sacred (*khekhe*), 147, 154–7, 159; *see also* sledge, inheritance
Ojibwa, 2, 7
onnir, 113, 115–7, 123, 125–7
ontology, 2, 7, 18, 34, 49, 64, 70, 71, 74, 108, 127, 139, 147, 163, 178, 189, 190, 196, 198
　pastoral, 152
　scientific, 147
orphan, 19, 32, 44n20, 134–7
ostensive communication, 88
other, *see* alterity
ownership, 13, 15, 16, 18, 29–42, 53, 60, 62, 90, 94, 127, 155, 177
　owner-master, 30, 109n6, 122

Paleo-Asiatic, 51
Parakanã, 30
pastoralism, 48, 198
Paumari, 39
peccary, 33, 71, 99, 102–3, 169
Pedersen, Morten, 49, 51, 57, 61, 62, 64, 142n7, 190
person, 2, 4, 36, 48
　distributed, 36, 53, 72, 73, 177
　extended, 172n3
　magnified, 29
　personhood, xii, 1, 14, 48, 58, 114, 131, 133, 136, 146, 148, 150, 154, 158, 162, 164–5, 167, 175, 177–8
　personitude, 172n2
perspectivism, xii, xiii, 4, 17, 50, 61, 75, 83–4, 92, 131–3, 136, 142n7, 163, 190

limitations of, 5–6, 13, 70
perspectivity, 172n2
transcendental, 7
and Siberia, 6–7
pet, 6, 18, 19, 30, 31, 75, 119, 130, 134–8, 163, 180
petrol, 86
phenomenology, xiii, 13
philanthropy, 186, 191
phratry, 149–50, 152–3, 159
Pijanakoto, 166
Pika, Alexander, 63
plant, xii, 2–4, 13–14, 15, 30, 32, 34–6, 42, 70, 71, 76–9, 99, 116, 123, 125
speech of, 197
symbolism, 69, 76
play, 115, 117, 123, 126, 127, 128n3
possessions, inalienable 155, 157–8
possessive individualism, 33
power, 30, 37–9, 43n10, 60, 74, 141, 146, 162, 164, 166, 176; *see also* ritual power
colonial, 39
creative, 49
sacred, 154
shamanic, 6
spirit, 190
predation, xiii, 7, 13, 18, 29, 33, 39, 53, 54, 56, 69, 97, 105, 109, 110n13, 131, 133, 136, 140, 175–91
explicit, 176, 178, 186, 187–9, 191
familiarising, 29
masked, 177, 178, 180–81, 183–4, 186–7, 191
prey, 30, 55, 98–100, 104–8, 120, 132, 133–4, 135–6, 177, 180, 184
primitive communism, 196
private property, 29
Prokof'eva, Yelena, 196
property relations, 33

recursivity, 13
rebirth, 61
reindeer, xii, 6, 16, 53–62, 113–20, 122, 124, 126–7, 154, 156, 157
religion, 3, 7, 72, 131, 177
remembering, technology of, 153
reversibility, 5, 13, 53, 55

Revunenkova, Yelena, 197
ritual, 8, 31, 38, 62–4, 70, 75, 77, 84, 88, 93, 113, 114, 116–7, 138, 157, 179, 183
action, 127
exchange, 165
flutes, 170–71
greeting, 33
hunting, 8
initiation, 6
knowledge, 30
power, 113, 115, 120, 122, 124–6
Rivière, Peter, 4, 5, 169, 191n7, 191n8, 198
Rousseau, Jean-Jacques, 1
rubber, 39, 98
Runa, 75–6
Russia, 147–9
Russian, 59, 150, 155
Academy of Sciences, 197
language, as obstacle, 196

sacrifice, 44n13, 51, 58, 62–5, 136, 157, 179
Sakha Republic, 51
Santos-Granero, Fernando, 13–14, 176, 178
scale, 175–91
sliding scale, 175, 190
schismogenesis, 93
secret, 84–6, 93
self-ownership, 33
self-realisation, 132
sentiments, conjugal, 152–3
shadow, 5, 124
shaman, 8, 20n9, 30, 31, 32, 35, 36, 38, 42, 58, 82, 85, 86, 87, 93–4, 97, 114–8, 122–4, 126–7, 155–6, 162, 168, 169, 170, 171, 176, 177, 181, 183, 188, 190, 196, 199
and death, 57
and healing, 105, 107
journey across chasm, 198
and shape-shifting, 49
text-reading, 176, 181, 183, 184
urban 159
and whites, 39, 41
shamanism, xii–xiii, 9, 12, 14, 16, 38, 99, 130–41, 147, 198
and hunting, 69, 108

horizontal and vertical, xiii, 16
shamanic arrows, 6, 105
shamanic cosmology, 6, 19
shamanic flight, 197
shamanic imagery, 154
shamanic script, 181, 182, 184
shamanic society, 1, 6, 38, 51
Sharanahua, 30
siblinghood, 41
singularity/multiplicity, 32
skill, 84, 85, 90
Skin, 97, 99, 103–7
slavery, 18, 33, 176, 186
   colonial, 39
sledge, sacred 154–7
Smith, Brian, 64
sociability, 163
social control, 37
social intelligence 77
socialisation, 86, 89, 90, 92, 94
soul, 2, 3, 5, 6, 13, 14, 15, 16, 31, 39, 52, 58, 61, 70, 79, 93, 97, 99, 100, 108, 114, 119, 121, 125, 129n10, 132, 155, 165, 169–70, 177, 180
   soul-spider, 181–5
Southeast Asia, 197
Southwest China, 176
space, 146–8, 152, 154, 159
species, 3, 7, 16, 32, 35, 36, 49, 69, 71, 73, 75, 76, 77, 84, 91, 99, 100–3, 105, 114, 117, 120, 123–4, 172n2, 176
   collectivity, 31
   ethnospecies, 70
   hyperbole, 30
spirit, 51, 130–32, 135, 176, 177, 179, 180, 185–91
   ancestor, 54
   auxiliary, 32
   evil, 51
   guardian, 186
   spirit-charge, 113–28
   spirit world, 65
   spiritual beings, 51
   superior, 56
   vampiric imps, 176–7
structuralism, xii, 12–13
subject, political, 146–7
subjectivity, 14

substitute, 55
suicide, 63, 64, 88, 177
Suriname, 162
Suyá, 30
Swancutt, Katherine
symmetry, 29
   symmetric affinity, 40

taboo violation *(khivy)* 150–51
tattoo, 167
Taylor, Anne-Christine, 180
taxonomy, 118–9
Terena, 40
things, theory of 146–8, 152, 158–9
Tishkov, 197
tobacco, 32
   vomiting, 198
tonalli, 125
Topolinoye, 51
totemism, xii, 14, 16–19, 21n19, 48–50, 54, 56–7, 62, 64–5, 90, 198
transformability, 164, 167–9
transformation, 131, 132
Trio, 162–72
tube, 169–71
Tungus, 51
Tupi-Guarani, 30
Turner, Terence, 5
Tylor, Edward Burnett, 3

Ulturgasheva, Olga, 53, 175, 191

Verkhoyansk mountains, 51
vertical, 50, 65
victimhood, 133, 140
violence, 130, 133, 140
virtue, 179–81, 187–9
vital substance, 166
Vitebsky, Piers, 54, 58
Viveiros de Castro, Eduardo, 2, 4, 12–13, 17, 50, 172n2, 180, 189, 190

Waorani, 130–41
warfare, 38, 44n12, 96, 101, 136, 139, 166, 167, 180
warrior, 38
Wayana, 162–72
Wayãpi, 30

Weiner, Annette, 155, 161
Whites, 40
wild, xiii
    animal, 35, 51, 53, 58, 90, 91, 97, 99, 113, 115–6, 119–24, 127–8, 185, 198
    boar, 89
    dog, 75
    fruit, 98
    pet, 30, 37, 38
    people, 134, 140, 163, 164, 171
    reindeer, 53, 55, 58, 119

Willerslev, Rane, 51, 63, 175, 177, 191, 197
Witchcraft, 130, 131, 135, 137–8
worship, 187–9

Xingu, Upper, 30

Yamal peninsula, 147–9
Yukaghir, 49

Zafimaniry, 75

www.ingramcontent.com/pod-product-compliance
Lightning Source LLC
Chambersburg PA
CBHW072153100526
44589CB00015B/2204